Rory Cellan-Jones was  correspondent until 2021.

Substack column *Always On*, and through this and his Twitter account @ruskin147 he spreads awareness of technological developments in the fields of medicine, health care and – more specifically – Parkinson's, as well as sharing the progress of #SophiefromRomania. Together with Jeremy Paxman and several others he hosts *Movers and Shakers*, a podcast about Parkinson's, which won the 2024 Broadcasting Press Guild's Podcast of the Year award. His other books are *Dot.Bomb: The Rise and Fall of Dot.com Britain*, *Always On: Hope and Fear in the Smartphone Era* and, out in autumn 2024, *Sophie From Romania: A Year of Love and Hope with a Rescue Dog*.

Praise for *Ruskin Park*

'Heartfelt, gripping … The former BBC correspondent's discovery of his mother's letters to and from the father he first met at 23 makes for a captivating family detective story – and a poignant social history of Britain.'　　　　*Observer*

'*Ruskin Park* is so much more than a memoir. It is a tribute to an individual woman and a whole generation and class.'
　　　　Justin Webb, *The Sunday Times*

'*Ruskin Park* is Rory Cellan-Jones's touching tribute to both his parents, but particularly to the mother he came to know more fully from the letters she left behind.'
　　　　Book of the Week, *Daily Mail*

'I loved this highly evocative, unpretentious memoir. It's a small-scale BBC drama in itself. Against the backdrop of an office love affair kindled at Television Centre, a baby conceived during a stolen weekend at the Three Crowns in Angmering-on-Sea, and a childhood of fish fingers prepared by a tired working mother in a south London council flat, it paints a Larkin-esque picture of the arc of one 20th-century woman's life, from passionate, ambitious and hopeful to lonely, depressed, nostalgic and "always a pain at Christmas".'

The Times

'Almost unbearably moving, but never sentimental. A fascinating, intensely personal story, courageously told with unflinching honesty.' Adrian Chiles

'The result is this enthralling memoir of his captivating, indomitable mother; his talented and ambitious father; and of the golden era of BBC drama and the glamorous milieu that was 1950s television.' Caroline Sanderson, *The Bookseller*

'Riveting, poignant.' *The TLS*

Reader reviews

'Rory is a terrific storyteller, and bringing that skill to the story of his indomitable mother and her battles against the mores of the post-war years, and her decision to keep Rory rather than have him adopted, makes this already compelling story an absolute belter of a book.' Daphne

'I loved this book, the social history, the strong will of Sylvia and the sense of family from all. Stephen, however, was the person who stood out for me – he seemed a wonderful, supportive son and brother. The sense of determination that Sylvia must have possessed at a time when society would have been horribly unsupportive of her is enviable. What a woman. Rory writes and reminisces beautifully.'   David

'An amazing treasure trove of letters have been interwoven with the memories of others to explain Sylvia's life journey. What a privilege it is to read a person's most intimate writings about their circumstances. Rory has not only paid tribute to his mother in this book but has painted a picture of society and its expectations of women, especially single women with children, during Sylvia's lifetime. Beautifully written.'

Heather

'I loved stepping back into the past, reading about how life was then and feeling grateful that so much has changed for the better. All credit to Sylvia for raising two sons as a single parent and holding down a career at the same time. I loved reading this book.'   Pamela

'What an amazing book. What a legacy left in the vast amount of letters and correspondence, and what a story brilliantly put together by Rory Cellan-Jones.'   Simon

'I eagerly anticipated the publication of this book and it did not disappoint. I cried, I laughed and felt bereft when I finished it. Combining social history with memoir, the source material made the story vivid and compelling. Rory allows the characters – his parents, family and friends – to speak for themselves. I was left in awe of Sylvia's spirit and Rory's gentle and honest introspection. Highly recommended.'   Cat

'What a compelling, bittersweet, tale. A fascinating tribute to both Mum and Auntie (Beeb) that is beautifully written. Rory's thoughtful account has many layers, making this in part a memoir, in part a voyage of discovery and in part an insight into life for single mothers in post-war Britain. A must-read!'

Mrs Evans

'I found this book deeply moving. What a remarkable woman! A wonderful read.'   Jim

'Gutsy, honest and riveting.'   Linda

'Touching, intriguing and beautifully written … I loved it.'

Mr Peach

RORY CELLAN-JONES

RUSKIN PARK

SYLVIA, ME AND THE BBC

3 5 7 9 10 8 6 4 2

This paperback edition published in 2024 by September Publishing
First published in 2023 by September Publishing

Copyright © Rory Cellan-Jones 2023

The right of Rory Cellan-Jones to be identified as the author of this
work has been asserted by him in accordance with the Copyright Designs
and Patents Act 1988.

Photo on page 90 from *Radio Times*, 6 November 1953.

Typeset by RefineCatch Limited, www.refinecatch.com
Printed in Great Britain on paper from responsibly managed, sustainable sources
by CPI Books

ISBN 9781914613616
Ebook ISBN 9781914613449

September Publishing
www.septemberpublishing.org

CONTENTS

To Sylvia and Stephen

CHAPTER 1

RETURN TO RUSKIN PARK HOUSE

On a showery Sunday afternoon in May 2022, I stood outside the south London block of flats where I had spent my childhood and wondered what I was doing there. Peering up at the second-floor flat, my home for 19 years, I could see the windows were open. Somebody must be in. But when I rang the mobile phone of the woman who had invited me over, my call went to voicemail – four times in a row. The rain started up again and I took shelter by the door to the block. It had been open to anyone when I lived here but now it needed to be unlocked by a flat owner's key. I felt conspicuous and not a little foolish.

An hour before, I had set off on a journey which I hadn't made for more than 25 years. Back then, it had become tediously familiar. Leaving the house in West Ealing where my family and I have lived since 1992, I travelled slowly down the traffic-clogged A40. I passed the old Hoover factory, now a Tesco superstore, and a string of some of the least attractive 1930s and 1950s housing estates, heading towards central London. But this time, driven by a sense that if I was on a journey into my past I had better go the whole hog, I turned off and drove down Wood Lane, past my former workplace, BBC Television Centre.

I had first visited Television Centre in the 1960s, taken to what seemed a magical place, more exciting than any theme park, by my mother, who worked in the drama department. As a child, I had delighted in spotting *Doctor Who* villains in the canteen or peering into a studio at a *Blue Peter* rehearsal. As an adult, I found that the asbestos-riddled complex where I practised my trade as a broadcaster had lost none of its glamour.

I drove on, retracing the route my mum had taken home in her little yellow Mini or later the MG Midget which I always suspected had been bought for her by an elderly neighbour who was an admirer. I passed the Albertine wine bar, just closed but for many years the scene of much BBC post-programme carousing. This had also been the location of my first meeting with my half-brother Simon in 1985.

Down, through Earl's Court to the Embankment, past the Royal Hospital. Across Vauxhall Bridge, overlooked by the postmodern fortress that is the MI6 headquarters, into grimy south London. Past the Oval cricket ground, where in 1968, aged ten, I had been left with a sandwich and a ten-shilling note, the price of entry to my first Test match. I sat on the grass by the boundary and watched England's John Edrich and Basil D'Oliveira – soon to be shamefully dropped from the team touring apartheid era South Africa – as they began to build a commanding first innings total against Australia.

Along Camberwell New Road, still choked with traffic but with some fine Georgian terraced houses that had since emerged from the blackened slums I had seen from the top deck of the number 12 bus in the 1960s and 70s. Then a right turn at Camberwell Green and up past the Maudsley Hospital, where in 1995 my mother and I had met the doctor to hear a diagnosis which frightened me but which she appeared to take in her stride. On past King's College Hospital, where she had been transferred the following year, and where her life had ended.

Finally, up Denmark Hill, turning off at Champion Hill, just short of the border with leafy Dulwich, to arrive at Ruskin Park House.

My mother, Sylvia Rich, had arrived here in 1955 with her 13-year-old son, my half-brother Stephen. She had written to a friend about the new home: 'It really is much nicer than the usual Council flats, central heating, constant hot water, quite new, and situated on top of a hill with a delightful little park just outside.'

It was, however, very small – Stephen had the one bedroom while Sylvia slept in the living room on a couch, or 'divan' as she called it, which became her bed each night. Then in 1958 I came along and, for a while, until Stephen left home to make his way in the theatre, it was even more cramped, with my cot joining his bed in the single bedroom.

From then on, it was just me and Mum, all the way until 1977 when I left the flat, first to live in West Berlin for six months, then to start my degree in modern and medieval languages in Cambridge.

When I picture the years I spent growing up at Ruskin Park House they have a stain of gloom. From very early on I was miserable there. At first, I suppose like most children of single parents, I had a strong bond with my mother. We would sit at

3

the dining-room table on a Sunday lunchtime eating one of her very limited repertoire of meals – poached eggs, fish fingers, occasionally a flavourless beef casserole – singing along to 'Puff the Magic Dragon' on *Two Way Family Favourites* or laughing at *Round the Horne*. The stately old valve radio, the centrepiece of the living room until we got a little portable black and white telly, is the one piece of furniture I still have from the flat. It sits in our attic, waiting for the day when the team from BBC's *The Repair Shop* brings it back to life.

But as time went on, Mum grew increasingly eccentric and possessive, before sinking into depression in my teenage years. Spending time alone with her in the flat as she began another rambling story about the goings-on at the BBC became a grim prospect.

I did escape during the holidays, when my mother, trying to hold down a demanding job with unpredictable hours, sent me out of London to stay with her family or with my godparents, whose house in a Wiltshire village had a long garden with a stream running through it. These were times of joyful freedom, while going back to the flat felt like a return to prison.

I escaped but my mum, who had at first so loved Ruskin Park House, did not. In the mid-1970s, the flat-dwellers, always encouraged to see themselves as a cut above most council tenants, were told that they had an opportunity to become homeowners. Under a Labour government, even before Margaret Thatcher came to power, the starting gun was fired on the privatisation of council homes. It was a revolution that gave thousands of tenants a valuable asset just as the 1980s housing boom got under way, and it would transform the politics and economics of Britain.

But Sylvia Rich was not going to be a part of it. She turned down the opportunity to acquire our flat for the sum of £5,000, despite – or perhaps because of – my brother Stephen telling her what a good idea that would be. He was exasperated because she was trapping herself in Ruskin Park House when she could have had a nice nest egg and moved somewhere better. 'It's all a con,' she would mutter under her breath when the subject was raised. She remained a Southwark Council tenant.

As the 1980s rolled on, the flats appreciated in value and a new breed known as the 'yuppies' moved in – after all, with Denmark Hill station just down the hill offering a ten-minute journey to Blackfriars, you could be in the City in no time.

By the early 1990s, one-bedroom flats like ours were going for upwards of £25,000, netting a tidy profit for those that had bought them in the 1970s for £5,000. Sylvia, however, appeared to have no regrets. After she died, I found a draft of a letter she had apparently sent around this time to the Conservative Party about a party political broadcast.

She wrote that while she was a Conservative voter she disliked the message in the broadcast about enabling tenants to have the 'dignity' of owning their own homes. 'Are you not equating "possessions" with dignity?' she asked, going on to claim many buyers had ended up having their homes repossessed. She ended by warning that if the 'misleading' statements continued, she would stop voting Conservative and she knew several people who felt the same.

I wonder who those 'several people' who shared her views on home ownership were? By this point, she barely knew anyone on the estate, although a young BBC radio producer who had bought a flat on her corridor knocked on her door from time to time to check that she was OK, letting me know if there was a problem.

One of my former BBC colleagues, Ellie Updale, who was born five years before me and spent her childhood in a three-bedroom flat in block B on the estate, has a different story. Her parents, despite some similar misgivings, did buy their flat. Then her father, a sub-editor on the *Daily Mirror*, died suddenly leaving her mother worried about meeting the mortgage. But things worked out: 'She'd always worked, my mother. She got through and eventually she sold it and moved to a little flat in Dulwich. And that was the making of her because she was pretty well independent.'

Now, on that rainy afternoon in May 2022, as I looked up at the flat, my mind went back to another Sunday more than a quarter of a century earlier. Then – as now – I had stood outside wondering how to get in. I had grown alarmed after failing to get Mum on the phone and had driven over to check up on her. When I got no response to knocking on the door and shouting through the letter box, I borrowed a ladder from the porter and climbed on to the second-floor balcony and through the open kitchen window. In my old bedroom, I found Mum and an empty bottle of sleeping pills. If she had meant to take a fatal dose she failed. The ambulance came and took her to hospital but she was home again within a few days. It was a stroke that killed her some months later.

A few days after her funeral in 1996, I again drove over to Ruskin Park House, this time to clear out the flat before it was handed back to Southwark Council.

I took the cramped little lift to the second floor and produced the key which we had found pinned inside my

6

mother's coat pocket after her death. She had always had a terrible fear of being locked out and when I was first given a key insisted, to my great embarrassment, that it was attached to my school trouser pocket on a piece of elastic.

Opening the door, the familiar smell of the overheated flat hit me, overlain with the extra layers of dust accumulated while it had lain empty for the last two months. Looking around, it struck me once again how sad a picture of her life the flat painted. Much of the furniture was cheap and flimsy, dating back to the 1950s when Sylvia and Stephen had moved in. Stephen's earnings as a child actor at the Old Vic had helped buy him a bed and a wardrobe but a tea chest served as a side table and old orange boxes as bookcases, and they were heading for the dump.

In the bedroom, the wardrobe was stuffed with cheap women's clothing, much of it acquired from charity shops, and some of my old school shirts, which Mum had taken to wearing – after all, they were only slightly shabby. But hidden at the back I discovered two extremely elegant 1950s evening dresses, one a long, white, silk number. We later handed them to a friend's two teenage daughters, who were delighted with their glamorous new party outfits.

It was as I began to open drawers, look under the bed and investigate behind the dressing table that I became aware that there was something far more valuable here. Everywhere, there were bundles of letters – hundreds, possibly thousands of them – along with folders full of BBC memos, my school reports and legal documents relating to custody battles and child maintenance arrangements. It seemed she had never thrown away any letter she had received and kept carbon copies of just about every one she typed, either in her BBC office or

Stephen's wedding reception, 1967. Sylvia in fur stole, with Joan, Rory and Bunty.

at home on the portable typewriter she had brought back from work.

I immediately recognised the handwriting in hundreds of letters from her two sisters, my aunts Bunty and Joan, who had attended her funeral days earlier. I had known that they had written to each other at least weekly – my mother used to read out selected items of family news to me while I stifled a yawn and pretended to be interested. What I had not realised was that she often typed her replies and kept carbon copies.

As I skimmed through some of these letters, a correspondence stretching over 50 years, I got the first inkling of something that was to become more evident when I looked more closely over the coming weeks. Yes, there was plenty of humdrum stuff – 'just bought a new winter coat from Lewis's'. But there was a total intimacy between the three sisters, Sylvia and Joan willing to share the details of their equally dramatic and sometimes disastrous romantic lives with Bunty, happily married but always with a kind word of comfort or advice. And between them they painted a vivid picture of what it was like to be a woman in Britain from the 1940s to the 1990s, especially one who wanted more from life than just domestic routine. What's more, I began to realise that my mother, who left school at 14 and had appeared to read little more than the *Sunday Express* when I was growing up, had a real gift for writing, her letters peppered with pungent descriptions of her colleagues and friends.

Next, a small, dark blue 1945 diary with 'B.B.C.' stamped on the cover fell out of one folder, and beneath it I found a sheaf of letters from the war. With her husband away in various non-combatant roles around England and then in Washington DC, she found herself a job in the radio talks department in Bristol. By day, she was mixing with poets and artists and giving her boss Geoffrey Grigson the benefit of her opinion of their scripts; by night, she was sheltering from bombs or going dancing with American officers. Oh, and taking a few weeks off in 1942 to give birth to her son Stephen.

There appeared to be mountains of letters telling the story of her separation from her husband, sparked by his distaste for her BBC job, and her move to London in the 1950s to work in television drama. I kept on reading, engrossed in the stories that unfolded about characters I thought I knew so well – my mother, my brother, my lovely aunts and cousins – but eventually I realised time was passing and I had to get on with the job. I scooped everything up and took it down to the car to examine more closely at home.

A few days later, I was trying to sort this sprawling archive into some sort of chronological order when I came across one batch of letters that made me catch my breath. They were in a small rectangular red box with 'Charmed Life by Kayser' printed on the lid, which must have once contained a pair of stockings. In blue biro, in my mother's familiar handwriting, I saw this: 'Keep for myself & Rory later.' Opening it, I first saw a brown envelope with another message: 'For Rory, to read and think about in the hope that it will help him to understand how it really was.' Inside was a bundle of love letters which told the story of how I came to be born and how I was very nearly given away to lead a different life under another name. But there were also clues to an entirely different woman to the one with whom I had grown up.

It would take me years before I was ready to undertake the journey this accumulated pile of paper invited me on. Years before I was able to begin to reconcile the greyness of my teenage years with a resourceful, beautiful woman working in those post-war years. But in 1996, with a young family and a career at the BBC which I felt at the time had stalled, it did not feel right to immerse myself in the past. Yes, I still had a whole series of questions about the circumstances of my birth but the answers might prove hurtful to at least one person I had grown close to in recent years. Better to leave well alone for now.

*

In 2021, a freelance journalist who knew a bit about my background contacted me about a story idea she was trying to sell to the *Telegraph*. Its letters pages had been full of people reminiscing about what they found when they cleared out their parents' homes – didn't I have a story about that? I told her my tale about the letters and it appeared in the *Sunday Telegraph* under my byline.

Writing the article sent me back to the filing cabinet stuffed with the letters I had not looked at for years. I wondered what had happened to the flat in Ruskin Park House and once Covid restrictions were removed, I sat down and wrote a letter, addressed to The Householder. I explained some of the story of my family's involvement with the flat and asked whether I might visit. I put it in the post and waited … and waited. Four weeks later there had been no reply. I decided on one more try, just in case the letter had not arrived, resending it with a covering note.

A few days later, my phone rang, an unfamiliar number flashing up on my screen. It was a young woman called Christina, who introduced herself as the girlfriend of Alex, who owned the flat. They had received my first letter but it had been a busy time and they'd not got round to answering – but yes, I'd be very welcome to visit the following Sunday. I put the phone down and did a little dance around the kitchen, excited but also a bit nervous about returning to Ruskin Park House.

But now I was staring up at the flat with a sense of anti-climax – maybe Christina and Alex had decided my visit was a bad idea after all? Then my phone rang. It was Christina, apologising – she'd had her phone on silent and missed my four calls. She rushed down to let me in and we made our way up to the second floor in the cramped lift, one of the few things that hadn't changed – apparently it still sometimes smelled of pee.

Along the familiar corridor – now carpeted – to the door. Christina produced a key and we were in. I had been bracing myself for a wave of emotion, perhaps even tears, but I felt … fine. Perhaps because the flat was almost unrecognisable. Gone was the battered furniture that took up far too much space and the threadbare living room carpet that had helped make it feel dusty, cramped and overheated.

A new wooden floor, minimal furniture and the windows and balcony door flung open gave the place a light, airy feel. They say that when you return to places you knew as a child they feel smaller but this felt like a bigger space. I wandered down the hall and peered into the galley kitchen where in December 1976, as I sat eating a boiled egg, my mother had handed me an envelope containing the news that I had won a place at Cambridge. I seem to remember her patting me on the shoulder but there was no great emotion from either of us at this momentous news which signalled that I would be escaping from Ruskin Park House.

Then I sat with Alex and Christina, showing them the few black and white photos I'd brought with me on an iPad – me as a small baby in my mother's arms looking out over the trees; me aged about four on the balcony blowing bubbles.

Then Alex explained how he had come to buy the flat during the pandemic in 2020 and had been just as delighted to move in as my mother and Stephen had been 65 years earlier. He, like Christina, worked in the arts and appeared to have a keen sensibility about architecture and firm ideas of what he wanted from his first home. He had seen another Ruskin

Park House flat featured on a website called The Modern House, aimed at design and architecture aficionados. It described the estate as 'a wonderful modernist development' and one of the few of its era 'to retain most of its period features, including Crittall windows, a laundry and exquisitely tended gardens'.

Really? I thought to myself. I'd grown up in a modernist masterpiece with white steel framed windows that had been period features, and I hadn't noticed? Yes, I did remember sitting in the basement laundry watching our weekly wash go round and trying to avoid the women who wanted to mother me, but as for exquisite gardens – well, a few municipal begonias was about it. Still, Alex's enthusiasm was genuine. 'It was the first and only flat that I saw,' he said.

But what did he like about it so much? I asked, trying to keep the tone of incredulity out of my voice.

'It is old and well built and was in a location that kind of had everything. It's next to a park, it's next to the hospital. It's next to the amenities and Camberwell – it's connected.'

As a cat meandered lazily down the hall and onto the balcony – Mum, no feline fan, would have shuddered – I reflected that he was right. The flat was desirable and he'd snapped up a bargain in the early days of the pandemic when the housing market briefly stuttered. He and Christina, a costume designer, had made it into a beautiful home with a calm, restful vibe.

But what a story the flat told of changing Britain. From the 1950s, when a woman with a teenage son arrived, probably to disapproving whispers – where's her husband? – which grew louder as she suddenly acquired another child without a man appearing on the scene. Through the 1960s, when the younger boy ends up with a place at a fee-paying school, funded by the local authority as part of a vast levelling up scheme. Then the 1970s, when he gradually wanders a little further afield into a London scarred by IRA bombs, while at home the power cuts of the three-day week see mother and son eating their evening fish fingers by candlelight. Through the giddy 1980s and 90s, the era of privatisation when the older residents died or sold up, replaced by young professionals, and into the twenty-first century, when Ruskin Park House is christened a modernist gem and my own children start looking at former council flats in places like Bermondsey, which my mother regarded as beyond the limits of civilisation.

When I picture the flat it is still in 1960s monochrome or the muddy Kodak Instamatic colours of the 1970s – somewhere to escape from, somewhere to be embarrassed about when the parents of friends with houses and gardens asked where I lived. But as I left Alex and Christina they looked relaxed and content in their perfect little home.

I had one last look around the estate, noticed that the playground where I once kept a nervous eye on rough kids who might push me off the roundabout had been replaced by a car park, and headed home. I felt relief. My journey into my past had been fine; I reckoned I had emerged emotionally unscathed. But there were questions and memories niggling at me. My mother had been dead for a quarter of a century; my father had died just a couple of years ago. I had two serious health conditions: a malignant tumour behind my left eye, which had been spotted in 2005 and had needed regular treatment ever since; and a recent diagnosis of Parkinson's disease. It felt like I needed to take stock of my life while there was still time.

I knew that if I wanted to understand my own story, how my parents came together and split apart, why my father disappeared from my life until I was 23, what had made my difficult, eccentric, cussed old mum such a captivating figure to him and others, and why the BBC had played such a big part in all of our lives, there was only one place to go. Back to that filing cabinet full of fading old letters.

CHAPTER 2

SYLVIA

Just before Christmas 1996, five months after my mother died, I was having a tearful moment in our kitchen in Ealing. The Christmas tree had been decorated and the turkey had been bought, but it had just hit me that Mum's annual visit wouldn't be happening. I do cry easily – at emotional scenes on TV or in films, when I heard I was to become a grandfather, even occasionally in the early days of my BBC career about work, to my great embarrassment. When I was a keen young producer on *Newsnight* in 1984, a report I was overseeing about the miners' strike fell apart on air, leaving the presenter floundering. Afterwards, a rather excitable programme editor bawled me out in front of the whole programme team and I felt the tears coming, managing to escape to the gents' loos in the nick of time. The next morning, I woke to the news of the IRA bomb at the Conservatives' Brighton conference hotel which had nearly killed Margaret Thatcher and when I arrived at the office in Lime Grove, I found the same programme editor in charge. 'Forget about yesterday,' he said, 'I want you to get involved in designing a model of the Grand Hotel for tonight.' And nothing more was said about my emotional moment.

But until that Christmas, I had hardly shed a tear over Mum. Perhaps it was because, since Stephen's sudden death in 1994, I had seen myself as head of the family, organising the funeral, finding out about the will and generally holding things together. But somehow the thought that I would no longer have to go over to Ruskin Park House to fetch her for Christmas lunch, sit through more meandering tales of her BBC career, increasingly incoherent with each new glass of whisky, and then drive her home again with the used wrapping paper she'd snaffled from the floor as we opened presents, got to me.

'She was always such a pain at Christmas,' I sniffled.

My wife, Diane, came over and gave me a hug. 'Sweetheart,' she said, 'she was a pain all year round.'

Which was true. She was difficult, demanding and increasingly eccentric. Whenever I want to remember how I thought about my mother in the last years of her life, I take a look at a photo from my wedding day. It was taken by the

official photographer and shows a group gathered on the steps of Ealing town hall in west London in April 1990. Diane and I have just emerged from the register office and are flanked by our parents. Diane's mum and dad, who met while serving on a gun site in London during the war and then brought up four children in a Lancashire mill town on meagre resources, are looking proud but slightly nervous. Diane says she remembers them feeling slightly socially awkward.

My father, a handsome man in his late fifties, has forsaken his usual open-toed sandals and corduroys for a sharp suit and tie, and a pair of highly polished shoes.

My mother, then 75, is wearing a dress I am pretty sure came from a charity shop and has a plaster above what looks like a black eye. Both Diane and I have broad smiles but I am clinging on to Sylvia's arm as if concerned that she might fall.

What is not clear from the photo is just how anxious I was that day. Not about getting married, or whether the wedding would go ahead smoothly. It was a modest affair – the ceremony at the register office followed by a lunch in a village hall in Richmond – because we were paying for it all ourselves, not wanting to trouble our parents for a contribution. No, the reason for my nerves was that this was the first – and it turned out the last – time that I saw my parents together in the same place. I had only met my father for the first time nine years earlier at the age of twenty-three, when I contacted him suggesting a meeting was overdue.

His wife, Maggie, and my three half-siblings were to join us later at the reception. My anxiety was not really about them, even though, like Diane's parents, I too felt a little awkward with my newfound family, who seemed rather posher than me, but about how my mother might behave. By then Sylvia was well into her batty old lady years – the Oxfam dress was an improvement on her usual wardrobe which relied heavily on those threadbare school shirts I had left behind when I moved out of our flat. She had always been superstitious, but now when I visited her in Ruskin Park House I would have to start by picking up any knives she had dropped on the floor. For her to retrieve them was apparently bad luck.

She had also become increasingly critical of every move I made in my life. When, four years earlier, I had given up my BBC staff producer job in London to chance my arm as a TV reporter on a contract in Cardiff, she had been appalled – I was throwing away my security in pursuit of a gamble that might not pay off. After a 40-year battle to bring up two sons on her own and give them the chance of some stability, she made it clear that my actions amounted to a betrayal.

As for my love life, it always seemed she only really approved of a girlfriend once we had split up. She was also remarkably prudish, embarrassed by any mention of anything even vaguely explicit on TV – 'This looks very boring,' she'd say, moving to switch channels – and seemingly disapproving of sex before marriage (funny, given my origins). A couple of weeks before the wedding, we had told her that Diane was expecting a baby in September and she had immediately jumped to the conclusion that this was why we were getting married. Pointing out that we had been engaged since the previous September cut no ice.

From the town hall, we were driven by my best man, David, a junior doctor proud of his black Ford Escort convertible, to the reception. David, already possessed of a soothing bedside manner, knew my mother and her eccentricities, and his next task was to keep an eye on her.

At the reception, a crowd of friends and family gathered outside in the spring sunshine for a glass of sparkling wine before a sit-down lunch of cold meat and salad. It was Grand National day and my family on my mother's side – lovely, warm, gossipy people who liked a flutter – promptly set about organising a sweepstake. Meanwhile, I watched nervously as my mother glided around with a drink in her hand, buttonholing people to deliver long anecdotes about her life at the BBC. (Or so I imagined – I learned later that another subject had been the merits of one of my previous girlfriends.) But fortunately, she mainly latched on to her Birmingham family, who nodded along tolerantly to stories they'd heard many times, rather than to my friends or, God forbid, my Cellan-Jones family. At lunch, she was seated between my new father-in-law, a quiet patient man who was deaf in the ear on her side, and my brother Stephen, well used to handling her. I tensed up when Diane used her speech to announce that she was keeping her maiden name and then, to roars of approval, that she was expecting a baby. I glanced along the table at my mother and saw her purse her lips momentarily before joining in the applause. After that, I relaxed and enjoyed myself and the day ended without any major embarrassment.

It strikes me, looking again at that picture, that embarrassment was the dominant emotion in my life from the age of around ten until my mother died. I was embarrassed about my home, about my lack of a father, about the clothes my mother chose for me, about the gloves on a piece of elastic running through the sleeves of my school blazer. Embarrassed by my brother, Stephen, who had a self-confidence I never had, dragging me backstage to meet actors he vaguely knew after a play – 'they won't want to meet me!' – or climbing over the fence at a smart golf club – 'we'll get caught!' – to play a few holes for free with me as reluctant caddie. But most of all I was embarrassed about my mother, what she would say, how she would behave.

Now in 2021, when I properly immersed myself in her letters for the first time, I realised that this recurring emotional spasm had warped my view of her. In 1996, a seed of doubt had been planted about my settled view of her when I skimmed through the story of her affair with my father. Twenty-five years later, as I dived deep into the picture the letters painted over the course of her adult life from the 1930s to the 1990s, I slowly began to understand just what a remarkable person she was.

It was the Imperial Airways air ticket to Le Touquet which immediately caught my eye as I was sorting through what I

thought of as the Sylvia Archive. It was dated 2nd September 1934, just a few days after her twentieth birthday, and on the cover was her name, Miss S. Parish. Inside were the stubs of vouchers which must have been used for what appeared to be a day trip to the fashionable resort on the French coast. It seemed the trip had started at London's Victoria station at 0900, with the flight from Croydon airport at 0945. The ticket cost £3 and 15 shillings and included entrance to the Le Touquet casino.

A little further research from me turned up an article in a 1934 copy of *Air Transport News*, which made it clear that these trips were Sunday excursions, begun in 1933:

The Sunday return trips to Le Touquet which were popular last year will again be operated by Imperial Airways, Ltd., this summer, and there is no doubt that the use of Handley Page 42s or Short Scylla-type aircraft, combined with the low fares charged and the excellent service, will make the Imperial excursions particularly popular.

The £3 15s fare might have included tea at the casino and dinner on the aircraft on the flight home, but whatever *Air Transport News* said it cannot have appeared cheap to a 20-year-old shorthand typist from Birmingham. And these were the very early days of leisure flights, so anyone climbing on board one of these noisy biplanes must have done so with a great sense of excitement and no little trepidation.

If a day trip to Le Touquet sounded more glamorous than anything I expected my mother to have been up to in her free time, so did my next two finds – invitations to Cambridge balls.

In December 1933, it was the university Medical Society ball, a grand affair with a menu in French, from *consommé royale en tasse*, through *mousseline de saumon* and *faisan en casserole*, to *trifle à l'Anglaise*. Six months later, she was at the First and Third Trinity Boat Clubs' ball, with another French menu and a separate dance card with a little pencil. One senses that this 19-year-old with auburn hair and a shy smile was not short of dance partners. Which young university man, I wondered, had invited her to balls, and had he also paid for her excursion to Le Touquet with Imperial Airways? None of this seemed to fit with the story I knew: a youthful social life mostly conducted in Midlands pubs, which swiftly led to a marriage to a rather dull man more than a decade her senior.

Sylvia Parish was born in Warwickshire in August 1914, the second of five children of Frank Cecil Parish – always known as Cecil in a family seemingly allergic to their first names – described on the birth certificate as a farmer, and his wife Alsie, née Jordan. In fact, the baby was christened Alsie Margaret Sylvia. My mother said the strange first name, which she never used, had been spotted on a circus poster by her grandmother. Perhaps she was just desperate for ideas, as her daughter Alsie was one of 17 children from a moderately prosperous Warwickshire farming family.

Sylvia's sister Cicely Joan, known as Joan, had been born in 1912, then Honor, later known by all as Bunty, came along in 1917, followed by Frank in 1918 and Derek in 1920. Joan, Sylvia and Bunty were extremely close throughout their lives, and later my two aunts played a vital role in my upbringing.

All five Parish children were born at Welford Hill, the 300-acre farm owned – or perhaps rented – by Cecil Parish. My mother made it sound idyllic, a home with a nursemaid for the children and a couple of farm labourers to do the heavy work. Among her papers I found a contemporary newspaper account of the 1910 wedding of Cecil and Alsie, which sounded like quite a grand affair. 'The presents were numerous and handsome' it declares. The bridegroom gave the bride a sapphire brooch and a bicycle; she gave him a gold signet ring and gold cufflinks. Among the gifts from guests were Venetian glass vases, a revolving soup tureen and a silver tea and coffee service.

But the Parish family was soon heading down the social scale. Sylvia talked to me with great affection about her 'dear old dad', while suggesting she had a more combative relationship with her mother. But she would also sigh and admit that an excessive devotion to the drink and the horses had been his downfall, seeing him slide from being a gentleman farmer to a farm labourer at the end of his life.

Some time around 1922, the Parishes left Welford Hill and farming, for reasons that remain unclear. Their departure followed the death of Sylvia's grandfather Frank Parish who is listed in the 1911 census as living at the farm with his two sons, Cecil and John. It is possible that Uncle John no longer wanted to carry on with the farm and so everybody moved on.

In any event, Sylvia always talked of Welford Hill as a lost childhood paradise. In a letter in the early 1950s, she described a visit to the farm with her friend Ethel:

We went up to see over our old home now owned by Stratford's ex-mayor. But it is not as Ethel and I remember it, the garden is uncared for, the creeper torn off the walls, and the farm buildings have been let go and are very ramshackle. It would upset Dad to see it like it is now I think. We remembered it as warm and comfortable with oil lamps and log fires and now it seems bleak with flickering Calor Gas (they haven't got the electric up the hill yet) – very bare. Maybe our memory paints it rose coloured, I don't know.

She had taken her young son Stephen – known for a while as Jo – on the visit:

I showed Jo the back stairs by the nursery where my nurse threw my doll down stairs and I screamed and tried to push her after it. We had a succession of nurses, some nice, some not, who left because of the too ardent attentions of Uncle John, who lived in the cottage. The nurses didn't object I don't think, but Mamma did.

One of Bunty's grandchildren got her to recount her childhood memories and, following her death at the age of 101, my cousin Susan, Bunty's oldest daughter, did some family research. From this account and some census details, Susan put together a picture of a family which, after years of early stability, was constantly on the move. She found that after the Parishes left Welford Hill they never seemed to stick anywhere for long through the 1920s.

Their first stop was the Welsh seaside resort of Borth, seven miles north of Aberystwyth on Cardigan Bay. Why they headed here is not clear, but soon they were back in the Midlands with a house in Malvern in Worcestershire. Then it was into

Birmingham and Handsworth, the site of inner city riots in the 1980s but at that time a quiet suburb. Next, outside the city to a bungalow in Barnt Green, and then off to Quinton in Warwickshire.

All this time, Bunty explained, both Joan and Sylvia were being sent to fee-paying schools. The older boy, Frank, had also begun a private school education. But at the next stop, a pub called The Talbot in the Worcestershire village of Knightwick, came the moment of crisis. Today, The Talbot describes itself as 'a traditional coaching inn which has been an institution of the local community since the fifteenth century', but I imagine that in the late 1920s, before the age of mass tourism, it was just a local drinking hole and far from a money-spinner.

What is more, running a pub cannot have been the best idea for a man with a taste for drink, and soon Cecil Parish was telling his wife that there was a problem. 'The money's all gone Alsie!' he is supposed to have said.

'Joan had to leave boarding school and Sylvia had to leave Worcester Girls Grammar, and they were both transferred to King Edward's Handsworth,' Bunty explained. 'Frank and Derek were sent to a boys' school. We came back to a different part of Handsworth.'

Their new home was a boarding house, mainly for men who were commercial travellers, and for the first time in Bunty's memory, she saw her father actually doing some work. At the farm he and his brother, Uncle John, had not needed to lift a finger. 'They paid people such terribly small wages – I think to do potato picking. The women got sixpence a day for a whole day's work.' But now Alsie, who was having to cook dinners for the commercial travellers, seemed to think it was time he pulled his weight and sent him out to do the food shopping each day.

Of all the five children, it seems Sylvia was the most affected by the constant upheaval, which by now meant that she and her two sisters were sharing a room for the first time. While Joan got her school certificate and then a job in a bank, and Bunty went as far as starting teacher training, my mother always used to tell me she had left school at 14 with no qualifications. She may have exaggerated her lack of education but what is clear is that there was a bust-up at home which led to her walking out some time in the early 1930s. It seems she had a row with her mother and found herself a bedsit in Birmingham. Her father, always the peacemaker, came to see her and said she could stay there as long as she promised to come home each week for Sunday lunch. Soon she was learning shorthand and typing and had got herself a job as a secretary.

But back to those Cambridge balls and the trip to Le Touquet. How did they happen, and who paid? There is no clue in the Sylvia Archive, although I thought I might find a hint when I came across an envelope postmarked Birmingham, September 1933, addressed in the most ornate copperplate to Sylvia Parish, Beach Hotel, Minehead in Somerset. It appears that the 19-year-old secretary had taken herself off on holiday.

But the letter was a disappointment. The handwriting is beautiful but the style is clumsy, repetitive and not a little creepy. Her correspondent appears to be an older admirer, styling himself Uncle Sam, although making it clear he is not a blood relative, and says he wishes he could be in Minehead too. It seems they are work colleagues, or at least he says he has been to her office many times and he is impatient for her return:

It seems quite dull without the one bright face to welcome me, however I shall be pleased to see you there again, I presume you will be there on Monday. Saunders is away on his holidays, I think Mr K will be at Shirley races on Monday so hope to have the pleasure of a little chat (this is of course private).

Why he wanted a private chat and why Sylvia hung on to this particular letter for more than 60 years was far from clear. There are some family rumours that she had a flirtation with a young man whose family ran Chad Valley, the Birmingham-based toy company, but 'Uncle Sam' was clearly not him.

After the Le Touquet ticket, there is a gap in the archive of a couple of years, and then in November 1936 comes the first letter from the man who was to play a key role in her story. It is written on the headed notepaper of the Merkham Trading Co. Ltd, purveyor of calculating machines and other office equipment with its headquarters at Bush House, London, and a branch in Paradise Street in Birmingham. It is from Leslie Rich, known to everyone as Richie, and is the first of many. In fact, there were more letters in the collection I found at Ruskin Park House from and to Richie than anyone else. Which was strange, in that she only spoke of him to me with exasperation and a certain disdain. This first one strikes what is to become a familiar note – it is an apology:

My dear,
I can't remember anything of last night – not even seeing you.

Judging from my condition this morning I must have been in a pretty hopeless state and I'm frightfully sorry.

I do hope after due consideration you'll decide to forgive me.

My hand is frightfully shaky so I don't suppose you'll be able to read this – I can't!!!
Love,
Richie

She obviously did forgive him but it seems he did not learn his lesson. Because next comes a note scrawled in capital letters on the pages for 24th, 25th and 26th December, torn out of a 1936 diary: 'DARLING I HAVE STAYED TOO LONG IN THIS PUB PLEASE COME AND RESCUE ME.'

From the following June, 1937, there is a rare typed letter (did he get a secretary at the Merkham Trading Co. to type it?) which strikes a saucier note:

Darling,
Herewith the bathing costume you so ardently desired. If you want any help getting into it please phone me. I have got a new film in my camera which is to be entirely devoted to pictures of your sweet self in this natty little costume.

Yours till the pubs close forever,
L Rich

Nothing then to suggest that the pub-loving amateur photographer was a great catch. She must have had plenty of admirers much younger than Richie, who at 35 was some 13 years older than her. Indeed, she used to talk wistfully to me of a boyfriend called Shadow, who sounded a lot more fun. But in August 1937, she and Richie were married at a

Birmingham register office. The marriage certificate describes her as a chartered accountant's secretary and Richie as a branch manager of a trading company.

Her father is listed as a licensed victualler, although by now he and Alsie seem to have moved on to The Bell in Alcester, with no greater success than at their previous pub. And now we have the very first letter in Sylvia's own hand. It is to her parents and comes from the Queen's Hotel in Burnham-on-Sea in Somerset, where she and Richie spent their honeymoon:

Dear Dad & Mother,
We arrived here quite safely yesterday. It didn't seem a long journey. Stopped at the Hop Pole at Tewkesbury and imbibed some more champagne.

We're having a lovely time – had two bathes – one in the pool last night & one in the sea this morning.
Hope you were allright yesterday – did you and Shadow go on the booze?

I liked your suit very much. Will you thank Joan for her letter and I'll write her later – also Bunty – the Roxy is working splendidly and is a Godsend.

We are both ever so happy and Richie is being absolutely sweet to me so in case you're worrying about that you needn't.

Please forgive scribble – in hurry
Love,
Sylvia

This letter, with the inevitable mentions of booze, seems to show a happy start to the marriage. But presumably Sylvia retrieved it from her parents' papers when they died, by which time she had long since separated from Richie amid some acrimony. In the early years, however, there is little hint of future discord, though I see everything through Richie's eyes – it was later that she began keeping carbon copies of the letters she wrote, as if determined to wrest control of her own narrative.

In the late 1930s they are living in the Edgbaston district of Birmingham and Richie is continuing to work for the Merkham office equipment company, travelling away from time to time as a salesman. After six years at the accountancy firm DM Saunders, Sylvia has given up work – 'I left this post on my marriage' she wrote later on several BBC job applications.

When Richie writes home he quickly resorts to baby talk – Sylvia is Baba and he is Dadda or Poppa, which may say something about how he sees the relationship. While Richie is away at an exhibition in Leicester with his friend and colleague George, Sylvia is given the task of finding them a better place to live in Birmingham than his bachelor flat.

His letters home are a tedious mixture of tales about pub visits and snooker games with excuses for not having written earlier because he is so busy – 'bad Dadda'. And it seems Sylvia's mission isn't going well: 'Sorry your house hunting has not been too successful but don't worry – we'll find something good sooner or later.'

Further letters, in which Richie and his colleagues are driving off for a drink at lunchtime or having a game of snooker – 'Dadda won!' – cannot have convinced Sylvia that her salesman husband was having a dreadful time. But my next find seemed to show that she was far from the meek little wife waiting at home. No, she was getting ready to serve her country in the skies above Britain.

A letter dated 19th April 1939 on the notepaper of the Midland Aero Club from its Castle Bromwich Flying Ground is addressed to Mrs S.M. Rich. It begins, confusingly, 'Dear Sir' but continues:

I am now pleased to advise you that your National Service Enrolment has been returned to me endorsed to the effect that you may be enrolled as a member of the Civil Air Guard and, under these circumstances, I am enclosing you herewith the necessary forms for your medical examination.

Enclosed is a form explaining that 'The Civil Air Guard has been formed for the purpose of giving facilities for flying training and practice at special rates to members of both sexes between the ages of 18 and 50 who are prepared in return to accept an obligation to serve their country at home in connection with aviation in the event of an emergency arriving from war or threat from war.'

Sylvia learned to drive only in her forties and was the most nervous motorist imaginable. She acquired a yellow Mini in the mid-1960s and drove it each day across London from Ruskin Park House to Television Centre, where it seems the first half hour of each day would be spent regaling her colleagues with the horrors of the journey. Apart from picking me up from the childminder in the evening, her only other regular use of the car was to take me on the 50-mile trip to stay with her sister Joan in Bedfordshire. For this, she applied to the AA for a route map. I would sit in the passenger seat reading out the instructions, accompanied by frequent cries of panic when she thought she had missed a turning or the dreaded Hyde Park Corner roundabout was approaching.

But when teased about her driving she always had a ready response – 'You may laugh at me now but I was training as a pilot and was about to make my first solo flight when the war broke out and all civilian planes were grounded.' I had never believed this story, such was her tendency to exaggerate to the point of telling downright lies. But it turned out to be true. And even if her application to join the Civil Guard went nowhere, the war was to change her life profoundly.

For so many women of her generation, the next six years would provide opportunities and freedoms they could never have imagined in peacetime.

CHAPTER 3

THE BBC

In October 2021, I left the BBC after a career which had started 40 years earlier with a 6-month contract as a researcher in the Leeds newsroom and culminated with 15 years in the most exciting job imaginable, as technology correspondent. My departure had been hurried along by the announcement that my post, along with those of 20 or so others working on technology coverage, was moving to Glasgow. For most of them it came as a terrible and bitterly resented upheaval, but for me, after the initial shock, it was good timing. I had been diagnosed with Parkinson's disease in 2019. So far, it had had little effect on my ability to work but it seemed sensible to leave Auntie's embrace and try a few other things while I was still reasonably fit.

So I left without any bitterness but determined to have a bloody good party. During the 18 months of the Covid-19 pandemic I had seen dozens of colleagues depart with a Zoom video call, a sad substitute for a real face-to-face celebration. Luckily, that autumn the virus was in retreat – though preparing to deal us a sideswipe with the Omicron variant at Christmas – and most restrictions had been lifted. So, at my own expense, I hired a big room in a conference centre just round the corner from Broadcasting House, ordered crates of wine and beer, and invited past and present colleagues to come and see me out of the door.

It was a fabulous evening, culminating in one of those leaving videos with which departing TV folks are both teased and celebrated. I'd made plenty of these myself over the previous years, including one with a scenario in which former business editor Jeff Randall, famously impatient with the perceived liberalism of the Corporation, had written a tell-all memoir called 'British Bolshevik Corporation'. I had suspected that something was afoot when Diane had asked me to unearth a sweary video of outtakes of me failing to master a self-parking car.

But the finished product was a masterpiece, with a running joke about my terrible driving (harsh but true) interspersed with tributes from everyone from Stephen Fry, the web creator Tim Berners-Lee and Prime Minister Boris Johnson (remember him?) to, best of all, the manager of my football club Brentford, the mighty Bees. Somehow they had coached Thomas Frank to say, 'Rory, less time with the Beeb, more time for the Bees!'

By the time I came to make a little speech to my friends and thank them for gifts, including a 1960 architectural plan of the new Television Centre, I was in a somewhat emotional state. But the main reason for that, as I explained to the crowd, was that for me, the BBC was, almost literally, family.

A few days earlier, the culture secretary, Nadine Dorries, in the latest of a series of attacks on what she perceived as the bias of the BBC, accused it of nepotism, saying it was staffed by people 'whose mum and dad worked there'. She must have been thinking of me, I joked, because my mother and father had both worked for the BBC for many years. But unlike Nadine Dorries' two daughters who had been employed in her Commons office, I had not got my first job at the BBC thanks to an intervention from a parent. At the time I applied for that researcher post in Leeds in 1981, my mother had been retired from the BBC for seven years. And as for my father ... I still hadn't met him.

It was in February 1941 that Sylvia Rich first went through the doors of the BBC's Bristol headquarters in Whiteladies Road, starting a relationship between the Corporation and my family that was to last 80 years. If she had found a different job, perhaps in another accountancy office, then she might possibly have stayed married to Mr Rich and I certainly would not be here today.

She was joining an institution yet to celebrate its twentieth birthday but which had quickly become an essential part of British life. All the more so in wartime, when its role as the principal provider of news, information and entertainment – closely overseen by the government and an army of censors – gave its employees a key role in the war effort.

The Bristol studios had opened in 1934 but the West Region's role was transformed in 1939 when war broke out and the BBC evacuated many of its departments from London. The BBC Symphony Orchestra, school and children's programmes, religion and variety teams were among those sent to Bristol, supposedly safe from German bombing raids. However, by the time Sylvia arrived the German bombers had turned their attention to Bristol, both a major port and the site of an important aircraft factory. What became known as the Bristol Blitz was at its height from November 1940 to April

1941, claiming nearly 1,300 lives and destroying over 80,000 houses.

Like a surprising number of her generation, Mum looked back on the war years with some nostalgia, speaking of a sense of community and shared purpose – not to mention evenings dancing with glamorous American officers ... When I was growing up in the 1960s and 70s, it still felt close, with bombsites yet to be cleared in parts of London and my comics full of Nazis shouting '*Achtung!*' and '*schweinhund Englander!*' as brave Tommies finished them off. Somehow, I never grasped the reality that life in Birmingham and then Bristol during the war was fraught with real danger, and she was probably at greater risk than her husband Richie, away at training camps in the English countryside.

I've struggled to work out how and why she came to leave the family home in Birmingham and end up at the BBC in Bristol. But a look at the register of all households conducted in September 1939 as a kind of stopgap census after war broke out provides a clue. When I first downloaded the entry from the National Archives all I noticed was that Leslie H. Rich was listed as manager of the Birmingham branch office of a firm selling calculating machines while Alsie M.S. Rich's occupation was simply 'unpaid domestic duties'. But returning for another look I noticed there was an additional column mentioning war effort activities such as air raid warden. It was blank for Richie – but for Sylvia the handwritten entry read 'Civil Air Guard (unpaid) Midland Aero Club'.

So she had told the official who called at the house in King's Norton a slightly tall tale – as she had not been allowed to take her first solo flight – but one which emphasised her desire to be part of the war effort.

If she wasn't going to be a pilot then maybe joining the BBC seemed almost as exciting and pivotal to the war effort. Among her papers is the first of many BBC contracts signed by my family: a job offer from the 'women staff administrator' at Bletchingdon Park in Oxfordshire. It concerns a post as 'Secretary-in-training in the General Office at our Bristol offices' and lists a series of terms and conditions beginning with this startling demand: 'You agree to devote the whole of your time and attention to the service of the Corporation.' She also had to promise not to disclose any 'information, processes or secret matters' which might come to her knowledge.

The remuneration was £3 10 shillings a week – about standard for a woman, though the average wage for a man was around £6 a week. On top of that was a 'cost of living bonus' of 5 shillings a week but the contract stated she would be 'billeted by the Corporation', for which there would be a billeting charge of 21 shillings a week. In other words, it was a bit like joining the army – she was told where she was going, had no choice over her accommodation and had to follow orders at all times.

Nevertheless, once inside the Whiteladies Road office it is clear that life was a lot more amusing than being in the army – or, it appeared, being stuck at home in Birmingham doing unpaid domestic duties. While there are very few letters from 1941 there are already hints that Sylvia was making an impression in audience research.

Most intriguing is a handwritten letter dated 10th October 1941 on BBC Bristol notepaper from a Robert Silvey. He begins 'Dear Mrs Rich' and appears to be so angry on her behalf that he feels like 'murdering somebody'. What about isn't clear but it sounds like some office gossip: 'It's the most damnably cruel thing I've come across in years – and, quite apart from that, it's so absolutely preposterous. As if anyone but a prurient-minded old spinster would "think things".' He says he doesn't know how this 'wretched thing' started but he's sure it didn't come from anyone in the department. (A Google search tells me that a Robert Spivey was a long-term member of BBC staff who pioneered audience research.)

He goes on to praise Sylvia's 'terrific guts' – what has happened? Aha, the mystery about the subject of the gossip seems to be solved when I turn the page and find that 'as the father of three girls' he understands the 'mysterious feelings of depression which mothers-in-anticipation have to put up with'.

In October, Sylvia must have been six months pregnant with Stephen who was born in January 1942. Presumably Richie must have had home leave in the spring just after she had started at the BBC, but perhaps someone 'prurient-minded' had suggested he was not the father? (Stephen turned out to be tall and skinny just like his father, so this was obviously nonsense.)

But in Richie's embarrassingly infantile letters to Sylvia in the last months of her pregnancy we see the first hints that her job at the Corporation will eventually drive them apart. Writing from St Anne's Hotel in Buxton where his Royal Artillery regiment appears to be billeted he starts:

First of all must apologise to posh BBC secretary wife for spelling 'Madeira' wrongly and thereby disgracing said P.B.B.C.S.W. in front of refined friends! After all am only a 'umble Dadda

Later, he asks about the arrangements for the arrival of 'Alfie', as they've taken to calling the baby she's carrying:

Urgently require to know by return what plans P.B.B.C.S.W. has made re birth of Alfie. Where is it taking place – have you reserved accommodation – if not, why not

In another letter, he complains that 'pooor Dadda' hasn't had a letter for nearly a week but 'suppose must expect it – Baba independent female with money of own and refined B.B.C. friends!'

Then more urgently as Sylvia sought to leave her billet and find a permanent home in Bristol:

If flats are so expensive, plus a nurse would be more than you could cope with, the extra expense cancels out any advantage you might gain by carrying on with the BBC.

The only thing seems to be to chuck the BBC job ...

I suppose Richie's views are pretty typical of a man of his background and era, but reading this barrage of nonsense, sometimes wheedling, at others just bossy, leaves me infuriated on Sylvia's behalf. But she did not chuck the job and it seems that she did make arrangements for the baby's birth – not in Bristol but in Birmingham, where her parents and her sisters Joan and Bunty lived. A telegram to the Bon Accord Nursing Home in Acocks Green reads: 'HEARTY CONGRATULATIONS FROM LISTENER RESEARCH PLEASE ENROL HIM AS A LOCAL CORRESPONDENT.'

If Stephen had not been a war baby, that would probably have been it for Sylvia's BBC career. If in peacetime women were not expected to carry on working after they married, then a mother with a young baby holding down a full-time office job would have been unthinkable. But Sylvia was soon back at work and making a move that was to mark the real beginning of her love affair with the Corporation. She moved out of listener research and into programme making, becoming a secretary in radio talks. During the war and afterwards, the Bristol talks department became the home to many of the leading cultural figures of the time. Poets such as John Betjeman and Dylan Thomas, and artists like John Piper were contracted to write and present talks on all manner of subjects, though while the war was on the censors were busy with their blue pencils erasing anything that might aid the enemy.

Among those employed in the talks department, as both a producer and broadcaster, was the poet and critic Geoffrey Grigson – then in his late thirties but with a reputation from before the war as a vociferous and cantankerous denouncer of anything he regarded as second-rate. It was as his secretary that Sylvia joined the department, so beginning a lifelong friendship with a man who was later to offer wise advice during the great crisis surrounding my birth, and who as my godfather – albeit a godless one – played an important role in both our lives.

In the flat at Ruskin Park House when I was growing up there were few books – a James Bond which I sneaked a look at in search of the racy bits, some Agatha Christies and editions of the *Reader's Digest*. But three or four books of poetry and memoirs by Geoffrey – never opened by me – stood out among the kind of middlebrow fare he would no doubt have despised.

When Sylvia talked of having left school at 14 and only

really got an education at the BBC, it was her four years in Geoffrey's office that seem to have provided a degree course – in literary appreciation but also in office politics, gossip and what today we would call banter but back then might have been described as a little light flirtation.

Sylvia's collection of letters is pretty thin during the wartime years – a couple from an American officer talking about taking her to dances, a postcard from the artist John Piper, the odd BBC memo about sending recordings of talks on the train to London to be played out from Broadcasting House. But in trying to piece together her life I have had two other very useful sources. A couple of weeks after Mum's funeral in 1996, I got a letter from Hilary Leeds, a lovely BBC colleague of hers from the Bristol days who used to send me presents every Christmas until I was around ten.

In 1943, aged 21, and very shy, Hilary arrived in the office Grigson shared with another producer and soon became friends with Sylvia, then a married woman with a one-year-old baby. Hilary kept a diary and her letter contained a transcript of all of the many entries which mention Sylvia – or Mrs Rich as she first called her – or Geoffrey Grigson. In her letter she described her impression of my mother:

Sylvia was slim and trim and fine boned with clear, almost translucent porcelain-skin, seductive cat-like eyes and lovely rich dark brown hair. She was always simply but smartly dressed and immaculately turned out – very attractive, very feminine. Though seemingly cool, calm and competent, she could be nervy and tense, and she suffered quite a lot from PMT – before the term was invented I dare say.

My other source is the BBC's written archive at Caversham. I had contacted the archive in the hope that among its vast collection I might find my mother's personnel file. The message came back that it had been destroyed, although they did still hold my father's file. I travelled to Caversham on a winter's day to read that and a pile of other documents I had ordered, including anything about the Bristol office during the war.

Hilary's diary makes clear what I had already gathered – that Grigson had a fearsome reputation as a somewhat irascible boss. You might think that Sylvia would have been intimidated but not a bit of it. By the time Hilary arrived, Mrs Rich had the air almost of a colleague rather than a subordinate of her boss, giving her views of scripts and arguing with him when she felt he was behaving badly.

Grigson's character comes across in his appearance on Radio 4's *Desert Island Discs*. His first job in the wartime BBC, he tells the presenter Roy Plomley, was at the monitoring service at Caversham, listening to enemy broadcasts and falling out with colleagues who he then sketched – 'I hated a lot of people in the monitoring service of the BBC, then I could draw them as the most appalling caricatures.'

Then he went to Bristol which was 'very pleasant ... one had a kind of kingdom which stretched from Southampton or thereabouts to Land's End.' And he says he was able to do quite decent drawings of people he liked. One of them turns up in Sylvia's papers, a caricature of a woman with a huge black hat and flowing hair sitting at a typewriter with a fierce expression. 'Dear Big Black hat,' reads the caption, asking her to please 'fill in the right amount for Musgrave and dispatch.'

Sylvia was soon confidently handling correspondence with contributing artists, from Walter de la Mare to John Betjeman, fixing up recording trips across the West Country and trying to keep her boss in check, all while looking after a toddler and having quite a boisterous social life. And all the time, the war was not just a distant event to be read about in the newspaper – with Bristol still a target for German bombs, air raid sirens would regularly send her to the shelter, whether at home or at work.

In the papers I found at the Caversham archive there were lengthy discussions about whether the Bristol studios should keep on operating during air raids. 'The studio has as far as possible been made safe against flying glass splinters, the most common cause of air raid casualties,' reads one memo. 'It is understood that many artists would prefer to be allowed to go on working through these air raid warnings as far as possible.'

Then again: 'The Corporation cannot ask staff to continue working during air raids otherwise than voluntarily and on this basis it has no legal liability. Staff contracts do not promise the grant of a year's salary in case of death or total disablement. This Grant is discretionary and ex gratia.'

A report marked 'TOP SECRET' says the War Ministry is concerned that if the sound of bombs is heard during a live transmission it could be of assistance to the enemy. The BBC seems impatient about this, asserting, 'We have come to the view that with a good scout outside there would be very little danger of transmitting a recognisable bomb explosion as the guns are all well outside this town. The chances of the enemy locating one of his raids by this method are at least 100 to 1 against.'

Overall, another report says, the BBC came through the Bristol Blitz relatively unscathed: 'The number of BBC personnel killed by enemy action at Bristol is one; the number injured 4, and the number bombed out 60.'

By 1943 when Hilary arrived in the office, bombing raids were much less frequent – the main danger of explosion came from Geoffrey Grigson. But her diary makes clear how shy she was: 'Mrs Rich said people thought I was standoffish and wouldn't mix. Absolutely flabbergasted. I only don't speak to them because I'm afraid to.'

We also get a glimpse of what it is like to be a working mother in the Second World War:

Mrs Rich brings her baby with her, as she says it's got a temp and the nursery won't have it. Told me later that she thought it has got whooping cough. Hope to goodness it hasn't as that would mean she would be away and I should have to cope with Eileen [her own producer] *and Geoffrey for a week!*

But soon 'Mrs Rich' becomes Sylvia and the older woman is introducing her to the delights of American officers:

Went down to the American Red Cross place. Sylvia and I went in together, and two officers came up and introduced themselves. Sylvia's captain turned out to be rather nice. Gave me a cheese sandwich and a Coca-Cola, (I think the first time I've had one!).

Later they are back again, with poor Hilary desperate not to be outshone:

Go to American Red Cross dance with Sylvia, calling at her flat for her first. An American came along who Sylvia seemed to know, and introduced to me as Captain Riesman. I liked the look of him, but was terrified he was going to ask Sylvia to dance and not me. Fortunately Linning came in and solved the situation by coming up and taking Sylvia away.

Linning appears later, with his 'uncouthness' remarked upon when he takes Sylvia to dinner.

There seems to have been a lot of drinking and dancing but it wasn't all fun – at one stage, baby Jo (Stephen's early nickname) and Sylvia were both in hospital for reasons that are unclear. She also came to rely more and more on Hilary and another BBC colleague for babysitting, even disappearing for two days on a work trip to London, having given the two women the key to her flat and left them to get on with it: 'Joy undressed him and I gave him his bottle, and then we put him to bed. He was very good.'

Soon, though, the war would be over and she would go back to being a respectable married woman, concentrating on looking after her husband and child. In Sylvia's sparsely filled little blue 1945 BBC diary the entry for 8th May reads simply 'V.E. Day'. Hilary's diary fleshes out the details:

Public holiday, but quite a lot of us were working – in fact we were pretty busy. Sylvia and I had a glass of sherry in the office and then we went over to the club for lunch, where most of the BBC had congregated, including Geoffrey and Eileen. Sylvia had Jo with her as the nursery is closed today.

Richie came home from what Sylvia always described as his cushy war and by October Hilary was organising a collection for her leaving present, amassing £2 14s 6d. At a 'large and cheerful gathering' a book token and a house plant were handed over. Sylvia left the BBC with this reference from Geoffrey Grigson, who was also departing:

MRS RICH worked for me as secretary in the talks department of the B.B.C. for several years.

She is an able shorthand typist, and a secretary of discretion and tact and a sense of order.

Her work at the B.B.C. demanded education and a wide knowledge and ability to handle people from all walks of life, from Fellows of the Royal Society to farmers and military censors. With all of them she was pleasant, sincere, and efficient.

She knew, as few other secretaries in the B.B.C., the complex administrative difficulties of wartime broadcasting: and it was possible to leave the management of the office to her with confidence.

She worked hard, well, and loyally and it was a bad day for my department in the B.B.C. when she left.

Within a year, however, she would be back – and soon afterwards her marriage to Richie would be over.

CHAPTER 4

STEPHEN

Some time in the late 1980s, I was driving Stephen, his wife Pat and my young nephew Sam home to west London from the airport when my patience finally snapped. I had agreed to keep an eye on their home in East Sheen while they were away on a holiday with Pat's family in Texas, and, as was his wont, Stephen had been continuously goading me about some failing on my part. I can't now remember what it was – maybe I had forgotten to reset the timer on the heating – but after 30 years of being bossed around I'd had enough. 'You are so bloody ungrateful,' I shouted from the driver's seat. There was a shocked silence in the car. Nobody said anything until Pat, ever the peacemaker, gently suggested we were all a bit tired and should try to chill out.

But something had changed in the dynamic between my adored but exasperating half-brother and me. From then on, in dark times as his marriage broke up, there seemed to be a reversal of roles, with him crying on my shoulder. Finally, he accepted that I had grown up.

For the first 23 years of my life Stephen was the nearest thing to a father I had. And in many ways he was wonderful.

When I arrived he was 16, fiercely devoted to Sylvia and adamant that he would look after her and me. He was as good as his word, sharing his bedroom with a noisy baby, changing my nappies and later driving me to nursery school in his battered old Riley, which needed to be cranked into action with a starting handle each morning.

In 1964 he left for the US to try to make his way in the theatre, he was 22 and I was just 6. I was heartbroken that this one constant male figure in my life had disappeared. But a constant stream of postcards and those blue aerogramme letters to Mum, always with a paragraph for me, painted a vivid technicolour picture of a land so much more exciting than the one he had left behind.

A few months after his departure on the *Queen Mary*, I went to stay for the first time with my godfather Geoffrey

Grigson and his wife Jane at their home in Wiltshire. Jane wrote to Stephen to compliment him on his parenting skills:

Geoffrey and I have been so touched by the way you care for Rory and bother about him; do keep this up even if you are in America for more than 2 years.

It means a great deal to him, and has evidently had a large part to play in making him such an enchanting little boy.

You and your mum have obviously done a marvellous job by him. Everybody took to him round here. He treasured the watch you gave him so much, and loved to tell me the time.

When he returned in 1966, having feared he could be drafted to fight in Vietnam, I was once again with the Grigsons for the Easter school holidays and he came to collect me. I sat in a window waiting with mounting excitement for the taxi bringing him from the station to appear, but when his reed-thin figure finally appeared I was tongue-tied and shy. He was still a loving presence in my life but was now more demanding, more critical of a sloppy piece of homework or what he saw as a lack of ambition on my part to get out of the flat, make new friends, learn to ride a bike, to break free.

Stephen brought me home to Ruskin Park House that Easter where, incredibly, he shared the one-bedroom flat with me and Mum for a few weeks. A letter from Sylvia to Jane Grigson after our return showed how much tension there must have been in the stuffy confines of number 147.

How did you think Stephen looked? I'm getting a bit more used to his thinness now but at first sight he looked very drawn and haggard. I suppose I'd expected him to have broadened out a bit with all those steaks and things he'd been having.

He seems very restless and tensed up and has SO much to say that I get glassy-eyed – sometimes I can only take so much America a little at a time!

Rory, she goes on, is:

... so excited and happy to have Stephen home again and I am too, though I'm anxious about his health and don't know how serious this ulcer business may be. He seems irritable and edgy, but I suppose it's a bit difficult for him to readjust and he's uncertain about what he's going to do next here but it's a bit exhausting to live with! I'm so used to Rory's calm tranquillity!

To my wider family over the coming years, it seemed remarkable that I retained that tranquillity as both my mother and my brother grew ever more neurotic and tempestuous. 'How come you have stayed so normal?' they used to ask with a smile. *Someone has to be*, I would think, silently. While I was not quite as untroubled a soul as they thought it was true that I somehow came through a sometimes difficult and lonely childhood to emerge as a calmer person than Stephen. But then I had not been at the centre of a constant battle between my parents over my upbringing.

*

Stephen – still called JoJo or Jo by his parents – had been five when in 1947 Sylvia left a letter for Richie on the table at their Bristol home:

My dear Richie,

I'm sorry to go like this, without giving you any warning, but I thought it over and it seemed the best way. We've said all there is to be said and more so many times, so it seemed useless to have another argument about it.

Jo is, of course, safely with me, and I think when you know the arrangements I have made for him you will agree that they will be very much for his good.

If you could ring me up tomorrow we could have lunch perhaps somewhere if you want to discuss things with me.

You know that I don't want to take Jo away from you but I feel sure that he is better with me while he is so young, especially now.

And I have tried to think of what would be best for him first, with the fact that I want him as the secondary consideration. About the fact that you and I personally both want him with us, wouldn't it be better if we could come to some arrangement whereby he spends say the next five years with me, and then five with you, with us both able to see as much of him as we could all through.

If you agree to come to some such arrangement I think it would be much the best. If not, then I suppose we shall just have to fight it out.

But feel sure that you must be able to see as well as I do that we couldn't have gone on as we have been doing much longer, both being unhappy, and seeing no prospect of anything else. You can't have liked this perpetual game of possum that we've been playing. It was only prolonging the agony.

Love,

Sylvia

P.S. I have taken a few things like blankets and linen for Jo – if you don't want me to have them, say so, and you can have them straight back. The suitcase that I borrowed I will return soon.

If Sylvia had expected calm acceptance from Richie then she did not know her husband, though I imagine she suspected they would not sort things out over a civilised lunch. Instead, he turned up at Stephen's primary school and tried to grab him from the playground. Sylvia then managed to spirit her child away to a boarding school in Devon for a few weeks, hoping that things would calm down. But Richie launched legal proceedings to try to obtain custody and Sylvia found herself a lawyer, Cecil Parker, who would represent her for the next 20 years as she battled over first Stephen's and then my future.

So what had gone wrong in her marriage? In a word, the BBC. Sylvia had left the Corporation in late 1945 but was still very much in touch with her wartime colleagues. One can imagine that life at home with a man who talked about his days with the civil service in India before they had met or his job selling office supplies seemed a little drab in comparison to the talks department at Whiteladies Road.

So when in December 1946 a job came up as secretary to Geoffrey Grigson's successor, Gilbert Phelps, she was back. What Richie thought of this we don't know. But given his evident contempt for the assortment of bohemian ne'er-do-wells who worked at the BBC and his suspicion during the war that they and what he described as his 'posh BBC secretary wife' were looking down on him, one can imagine he wasn't best pleased.

When, just six months later, Sylvia left home, her sister Joan thought she knew what was behind the breakup. Writing to her in June 1947, she has some sympathy for her discarded husband:

> *I get on all right with Richie but can quite see he can be completely irritating. In fact his anti BBC complex must be maddening and even gets me down! However, I think it is all because he blames the BBC for luring you away from him. If it were another MAN he would feel he could perhaps fight for you and win you back but he (I imagine) feels completely at a loss to hold his own against such an inanimate thief of your affections as your job and all it implies.*

Joan, who had married at 18, was bringing up two teenage daughters Anne and Dawn on her own. When they were still very young her husband Bert set off for work one morning and never returned. Now, in another letter, Joan warned Sylvia about the impact of the breakup on Stephen: 'Even Anne and Dawn – babies as they were when Bert went – always resent being as they say "without a proper father like the other girls".'

She goes on to make an impassioned plea to her sister to think again for the sake of her child:

> *What has Richie done to you that you should break up your home. Has he cheated and lied to you, is he*

unfaithful? Does he get heavily into debt, is he mean and unkind or neglectful or does he get drunk and knock hell out of you. My dear I've had all this and still say a woman needs a man in the house no matter what. If only to argue with so to speak and I don't mean physically!

Of course Mother says you have always been self sufficient but I can't believe you're really so different from the rest of us when your back hair is down!

But above all, she warns, Stephen must come first:

One thing you'll find as I have in the times in the future when you're blue or perhaps worried or lonely NOTHING will mean as much to you as your child – no man or job or pleasure can ever take the place of this mother love.

Reading these letters again over 75 years on, I am struck by how vivid and honest my aunt's letters were. By the time I knew her she was living in a Bedfordshire village with my Uncle Barry, the only reliable and kind man in a romantic life which seemed to veer from one disaster to another. I knew nothing of that, of course – to me she seemed the acme of respectability, a pillar of the Women's Institute and of the Mid-Bedfordshire Conservative Association. She once recruited me to help at the party's tombola stand at the village fete which, aged ten, I thought was tremendous fun.

But in 1947, Sylvia, however close she was to both Joan and Bunty, who also cautioned against leaving Richie, was going to go her own way. The battle for custody of Stephen was fierce, with Richie insinuating that there was another man in the picture and that Sylvia was an unfit mother.

'I've reviewed my past life pretty carefully and it all seems fairly innocent,' she wrote to an older friend, Edna. 'Of course I went out quite a bit during the war – but I should say nothing like so much as Richie did in America – and I always told him about everyone I went out with.' After a few years at various bases in England, Richie had been posted to Washington DC in some kind of military liaison job and Mum always suggested he'd had a 'high old time' far from the action.

Unsurprisingly, she won the custody case – no court was going to take a child away from its mother. From now on, it was going to be Sylvia and Stephen battling to make their way in the world.

If Sylvia was fierce in her devotion to her child – yes, that mother love that Joan talked about was strong – she was also ambitious to pursue her own career. That meant leaving Bristol for London and, after three years, and a number of failed attempts, she made it. And not only was she leaving a provincial city for the capital, she was departing radio for a brash new medium: television. In 1950, the year she turned 36, she was appointed secretary to Joan Gilbert, editor of *Picture Page*. A BBC memo shows this meant a pay rise from £5 15s 6d to £5 17s 6d a week.

A rise of two shillings was hardly going to be enough to cover the difference in the cost of living between Bristol and London and immediately two new battles began – to find an affordable home and to fight off renewed attempts by Richie to take Stephen away from her. He was furious that she had taken their son off to the fleshpots of London without consulting him and tried to challenge the custody order on the grounds of changed circumstances.

News of this latest confrontation came just as she was writing to Geoffrey Grigson about having taken his advice to screw up her courage and move to London. 'I've found an attic in Maida Vale for Jo and me,' she tells him. But then there is a postscript:

PS Bombshell. I've just had a phone call to say that two summonses are being issued against me in the light of changed circumstances for reconsideration of Jo's custody (because of the move).

R. came to see me last night and seemed to accept it – but apparently not.

What shall I do now – fight it, or give way and stay in Bristol and show I'm afraid, with a pistol at my head for the rest of my life? I don't know. I feel 90 per cent sure I should win but I'm so afraid of the other 10 per cent.

A couple of months later, in another letter to Grigson, it becomes clear that she did fight and win, with the help of some hardball tactics from her solicitor Cecil who made it clear to Richie's lawyer that his client could end up having to increase his weekly maintenance payment from £1 to 30 shillings a week.

He advised R. to withdraw, which apparently after much Indian Army gnashing of teeth he agreed to do. Anyway, my solicitor now says that I should have no further worry about this, as long as I stay in England, so I can start looking for a less expensive flat. Jo is very happy and loves it here.

The expensive flat was that attic in Maida Vale – in fact, a room in a boarding house in Randolph Crescent – and it was to be five years before she and Stephen managed to move on to the flat in Ruskin Park House when they finally came to the top of the council waiting list. Whenever I used to express even the mildest complaint about Ruskin Park House, Mum would tell me what a paradise it was compared to the grim room in Randolph Crescent, where there were mice (always a phobia of hers) and taking a bath meant a walk down the corridor to a freezing shared bathroom.

Whatever life was like at home in what was then an unfashionable part of London still scarred by bomb damage (today, the average house on Randolph Crescent sells for £4.5 million) it seems that both Sylvia and her son were determined to enjoy London. Friends took them that first summer to watch the Wightman Cup tennis tournament and then a Test match at Lord's. 'I had a nice doze and clapped at all the wrong moments,' wrote Sylvia, but for eight-year-old Stephen it started a lifelong passion for cricket. Nearly twenty years on, he would be taking me, at eight, to Lord's to my first cricket match, passing on the bug.

On the face of it, Sylvia and Stephen thrived, arriving just as the city was finally emerging from the war, with rationing coming to an end and the 1951 Festival of Britain reshaping the South Bank of the Thames and signalling a new era of architectural renewal. Sylvia's letters to Cecil Parker convey both her enjoyment of London and her struggle to make it work financially. In November 1950 she writes: 'Anyway you really ought to come to London to see Father Christmas and his reindeers dashing madly lit up all over Oxford Street.'

But then there is this: 'PS. Ponder in passing from time to time, and think if you know any rich landowners in London who might have an attic to let. I'm still paying double the rent I can afford.'

In the summer of 1952, she writes that they are still in Randolph Crescent:

But London is so fascinating – though not always easy. Mozart in that delightful Festival Hall – and always the river.

I'm going to Glyndebourne on Friday – with a borrowed evening dress, and some prop jewellery from TV Wardrobe. It was wonderful last year.

As I read these letters with their glimpses of a cultural and social life I never associated with my mother, my picture of her shifts again. I think back to our flat in the 1960s where the only music came from the radio and was limited to Tommy Steele singing 'Little White Bull' or the Adams Singers on the dismal *Sing Something Simple*. No Mozart then and certainly no Glyndebourne – as if Sylvia had decided such delights were now beyond us.

But it was Stephen's schooling which was a worry and such a big one that just weeks after arriving at her exciting new job in London she was contemplating throwing it all in and moving with her child to Devon. The lure was a job as secretary to the headmaster at Dartington and with it a place at the progressive private school. The idea had been suggested by Geoffrey Grigson, whose children attended the school, and other friends thought it was a practical solution to all her problems. But in a 1951 letter to Lindsay Fraser, a Scottish businessman with whom she appeared to have some kind of relationship (later he sent us a turkey through the post every Christmas), she makes it clear that London and the BBC have won:

I regard the BBC as my father and mother, and don't think I shall have the courage to break away from home so to speak. [Stephen] also feels tied to the BBC and would hate me to leave he says. I'm rather relieved as I was all prepared to burn my boats for him, and yet half terrified at the thought it might not work out.

His progress in a state school in Marylebone may have been patchy, and there were concerns that he was picking up a cockney accent, but Stephen appears to have been a strong and independent-minded character. In March 1951, aged nine, he received an acknowledgement of a letter he had sent to Winston Churchill. Who knows what Stephen had written to Britain's wartime leader, then leader of the opposition Conservative Party and preparing for a general election which would see him return to Downing Street as prime minister that autumn. Certainly he had a lifelong fascination with Churchill which he passed on to me. In the 1970s, he rushed to buy each volume of the official biography by Martin Gilbert, which I would then devour after he had read them.

And if history was happening around him he was determined to be a witness to it. One story from that time that my mother told me many times was of how in 1952 when George VI died, Stephen decided he wanted to go to the monarch's lying in state in Westminster Hall. The queue was immense – Wikipedia tells me more than 300,000 people passed by the coffin over three days, more than queued for the Queen's lying in state in 2022. But it seems a kindly policeman ushered Stephen to the front. Nevertheless, Sylvia told me, she was beside herself with worry waiting for him to come home. But what strikes me now is that a ten-year-old was allowed to travel across London on his own, especially one whose mother was later paranoid about her second son's safety out and about even when he was a teenager.

The Old Vic theatre, which had been badly damaged in the war, was getting back on its feet in the early 1950s and had for several years been the place to see productions of Shakespeare plays in repertory. The company included the young Richard Burton and Claire Bloom, along with a clutch of other names later to become familiar – Robert Hardy, Eric Porter, Virginia McKenna and John Neville. Another member of the company was Stephen Rich. At first, he understudied for an older child actor, Bunny May, then played roles such as Moth in *Love's Labour's Lost* and the young sons of Macbeth and Coriolanus.

It had all started when Sylvia sent him to classes at the Italia Conti drama school, mainly because she wanted the hint of cockney she had detected in his accent drummed out of him. But soon he was auditioning for roles as a child actor and then came an opportunity to join the Old Vic company. It was an early start on a career which would be an immense support to the family's fragile finances.

In 1954, afternoons and evenings at the theatre in Waterloo quickly became part of their routine, as Sylvia described to her old friend Ethel in a letter written from her BBC office:

I thought you might be interested to see that Jo is progressing in his 'career'! It's been rather hard going for him (and me) this month, as he's been there every night and two matinees a week, and only has permission from school provided homework and school attendance are up to standard. I try to help him but really the maths are quite beyond me. Have to go to the theatre every night to fetch him after the performance so I never get any housework done except on Sundays – it's hardly worth going the round journey from here home first and then on to the Old Vic. So I get a lot of extra work done at the office which is one good thing.

Stephen's first season at the Old Vic seems to have been a success: 'His accent still needs a lot of improving tho Miss C. [Conti] says his acting's splendid,' Sylvia wrote to Joan. There was talk of another season with less understudying as Bunny May was going off to do *Noddy in Toyland* on TV. The only issue was that his schools, first in Marylebone then later at Alleyn's in Dulwich, were none too keen on this distraction from his education, though they appeared mollified when Stephen hauled himself up from his position at the bottom of the class.

And there was someone else who was not convinced that it was a good idea for a child to be treading the boards. While Richie had lost the two custody battles, he continued to have access to Stephen, who travelled down to Southampton to stay in the boarding house where his father was living, the landlady putting up a camp bed in his room.

Sylvia's letters to Richie through the 1950s are surprisingly chatty. They often begin with arrangements for Stephen's visits but they are far from perfunctory, containing long descriptions of her life at work and home. But it is clear they didn't see eye to eye about his acting career. In 1954, after telling Richie what train to meet, she pleads with him to be more positive about the Old Vic:

He did a very good job of work on Saturday, with very little rehearsal and I felt very proud of him. He takes a lot of exercise during the course of the performance. I wish you would try and take a little interest in this, as it means so much to him.

It really is quite something, and I think neither of our families has ever achieved anything like this before – probably perhaps more by chance and luck, than actual achievement – but still something for him to remember with pleasure when he's perhaps a bank clerk or something later on. Don't spoil it for him by belittling it.

His reply can hardly have reassured Sylvia:

Don't think for one moment that I will belittle his efforts – on the contrary I'll demand a full account and applaud at all the right places! I wish you would send me a full account of the rehearsal and tell me about the 'exercise' he has to take.

It's just that I don't want him to get effeminate and affected and spoilt. Frankly, I'd rather see him mending a bike with oil up to his elbows, or making some weird contraption and probably dangerous which might (a) break down or (b) blow up or (c) fuse the lights!!! Get me? I want him to be a real honest to goodness BOY.

Sylvia did not give up on trying to convince Richie that acting was good for Stephen. Her next letter gave a rather brilliant and detailed summary of the plot of *Coriolanus* and tried to persuade Richie that the energetic staging would be good for their son's athletic stamina, among other things.

> *Jo's part in all this is of course in the mob scenes, of which there are a great many; the set in Rome consists mostly of terraces and lots of flights of steps, which the mob dash up and down, or creep depending on the state of emotion. This is where all the athletic exercise I mentioned comes in.*

It cannot have been easy for Stephen to maintain good relations with both parents and it is evident from a note at the end of this letter that his visits to Richie were not something he looked forward to:

> *Jo seems to like Southampton much better now that you've changed your digs. He says the previous ones had an 'atmosphere', he can't explain what he means, but I expect you will know. This was the first visit to Southampton that he has come back from saying he 'thoroughly enjoyed it all'. He says your present digs are much nicer in every way, so I was very glad.*

Richie was old-fashioned in his views, even for the 1950s. One incident casts a light on his views on race, though Sylvia does not come out of it much better. In 1953, with London packed with visitors in the run-up to the coronation of Queen

Elizabeth II, she writes to Bunty about the latest contretemps with her estranged husband.

Stephen had a week of his Easter holiday with Richie but was sent back earlier than planned because R's landlady took in some negroes much to R's wrath, and he didn't think Stephen should mix with them. Oddly, the same evening he came back, my landlady came up to see me and said she'd had difficulty in letting one of the flatlets and was thinking of taking coloured people, and would I mind as she felt that as the oldest tenant, I ought to be consulted. I found it difficult, as in principle I don't believe in colour bars, but in actual fact I wasn't at all keen (not having the courage of my convictions) and also thought R. would raise hell if he got to know.

These were the days when the Windrush generation was arriving in Britain from the West Indies to fill jobs where there were labour shortages and found signs in the windows of Notting Hill boarding houses reading 'no dogs, no Irish, no blacks'. Sylvia uses Richie's bigotry as an excuse for her own, though at least she seems aware of her hypocrisy and later seemed to me to be more tolerant in all sorts of ways than many of her generation.

I got a glimpse of what shaped Richie's view of the world from two of his photo albums which were passed on to his grandson, my nephew Sam, after the death of Stephen. They feature page after page of pictures from his time in India in the early 1930s – parties, golf games and hunting expeditions, with native servants standing respectfully in the background. Next, there are plenty of photos of Stephen from five onwards, on his own playing on a beach, or later as a teenager with Richie standing by his side, both dressed similarly in quite formal attire – tweedy jackets and shirts, open necked for Stephen, a tie for Richie. Interspersed with these is an endless series of photos of social gatherings, often featuring Richie and other chaps posing with pints outside pubs. A few women pop up from time to time, notably Sybil with whom he lived from the 1960s after finally accepting that his marriage to Sylvia was over. Of the mother of his child, the woman he plainly adored and hoped to win back for at least a decade after she left that letter on the table in Bristol, there is not a trace.

But right at the end of the two albums comes a surprise. A series of professionally shot photos depict a dapper elderly man in a trilby striking various poses, holding an umbrella or puffing on a pipe. With them is a printed card from Rose Enterprises, evidently an actors' agency, offering the services of Peter Rich, aged 70, height 6'1½", waist 31", complexion

Peter Rich

Age	70	70
Height	6'1½	1.86
Chest	38	96½
Waist	31	79
Hips	37	94
Inside leg	34	86
Shoe	8	40½
Collar	14½	37
Hat	6¾	56
Glove	8	8
Eyes	blue	
Hair	dark brown/grey	
Complexion	Healthy	
Drive	Yes	

Rose Enterprises,
54, Pembroke Road,
Kensington,
London, W. 8.

Phone-603-9394 and
603-8441

healthy, and able to drive. It seems that in the late 1970s – that 'aged 70' was definitely an approximation – with Stephen then moving from the theatre and TV to the Bar, his father had finally come round to the view that acting was neither effeminate nor affected and offered himself up for work as an extra.

I only met Richie once, when Stephen took me to the small council flat he and Sybil shared in St John's Wood when I was about ten. He shook my hand, gave me the once-over and said to Stephen, 'Poor little lad!' I suppose he meant that, unlike his son, I was growing up without the benefit of a father. But I could not help thinking then, as now, that I was getting the better end of the deal.

CHAPTER 5

CELLAN-JONES

'For God's sake, boy, you can't even pronounce your own name!' I was nine and a new teacher, Mr Llewellyn, was exasperated. He had gone round the class asking us to introduce ourselves and when he got to me he was not impressed with the way I said the Cellan in Cellan-Jones. I knew it was 'Kethlan' rather than 'Sellan' as most people seemed to assume, but Mr Llewellyn tried to coach me to put my tongue on the roof of my mouth to deliver a proper rolling 'llllllllan' sound. My efforts continued to disappoint him but I did not really care. Back then, I did not have any sense that I was Welsh.

Indeed, through my early years, I was convinced I was not a Cellan-Jones but a Rich or rather a Parish, part of a big, warm Midlands-based, very English family. After all, I had never met the man who had given me my complicated surname while my mother's relatives played a big part in my upbringing. The highlight of my year was escaping from Ruskin Park House for Christmas in Birmingham with Aunty Bunty, Uncle Bill and my three older cousins, Susan, Christine and Jane. On Christmas Eve, a day of almost unbearable excitement, we'd leave a mince pie and a tot of whisky outside my bedroom door for Father Christmas. Early the next morning I'd wake and feel the satisfying weight of the stocking – no sacks back then – at the foot of the bed. Inside, there would be a tangerine, a pair of socks, maybe a Dinky toy car and once a Puffin diary for 1968 inscribed 'TO RORY FROM FATHER CHRISTMAS' in handwriting which, bizarrely, resembled that of my mother.

I would creep downstairs to find Uncle Bill in his dressing gown inserting a giant turkey into the oven before returning to bed with a cup of tea for him and Bunty. The women would spend hours preparing roast potatoes, bread sauce, gravy, carrots and the dreaded Brussels sprouts, which I would try to avoid when they were passed to me. Aunty Sylvia, known to be a hopeless cook, would be given some simple task such as cutting an x into the base of the sprouts, which she executed at a snail's pace while keeping up a constant stream of chatter, often about people at the BBC nobody else knew or was interested in, while her sister and nieces smiled and rolled their eyes.

At around midday, Uncle Bill would round up any men in the house and drive them off to the pub for a couple of pints before lunch and sometimes, if I'd been good, I would go too – not into the pub, but left in the car with a Coca-Cola and a bag of crisps fetched by one of the adults.

The turkey would emerge from the oven rather overcooked at two o'clock, ready for Bill to carve and every adult to exclaim, 'Ooh, what a fine bird!'

At teatime, we would all gather around the giant Christmas tree in the sitting room for the handing out of presents, with Uncle Bill presiding as Santa and Mum, to my embarrassment, carefully retrieving and folding up sheets of wrapping paper to use again the following year. Then after tea, the drinks would come out – never wine, but bottled beer, sweet sherry or whisky, my mum's favourite tipple. And all the while, constant chatter in this most talkative of families – memories of Christmases past, of Sylvia and Bunty's dear departed dad and his love of a drink and the horses, of the lost paradise of Welford Hill, of their mother, Alsie Jordan, and of various Jordan cousins who had somehow stayed in farming and prospered while the Parishes ended up in cramped Birmingham houses.

What this all told me was that I belonged to a clan and a very English one. England was where I was born; English history – from 1066 to two world war victories – and English geography was what I was taught, once diligently tracing a map of all the English counties at my Aunty Joan's house and getting into trouble because the outline came through on her best dining-room table.

And above all, I was English when it came to sport. I was at Joan's home in the village of Silsoe in Bedfordshire during the latter stages of the 1966 World Cup. I wasn't allowed to stay up for the semi-final against Portugal but scoured their copy of the *Daily Mail* the morning after to read of the two goals scored by my hero Bobby Charlton. Then on the Saturday I squatted on the carpet in front of the television absorbed in the drama of the final against Germany – 'They think it's all over … it is now!' – while the adults, only mildly interested, chatted in the background. At home, when a little portable TV arrived in 1967, I would cheer on other English sporting stars – David Hemery in the Mexico Olympics, England's cricketers Colin Cowdrey and John Snow valiantly going down to defeat against the West Indies.

Nearly 60 years on, I am writing this from an Airbnb overlooking Cardigan Bay on the west coast of Wales. We've been coming to this part of the world for years, partly because it is beautiful but also because I like how very Welsh it is. This is an area where the language is still strong and you hear people speaking it as you pass them on the coastal path or wander around the Cardigan county show. As I waited for our lunch in the chip shop above the beach just now, the television was tuned to S4C's coverage of the National Eisteddfod, happening a few miles away.

Beyond a couple of phrases – *bore da*, *iechyd da* – I do not speak a word of Welsh but I like to hear it spoken. It is nice, too, to hear the Cellan in my name pronounced properly – something I only really learned to do as an adult.

Over the years, as I have heard English people mock the language, moan about its appearance on every road sign or, worse, tell that stupid apocryphal tale of arriving as strangers in a Welsh pub to find the boorish natives instantly switching from English to Welsh, I have become clear which side I am on. These days, when England play Wales at any sport it's Wales I cheer on. I go jogging – or rather ambling – in an old Welsh rugby shirt and when attending the Last Night of the Proms a few years ago and offered a choice of flags to wave, I chose the Welsh dragon.

This Welshness came on gradually, accelerating when at 28 I threw up my secure job as a producer in the London TV newsroom – to the despair of my mother – and moved to Cardiff to be a reporter on a two-year contract for *Wales Today*. My news editor appeared surprised to discover that his new reporter with the authentically Welsh name had an accent more south London than South Wales. The BBC

Llandaff newsroom had a corridor down the middle – on one side, English speaking journalists served the daily TV news programmes and the news bulletins on Radio Wales; on the other, they produced news in Welsh for Radio Cymru and the nightly *Newyddion* programme on S4C. The two sides shared resources such as camera crews and (mostly) got on well.

On my first couple of days, the new boy was sent out on the road with other reporters, either with a veteran correspondent from *Wales Today* or a keen as mustard young reporter from *Newyddion*. Stories ranged from the closure of Merthyr Tydfil's Playtex bra factory to a Cardiff house fire and my two tutors seemed massively self-assured, directing the crew – often a grumpy Scotsman and his affable young Welsh sound recordist – on the shots they wanted, then delivering a confident piece to camera in just a couple of takes. Then they got me to have a go, coaching me in how to stand, how to speak and how to imagine I was just explaining the story to a friend rather than ADDRESSING THE NATION. They watched as I stumbled through half a dozen takes before saying 'that'll do' and giving me a lift back to Broadcasting House in Llandaff.

Over the coming months, as I roamed my patch from Swansea in the west to Newport in the east and north to Brecon, my performance in front of the camera gradually improved. But I never achieved the fluency of my colleagues – people like Gail Foley, who I first encountered changing the nappy of her infant son on her desk in the *Wales Today* reporters' office.

My progress in Wales was not without its hiccups – viewers spotted the deficiencies in my pronunciation of difficult place names such as Machynlleth and Pontllanfraith, for a start. But, just five years after meeting my father for the first time, I was now in a place where my name seemed to fit me and was accepted rather than seen as an oddity. 'You got a connection with Cellan down near Lampeter?' people would ask. I didn't know and thought I should find out whether there was a family link, although it was many years later before I did anything about it. Once, when I was filming in Cardiff's giant University Hospital, an elderly patient asked me if I was related to the Swansea surgeon. When I confirmed that he was my grandfather, he replied, 'He took my leg off in 1938.' Which was something of a conversation stopper.

After nearly three years in Wales I returned to London where I have lived and worked ever since, but something had changed – I now felt at least half Welsh. For one thing, my best friend, a trainee doctor I had met at Cambridge, had come to live in my Cardiff house while he started a new job at University Hospital. He was to stay in Cardiff for the rest of his life, buying a big house on the fringes of the city, which gave me the excuse to return frequently to Wales. Plus, many of my friends in Welsh broadcasting also made their way to London, where we would meet up for what we described as 'Taffia dinners'. Having been treated by them as an Englishman in Cardiff, I was slowly upgraded to a Welshman back in my home town.

But the first stirrings of my Welsh identity had come much earlier, mainly because of rugby but also as I became aware of who the man was who had given me my surname. (Actually, that was my mother not my father, but we'll come to that later.) In the late 1960s and early 1970s, the Welsh rugby team was entering a golden era with the likes of J.P.R. Williams, Gareth Edwards, Barry John and Phil Bennett playing the game with great verve and flair. Even on our little black and white portable TV it was clear to me that the men in scarlet were superior beings. As I watched them run rings around dull old England I soon decided I was Welsh and a Cellan-Jones when it came to rugby.

When I was ten, that name, my name, started appearing in newspapers, all because of my father's role in a television phenomenon. *The Forsyte Saga*, an adaptation in 26 parts of the series of novels by John Galsworthy, was a hugely ambitious and expensive project for the BBC, the last major drama shot in black and white, with what was then a huge budget of £10,000 per episode. James Cellan Jones, then 36, directed the middle episodes featuring many of the most striking scenes, including one where Eric Porter as Soames rapes his wife Irene, played by Nyree Dawn Porter.

The series was first broadcast in 1967 on BBC2 but as only a small proportion of viewers had 625 line sets which could access the new channel, audiences were modest. The following year it was shown on BBC1 and gripped the nation, with 18 million watching the final episode and, if you believed the newspapers, vicars adjusting the time of evensong rather than lose their entire congregation. And it was now that my name, and the fact that it belonged to a person who was my father, who also worked at the BBC, became clearer to me.

My mum, still employed by the BBC drama department and presumably brushing past Jim in the corridor of TV Centre from time to time, was among those addicted. I was often shooed out of the living room if scenes got a little too adult but returned to watch the closing credits, waiting for 'Director James Cellan Jones' to roll up onto the tiny screen and wondering why he was missing the hyphen in the name I inscribed in my school books. A smile passed across my mother's face, but she said nothing and it was off to bed for me.

But my childminder, Mrs Gregory, knew about my father and spotted a short piece about him in the *Daily Mirror*. It featured a photo of the director sitting in an armchair with a dog on his lap, and when she showed it to me that was what I latched on to. 'He's got a dog!' I cried. I can't remember why I said this. While later in life I grew to love dogs, at that stage I was rather scared of them, and it was obvious that we were never going to have a pet at Ruskin Park House. Perhaps the truth is that, faced with this picture of the dad I had never met, I felt I had nothing to say – and the dog was my only conversational gambit.

Mrs Gregory shook her head, turned to her husband in his wheelchair and said, 'Ain't it a shame?' Which was strange – many of the children who passed through her crowded flat didn't have a single parent, let alone two, yet she seemed to feel that I was more deserving of sympathy.

At that stage, I did not feel in need of pity. While I did not have a father at home, and was beginning to be mildly embarrassed about that, I had my mother, my exciting and adored brother Stephen and his new wife Pat, lots of loving aunts, uncles and cousins, and my godparents the Grigsons. But gradually, as that Cellan Jones credit kept popping up at the end of more BBC dramas – *The Portrait of a Lady*, *The Roads to Freedom*, *The Golden Bowl* – I began to be more curious about the other unknown side of my family tree. I did not want to talk to my mother about this, though she always spoke warmly about my father, blaming others for how things had turned out. As I entered my teenage years I was ever less keen to discuss such sensitive matters with her.

She did once pull a trick, however, which still makes me wince with mortified embarrassment when I think about it 50 years later. It was on one of my regular trips with her to Television Centre and I must have been around 12 or 13. We were in the habit of descending from her fifth floor office in the 'doughnut' section of the building to the second floor, where you could tour the observation galleries for each studio. There, you could stand at a sheet of glass looking down at the sets for a drama or a sitcom or, if you were very lucky, the rehearsal for *Blue Peter*, while listening to the chatter from the control room over a loudspeaker – 'Let's go in a little tighter please, camera two ... where's Ronnie? We need him on set now or we'll hit the tea break and a massive overtime bill.' It was compelling and often Mum would leave me to wander for hours around the circular corridor, diving into each gallery behind some official tour.

But this time was different. 'Let's go and look in a control room,' she said. We came out of the lift on the first floor and she ushered me through a door with an illuminated sign saying 'On Air, No Entry'. 'We're not allowed in here, Mum!' I protested, but she brushed that aside.

Inside, it felt rather like the bridge of a battleship, with the director in command of a crew of lighting and sound operators and a cast of actors or presenters. We stood at the back looking at a row of heads silhouetted in front of banks of monitors. It seemed to be the recording of a drama but it was all a bit low-key, with the curly headed figure in the middle – obviously the director – sharing a joke with his assistant while they waited for the actors to take their places for the next scene. After a few minutes, Mum decided we'd seen enough but as we left she murmured beneath her breath, 'That was your father.'

My ears were burning and I felt almost physically sick as I imagined with horror what would have happened if he'd turned around and seen me standing there with Mum. Is that what she'd intended? What was she playing at? I could not get out of there quickly enough. Of course, I said nothing to her and tried to stop thinking about my dad. By this time, however, as a teenager getting to grips with my identity and increasingly impatient with the single parent I had, it was hard to shut out the insistent drumbeat of questions. What had happened between my mother and father, what kind of man was he – and why did he have so little interest in me?

It was to be many years before I got some answers and even longer before I learned much about the Cellan-Jones side of my family tree.

In 1931, as Sylvia was turning 17, Alan James Gwynne Cellan-Jones was born in Swansea in South Wales. His mother, Lavinia, was 39 – quite old back then for a first birth, and there were to be no more children. His father, Cecil, was 34 and a surgeon at Swansea General Hospital. Lavinia had been a sister at the hospital when the young doctor met her.

In 2021, as I explored the Cellan-Jones family tree, I was contacted out of the blue by a distant relative. Mary Evans emailed me from her home near Aberystwyth to tell me we shared a great-great-grandfather. Research by her daughter Sian, who worked for the National Library of Wales, had identified a Benjamin Jones, born in Carmarthenshire in 1842. Mary and Sian were descended from Benjamin and his first wife Jane, while my father and I were descendants of Evan, Benjamin's son by his second wife, Mary. Evan was the father of Cecil.

Sian had uncovered all sorts of colourful material from the National Library's archive of nineteenth-century Welsh newspapers. It seems that Benjamin, a blacksmith, had fallen out with his first wife's family over the ownership of a field and had been involved in a fist fight over the matter.

Armed with this information, I started searching various genealogy sites myself and found an entry in the 1881 Welsh census. There, in a property called Fountain in the village of Cellan, we find Benjamin, a 49-year-old blacksmith; Mary, 'smith's wife', aged 37; daughter Margaret from his first marriage, 20, described as 'farm servant indoor' and two sons, Evan aged 9 and Timothy, 3. At this stage, all of them are still just plain Jones, no Cellan.

It is Evan who changes that. In the 1891 census he is still listed at home in Cellan, aged 19, but is now described as a schoolmaster. But just six years later, his first son, Cecil John Cellan-Jones, is born in Newcastle upon Tyne. By then, he had been married to Sarah Davies, a Carmarthenshire woman five years his senior, for a couple of years.

Their child is the first to be christened Cellan-Jones, which seems strange because Evan and Sarah were to spend the rest of their lives in the north-east of England where there was not such a need to differentiate yourself from all the other Joneses. But maybe they wanted young Cecil and the children that followed, Katherine, Gwynne, Timothy and Alan, to have a name reminding them of their Welsh heritage.

Evan, the blacksmith's son, appears to have prospered in the north-east. The 1911 census finds him at 39 the headmaster of a secondary and technical school and living with Sarah, their four children and now two servants at their home in Consett in County Durham. Cecil is by now 13 and at school – though whether the same one where his father is head is not clear.

A decade on, they are all in the same house in the 1921 census. Evan is listed as the principal at the secondary school while 23-year-old Cecil is now a medical student. Two of his three siblings are going down a similar route – his 16-year-old brother Alan is already a dental student and at 21 his sister Katherine is another trainee doctor, quite a pioneer at a time when women were only just beginning to get a foothold in medicine. The exception is Katherine's twin brother Gwynne, listed on the census form as 'coke ovens apprentice' at the Consett Iron Co.

But it was from his obituary in the *British Medical Journal* in 1966 that I got the most detailed picture of my grandfather's life and what the eminent and lucrative career that he built himself must have meant for my father's upbringing. The *BMJ* said Cecil 'served during the First World War, and after demobilisation took up his medical studies at the universities of Edinburgh, Durham, and Vienna'. Quite a ritzy education for a schoolmaster's son who, we learn, 'obtained the Diploma of the University of Vienna in 1925, proceeding M.D. with gold medal in 1927'.

Then, after a short spell at Newcastle General Infirmary, he arrived in 1928 at Swansea General and Eye Hospital where he was to spend the rest of his career. He was 29 and it struck me that he arrived in Wales even less of a Welshman than I was when, nearly 60 years later, I started my job in Cardiff as a reporter on *Wales Today* at 28.

What was it that kept this ambitious young surgeon, educated in Durham, Edinburgh and Vienna, a veteran who had served in the war, in Wales for the rest of his life? Perhaps it was Lavinia, who he met on the wards in Swansea. She had been brought up in Devon, the daughter of a coastguard officer, and they married in 1929 at a church in Waterloo in London. In Cecil's obituary, his wife is described as 'a woman of great character' which feels like code. Certainly, she was the older and more dominant figure in the marriage – as we'll find out later in her correspondence with Sylvia. I never met either grandparent but Cecil sounds a lot more fun, if the *BMJ* is to be believed:

Cellan, as he was known, was one of the most popular men in Swansea, and was always ready to help anybody that he could. He had a great fund of humour, and was asked to innumerable functions, proving among other things to be an excellent after-dinner speaker.

The couple settled in Uplands, a prosperous area of Swansea with substantial Victorian villas, many with views over the Bristol Channel. The city, with its thriving port handling coal, steel and copper, had grown rapidly in the first three decades of the twentieth century, but then in the 1930s the Depression arrived, with a savage impact on jobs. Unemployment across South Wales topped 40 per cent in some places and in Swansea was described as 'horrifically high' by one local historian.

'Men were standing on the street corners not knowing what to do with themselves,' one woman remembered, looking back in 1985. Progress in improving the health of the population seemed to go into reverse. When an epidemic of scarlet fever broke out in South Wales in 1933, one chief medical officer was clear about the causes: 'The general want of resistance to attack and the severity of the symptoms were, in my opinion, due to general malnutrition among the children, the result of the unfortunate economic conditions in South Wales.'

But in Swansea it was a tale of two cities. For middle-class families like the Cellan-Joneses, who had a fast growing income as Cecil rose to the title of honorary surgeon at the hospital, life was very comfortable. According to a book about the redevelopment of Swansea after the war, a survey of the town in 1936 counted no fewer than ten department stores and a host of specialist shops and car showrooms, selling everything from fine art to corsets to Rolls-Royces. The grand old David Evans store even installed a replica Indian village, with staff from the subcontinent in traditional dress and a jungle replete with live monkeys.

One of those Rolls-Royce customers was the dynamic young surgeon Cecil Cellan-Jones. Apart from his father's taste for luxury cars and an unlikely story about the people of Llanelli going up a hill on evenings during the war to watch and cheer as the bombs fell on Swansea, Jim told me little about his childhood and, unlike Sylvia, left behind few letters. I learned a little more when in his seventies he wrote and self-published an autobiography. But *Forsyte and Hindsight* is mostly a string of anecdotes – 'a funny thing happened on the way to the studio' – without a lot of self-reflection and sailing lightly over his early years.

The first trace of him I can find in official records is the 1939 census which finds the Cellan-Jones household at 1 St James Gardens in Uplands. In that same extra column added during the war years where Sylvia's volunteer civil air guard post was recorded, Cecil is listed as 'ARP Emergency Medical Service' and Lavinia as 'Commandant, Civil Nursing Reserve'. When I travel to St James Gardens via Google Street View I find a pleasant tree-lined street of substantial Victorian houses around a square – until I arrive at number 1, which is now St James Court, a small development of modern homes. Was the house damaged by a bomb or just demolished in one of the many post-war development schemes which transformed Swansea, mostly for the worse?

What is clear is that the war had a major impact on the city and on the Cellan-Jones family. Aged 42 when it broke out, Cecil was too old to fight but he did join the Royal Army Medical Corps and spent considerable time in Malta, rising to the rank of lieutenant-colonel and being mentioned in despatches. Malta may have been safer than Swansea, which, as a key industrial city, like Bristol, faced devastating air raids. The raids started in 1940 and were at first sporadic but then in February 1941 came what was later dubbed the Swansea Blitz. Over three nights, German bombers rained destruction on the city, many of the bombs missing the docks and laying waste to the residential and shopping areas at the centre – 227 people were killed and around 400 injured, with approximately 11,000 properties damaged or destroyed.

It sounds as though this might have had a profound effect on young James, returning in the holidays to find whole streets gone, but apart from the jokey story about the people of Llanelli watching the fireworks display from on top of a hill he never mentioned the war. Perhaps that was because, as his autobiography reveals, he spent most of it at boarding school in Oxford. In 1940, with his father away with the army and his mother commanding the local Civil Nursing Reserve, he was sent to the Dragon School, a smart preparatory school which in Jim's words was 'an extraordinarily liberal establishment'. It took a small number of girls, and Antonia Pakenham, later the writer Lady Antonia Fraser, was one of them. She played Lady Macbeth in a school play, with Jim playing Ross. 'I was wildly in love with her,' he writes in his autobiography. 'I used to stand in the wings and sigh a lot.'

From there, he moved on in 1944 to Charterhouse, which he spoke of with no affection, though it was there that he befriended Frederic Raphael. In his autobiography, he describes, with great shame, how boys would mock Raphael for his Jewishness – and admits he joined in. Which makes it all the more remarkable that the two maintained a long personal and professional friendship. Raphael wrote a television play, *School Play*, which was a thinly disguised and unflattering portrait of Charterhouse. Jim directed this and also most of *Oxbridge Blues*, a 1984 TV series written by Raphael.

Growing up in Ruskin Park House, I had only the fuzziest sense of my father, informed by a few photos that my mother took to putting on the mantelpiece or bookshelf when I was in my teens. The first was one of him at a graduation ceremony outside the Cambridge Senate House, where I was to graduate in the presence of Mum and Stephen in 1981, just weeks before my first meeting with Jim. At a later stage, a snap of him in

military uniform with a beret appeared, along with a smudgy shot of a parachutist landing. A student and a soldier, both extraordinarily good-looking. My mother still gave away very little about their relationship but when she did speak about my dad it was always with affection and she never showed any bitterness towards him. Perhaps the photos were a way of seeding in my mind that one day I should make contact with him, but at that stage he was just another embarrassing subject that I did not want to discuss with Mum.

Many years later, it became easier for me to decode the two pictures when I read *Forsyte and Hindsight*. The graduation can't have been a happy event – Jim had just scraped a third, having put all of his energies into drama and the Footlights rather than the studies which were supposed to set him on the path to a career in medicine. Even worse, he had just told his father that he had no interest in becoming a doctor and instead had set his heart on a career in television. 'My poor father, a surgeon and an emotional Welshman, cried for five days without stopping,' he writes, which sounds, like many of his stories, both charming and a little far-fetched.

As for the photo of the young man in his beret, and the one of him parachuting, they had left me feeling slightly uneasy when I was shown them as a teenager. I could not imagine jumping out of a plane or serving in the Korean War, as Sylvia said Jim had. Was growing up without a father making me a bit soft? His memoir, however, made it clear that he had done his National Service in Korea after the war there was over. It turned out that the parachute jumping happened later when he joined the Territorial Army while awaiting the results of various BBC job applications. 'The five seconds before a parachute jump are one of the most terrifying moments in the world,' he writes. By the time I read that, I could think of more terrifying moments – like waiting to go into a BBC board or to hear the results of an MRI scan.

After Jim died in 2019, and I started thinking again about the big empty spaces in the picture I had built up of his life and his relationship with my mother and me, I realised that one organisation had very detailed records on all three of us. The BBC has always loved writing things down on paper – memos, scripts, internal reports, personnel records, all filed away, with much of it kept secret for years. George Orwell, who worked at the BBC from 1941 to 1943 when it was an essential weapon in the propaganda war, is thought to have taken inspiration from his experiences at the Corporation when writing *1984* a few years later.

In the BBC Written Archives at Caversham a vast mountain

of paper is stored. The archive – or at least its reading room – is kept somewhat incongruously in a small white bungalow a few hundred yards from Caversham Park, the great nineteenth-century pile which until 2018 was home to the monitoring service, first established during the war. (It was here that Geoffrey Grigson feuded with several colleagues before moving to the more agreeable surroundings of the talks department in Bristol.) On a chilly day in December 2021, I sat down at a desk next to a trolley laden with my chosen files, accompanied by instructions to make notes only in pencil and refrain from eating or making loud noises. I had enquired why Sylvia's file had been destroyed. 'That is not surprising or unusual,' the archivist had written to me, 'only a very small percentage of staff files were selected for permanent retention.' That small percentage, however, included my father's file – his staff record and some papers on his time as a freelance director had been retained. I was allowed to use my smartphone to take photos of documents but only if I disabled the artificial shutter noise.

My father's bulky file, the detailed history of his career at the BBC, began in 1955 with the kind of job application form I was to become familiar with many years later. Jim – or rather Mr A.J.G. Cellan-Jones – listed his education at the Dragon School, Charterhouse and St John's College, Cambridge. Then off to Korea for National Service. Under qualifications, degree in natural sciences (no mention it was a third), languages French (excellent) and German (good); referees a Swansea doctor (presumably a colleague of Cecil's) and his Cambridge tutor. 'State kind of post wanted – Outside Broadcast department.'

Then the key bit, which had me chewing my pen for hours – 'additional space for applicant'. In other words, give us some compelling reason why we should give you one of our highly prized if poorly paid jobs. This vast empty space was occupied by just two brief sentences.

Previous experience: almost nil except appeared on Cambridge Univ Footlights Television Show 1951

Sport (if required): Was captain of university swimming club 1952. Represented British Universities at Luxembourg 1951

It does not look like a knockout application but it seems to have worked. The next item is a letter to someone in the BBC administration department from Lavinia Cellan-Jones on headed notepaper from The Knoll, Uplands, Swansea:

Dear Sir,

My son is away from home at the moment and will be returning at the end of the week. I am sure he will be most anxious to accept your invitation and he will write to you on his return, with regard to the time and date of appointment.

Jim's memoir recounts that when he told his parents that he was not going to pursue a medical career, the forceful Lavinia had said 'this will kill your father', but now she seemed eager to propel him into the arms of the bunch of ne'er-do-wells in television.

October saw Jim interviewing in London with a BBC manager. The account in the Caversham file records a rave review:

After a short interview with Mr Cellan-Jones I was left with an extremely favourable impression. I found him to be pleasant in manner, well educated and having an alert mind. His army service has obviously given him experience of authority and handling of men, but at the same time this is in no way aggressive.

In view of his complete lack of experience I pointed out to him that in all probability, he could hope for nothing more than Call Boy. He readily agreed with this and felt it only logical that he should start at the bottom. He is very keen indeed and anxious to learn all he can.

'Call boy' was a job imported from the theatre, the dogsbody who would knock on the actors' dressing room doors to tell them they were due on stage – or in television, on set. It was indeed the very bottom of the ladder at a time when bright young things were being recruited from Oxbridge direct into jobs as trainee producers. But there was the possibility of a career path, from call boy to assistant floor manager to production assistant to producer – in the early days of television there was no separation between the roles of producer and director, which later came to mean the more creative job, in charge of the look of a programme.

Following this enthusiastic recommendation, Jim was offered a call boy job at £5 12s 6d a week. He had obviously impressed the BBC manager with his eagerness to start at the bottom – but there turned out to be a bit more to this story of success at first attempt in getting a foot in the door. At the top of the account of the interview was the line 'previously seen by Sir George Barnes'. As I burrowed deeper into the file I found a letter from Jim on 'The Knoll' notepaper thanking Sir George for seeing him and enclosing his BBC application form.

I knew all about George Barnes, who was director of television at the BBC from 1950 to 1956. Among Sylvia's letters, there are a clutch from him in the late 1940s and early 1950s when she worked for him. When the Queen came to visit Lime Grove in 1953, she knighted George in a studio and in a photo Sylvia can be seen smiling in the background.

What connection Jim had with Sir George that allowed him to approach him about a job at the BBC in 1955 is not clear, though it had nothing to do with Sylvia, who by then had moved on to the drama department. In November, Jim started his job as a call boy, working for the outside broadcast department and instantly making a good impression. In February 1956, a memo says he 'has made a very good start as Call Boy and is a keen and willing worker. As a result of recent

boards he has been given a chance as Holiday Relief A.F.M. [assistant floor manager] in the Drama department.'

By the summer, as he turned 25, he had been assigned to *Who Goes There!*, a comedy which would be broadcast live from Lime Grove on an August Sunday evening. And as a holiday relief AFM he would be working under someone else who'd had a temporary promotion. The studio manager was a Mrs Sylvia Rich.

CHAPTER 6

TELEVISION!

From a very early age, I was in love with television, all the more so because we did not have a set at home until a little black and white portable arrived in 1966. But regular trips to my mum's office told me that this was a world of enchantment, somewhere I wanted to be. When I was eight and my school set a handicraft challenge of constructing a model building, I took a cardboard box and turned it into a studio like those I had seen, with cameras made of blocks of polystyrene and lights strung across the top. (Sadly, my artistic limitations were such that I had to explain to the teacher exactly what it was.)

But I hardly dared dream that I would end up with a job on television. So I had to pinch myself when, one day in 1983, I arrived at what had always seemed to me the world's most glamorous workplace, Television Centre. After 18 months in regional TV in Leeds, I had won a job as a sub-editor in the London TV newsroom. It was a time of rapid expansion with the launch of Britain's first breakfast television programme, *Breakfast Time*, and my job involved a mix of working for the daily national news bulletins and doing night shifts preparing the breakfast news summaries. At first, the job proved deadly dull, mainly involving writing short intros which the newsreaders would rewrite. But then I wangled a transfer to the production team of *Newsnight* and things got a whole lot better. For one thing, *Newsnight* producers were actually encouraged to do some journalism – make phone calls, go out with camera crews and design complex graphic sequences to illustrate the rise of Gorbachev or the economics of the coal industry.

For another, the programme's offices were in Lime Grove, a building steeped in BBC history and quite possibly the place where the office love affair which produced me began, although I was not aware of that at the time. It was also the most ramshackle, run-down and mice-infested building imaginable, a confusing warren of endless corridors and staircases which appeared to lead nowhere, like something out of an Escher illustration. The only fast route from the *Newsnight* office to the studio several floors away was up an external fire escape, which saw young producers dashing up in rain or snow with a late script for the presenters. Escorting eminent guests to the set was another challenge. I once collected a famously dyspeptic Labour MP from reception and somehow led him into the wrong lift. We emerged in some far flung corner of the building apparently abandoned some years before. As the time for his interrogation approached and it became clear we were hopelessly lost, the MP became so enraged that I feared he might eat me.

But my year at Lime Grove on *Newsnight*, just three years into my BBC career, was a magical time when everything seemed to click. In the young 'on-the-day' team there was a sense of unified purpose – we worked three long days a week, arriving at ten each morning and leaving at midnight after the post-programme drinks. In between, we'd compete furiously at the editorial meeting to show we were on top of the news agenda – 'the 0400 World Service bulletin had an item on trouble brewing in Burma'. We got to work with journalists of the calibre of Charles Wheeler, Peter Snow and Joan Bakewell; see our story ideas rise to the top of the running order or, more likely, fall off the bottom; put together taped packages with skilled and apparently nerveless video editors, finishing them at the very last second, then stand at the back of the gallery, hoping that the piece would not fall off air and that maybe the programme editor would swivel round in her seat at the end and say 'nice work'.

At a time of fast changing technology with videotape replacing film and the first crude computer graphics coming into use, working in live television felt like walking across a tightrope knowing that you were bound to fall off at some stage. But if I felt that way in 1984, how much more dangerously exciting must television have seemed to Sylvia when she arrived in London in 1950, child in tow, to start her new job?

She had spent three years on her mission to move away from Bristol to the capital, applying for jobs ranging from secretary to the head of the overseas service – 'I am interested in European and World affairs, though I should like to know a lot more about them than I do at present' – to secretary to the director of spoken word, George Barnes. She did not get either job but Barnes wrote her an encouraging letter: 'I hope you will find other ways of promotion. Always let me know if I can help, and should you come to London again on business or pleasure I rely on you to look me up.'

He was as good as his word, putting Sylvia in touch with

the BBC's founder Lord Reith who had left the Corporation in 1938 but thought he might need a secretary to organise him in his various activities. There followed a surprisingly long three-way correspondence between Barnes, Reith and Sylvia.

'George' wrote to 'Sylvia' – no longer Mrs Rich – giving her a long reading list, starting with Reith's autobiography, followed by a menu of great novels, from Tolstoy to Henry James and Turgenev. Sylvia wrote to Lord Reith, complimenting him on his memoir, and the austere, decisive, short-tempered founder of the BBC wrote her a series of affable handwritten notes in which he hummed and hawed and havered about whether to give her a job before deciding he probably didn't need a secretary after all. It was a lucky escape – Reith did nothing particularly interesting or noteworthy after he left the BBC and told an interviewer in 1960 that he did not listen much to the radio and watched almost no television.

Instead, success came with an application to be secretary to Joan Gilbert, editor of what was almost certainly the kind of programme Lord Reith would have abhorred. *Picture Page*, the first television magazine programme, was the precursor of everything from *Nationwide* to *The One Show*.

It had gone on air surreptitiously nearly a month before the official launch of the BBC's television service in 1936 and had rapidly become the biggest hit among the tiny group of people with TV sets. In his book *The BBC: A People's History*, David Hendy describes *Picture Page* as 'a mix of the traditional variety show and appearances from an eclectic array of topical guests'.

When television returned in 1946 after the wartime shutdown, it was inevitable that *Picture Page* would be chosen as one of the flagship programmes. Joan Gilbert, who had been a reporter on the programme before the war, was appointed editor, but after months of auditions no suitable presenter could be found, so she stepped into that role too. By the time Sylvia arrived as secretary to this formidable woman, *Picture Page* had become the world's longest running TV programme, but its host was apparently dividing viewers, an article at the time describing her as 'effervescent but unpredictable'.

Television was still very much in its infancy in 1950. A 17-inch screen Murphy set cost £80 – far beyond the reach of the likes of Sylvia, for whom that would have amounted to three months' salary. What's more, the audience was concentrated around London and south-east England because government austerity measures capped BBC capital expenditure, meaning only one new transmitter could be built each year. It was only in October 1951 that television reached the north of England, when the Holme Moss transmitter was switched on. The high command of the BBC at Broadcasting House still viewed radio as the Corporation's main mission – even when I joined in the 1980s some radio old hands still referred to it as the 'senior service' – and that meant budgets for improving facilities at television's home, Alexandra Palace, were tight.

But all this must have bred an 'us against them' pioneering spirit in the small team which prepared, rehearsed and then broadcast live the hour-long weekly edition of *Picture Page* from Ally Pally. The programme involved assembling a cast of the most interesting and newsworthy people of the week and interviewing them live. On a TV history website Teletronic, Laurence Marcus described the weekly routine:

> *Each weekly edition of* Picture Page *was rehearsed from about 4.30pm on the day of transmission. Joan*

Gilbert and interviewer Leslie Mitchell met up with the personalities who were to appear in the show and, with the producer, they ran through the order and general presentation of the programme giving each guest the opportunity to become familiar with their surroundings as well as (this still being the early days of television) the paraphernalia in the television studio, so as not to feel intimidated during the live broadcast. Following a break of about thirty minutes Joan would then break the ice a little further by inviting everyone into her dressing room for a pre-transmission drink.

The process of choosing and booking guests sounds as though it was something of a logistical nightmare, with Joan Gilbert apt to change the running order as late as the night before transmission if something newsworthy came along. Presumably, the novelty of a visit to a television studio was an attraction for many guests – until you found yourself tongue-tied and sweaty under the lights, wondering why you had accepted that second glass of whisky from Miss Gilbert.

It was a very different world to the radio talks department in Bristol, but in a letter to Geoffrey Grigson Sylvia appeared to be having a whale of a time:

My new programme 'Picture Page' is fun, wild panic, and very bespattered with titles, and Ava Gardner's bullfighter, and decayed film stars and snakes, frogs and baby alligators. They wind their way out of innocent looking handbags while I'm doing things with scripts. All very shattering at first, but you get used to it.

A long, complex memo from 'secretary to Joan Gilbert' about transport arrangements for one edition gives a flavour of the programme. Four large cars have been ordered, along with a van and a 'brake' – presumably some kind of 1950s minibus. It all starts at 2.30pm with a car picking up Joan Gilbert and Sylvia Rich from the production offices near Baker Street and taking them to Alexandra Palace. Later, Sir Harry Brittain is collected from St James's Street, Charles Chilton from the Schoolboys' Exhibition at the Royal Horticultural Hall and Frank Owen from the *Daily Express*, and delivered to the studios. At 4.45pm, the brake is despatched to the Norwegian Embassy in Belgrave Square 'to collect ten Norwegians (in charge of Mrs. Temfjord)' and at 6pm the van goes to the show manager's office at Olympia to pick up dogs from the National Dog Show.

Until 1951 the technology was not available to record television programmes for posterity, so we cannot know whether this eclectic mix of politicians, writers, newspapermen, dogs and ten Norwegians added up to compelling viewing. But at 10pm the BBC ferried them all home again, with one car taking several guests plus Joan Gilbert and Sylvia Rich to the West End. Presumably from there Sylvia made her way to her shabby lodgings in Maida Vale, though who if anyone was looking after eight-year-old Stephen isn't clear.

There are only a few glimpses of her nine months at *Picture Page* in Sylvia's collection of letters and documents, but they certainly don't show her overawed by television or her job with a demanding boss. Take this memo to the complaints unit about a young viewer called Leila, who is cross because she thinks a female tortoise has been mistakenly identified as male on the programme:

Secretary to Joan Gilbert
Subject: How to tell the female tortoise
Miss Gilbert is still away on sick leave and I don't really want to bother her with this and don't feel she could help in any case. It doesn't seem worth ringing up the Zoo and digging up the particular keeper, who will not really remember what he said. I expect what happened was that the keeper either said it the right way round and Leila misheard him, or he just got mixed up. Could you think up one of those nice non-committal answers to send her? I'm sure she's right with all her overwhelming evidence. But why do they always want to prove it. I suppose when you're young and an ardent tortoise fan the shape of their breastplates is of world-shaking importance. Me, I went in for rabbits. Much simpler – and no possible room for doubt!

These days, the young viewer would be on to Ofcom like a shot, outraged that her complaint was not being taken seriously, but I find the breezy, funny, self-confident tone of Mum's memo immensely refreshing. I showed it to a friend who works in the BBC's complaints department and she hooted with laughter, especially at the line about 'one of those nice non-committal answers'. Seventy years on, the same approach is tried but often with less success.

But behind the breezy, self-confident front, this incredibly capable professional woman was struggling, with money a constant worry – 'I find my present high rent absolutely crippling, and am having to borrow in order to make ends meet, which I hate doing,' she wrote to a BBC personnel officer in November 1950. That meant she was already hunting for new jobs with better pay. She applied to be a trainee producer on *Children's Hour*, writing on her covering letter, 'I realise that I'm probably being over ambitious, but secretaries have been known to become producers and it seemed worth trying.'

Her application failed but in January 1951 she started a new job – as second of three secretaries to George Barnes, with whom she had shared an increasingly intimate correspondence since that first letter following an unsuccessful job interview. Sample note – 'My dear G., I think I was petulant last week. Very childish of me. Please forgive. It was only because I was so disappointed not to be able to see you.'

In 1950, Barnes had been plucked by the director general from his post as the high-minded director of the spoken word and made the first director – as opposed to controller – of television, a scrappy adolescent medium of which he had no experience. Like many BBC appointments over the decades, this baffled and angered staff who had thought the job would go to an executive who had been running the service with verve and enthusiasm. 'Barnes was humane, clever, high-minded, and supremely well-connected in Cambridge-Bloomsbury circles,' writes David Hendy. But insiders were certain he was not up to the job, one declaring, 'You might as well put Isaiah Berlin in charge of Chipperfield's Circus.'

Still, for Sylvia it meant a big office in Broadcasting House, often a chauffeur-driven car picking her up on the way to collect the director of television, and a substantial pay rise – by late 1951 she was earning over £8 a week. Sitting in on all of George Barnes's meetings to take the minutes, accompanying him on visits to Alexandra Palace, to the new Lime Grove Studios and to outside broadcasts of sporting events at Wembley, she must have had a panoramic view of television at a formative stage, two years before the 1953 coronation provided the lift-off moment.

Despite all this, and the pay rise, she was unsettled, still struggling to make ends meet in the capital and still wondering whether she ought to follow the advice of Geoffrey Grigson to chuck it in and go to work for the headmaster of Dartington School in Devon. She sought the views of everyone on this, even Director General Sir William Haley, as she told her sister Joan, describing her week:

Thursday a.m.
9.45 am. Looking, I hope, my best, go to D.G.'s sanctum to receive my ten year bonus (sadly depleted by deduction of £15 income tax, which I shall query like mad as it seems quite wrong to me) left with about £27 in all. Have cosy chat with Sir William, ask his advice about Dartington: he feels I should accept, as education is about the one thing one can give a child these days. Have ten minutes over my allotted time!
10.15 Have coffee in Light Programme Continuity suite with Alan Skempton – he advises accept Dartington.
10.30 Ditto with Gil. In canteen. Ditto.

Thankfully, she rejected the advice of all these men who wanted her to leave the BBC – otherwise I would not be here writing this. But soon she was looking for a new job. George Barnes decided that three secretaries was at least one too many and Sylvia had to move on, though the two stayed on good terms.

Her next move was to the department where she was to spend the rest of her career, to join a group of brilliant people pioneering a brand new art form, television drama. She joined it at a moment of crisis. There had been all sorts of arguments about how much drama should be broadcast and what form it should take. Was it aspiring to be a new form of cinema with the emphasis on the visual or was it the words that mattered and should it just be radio with pictures? When Val Gielgud, another great radio man and brother of the actor John, was appointed to run TV drama, it was no surprise that he favoured the latter approach. But in 1951 he gave up and returned to radio drama, shortly after writing this:

> ... it has not yet been possible for television drama in this country to achieve what can be called genuine professional status. The space has not been available. The gear has not been available. More important than anything else, the camera-rehearsal time has not been available.

But his replacement, Michael Barry, had more cinematic ambitions for television drama and soon things began to look up. New talent began to arrive in the department, people like the writer Nigel Kneale and the directors Rudolph Cartier and Alvin Rakoff. In 1953, Kneale and Cartier teamed up to make the groundbreaking sci-fi drama *The Quatermass Experiment*, the first example of a watercooler hit in British television. Its terrified audience grew from 3.4 million viewers at the beginning to over 5 million for the final episode of the six-part series. That must have been just about the entire population of television owners and, despite a horrendous technical cock-up in that final live episode, the drama lived long in viewers' memories with the word 'Quatermass' entering the language, signifying something scary but futuristic. A few years on, Sylvia described walking past the 'Quatermass' building site where the new Television Centre was taking shape.

This, then, was the world Sylvia entered in 1952, first as secretary to Michael Barry, then as assistant to the producers – soon to be renamed directors – who were shaping this new form of drama.

'I'm no longer on the august third floor at B.H. but at Lime Grove Studios working for television drama, and enjoying it immensely,' she wrote to Geoffrey Grigson in March. She was particularly enjoying her involvement in the casting process, though she observed it with her usual waspish eye:

We're spending today seeing, at 10 minute intervals, handsome young men who feel that their art is being outraged at being asked to play the back legs of a horse in 'The Taming of the Shrew' – 'I, who played the gloomy Dane at Sutton Coldfield ...'

Now, even though she may have had her views, it certainly wasn't her job to choose who would play the back legs of a horse, or more prominent roles. So what exactly did a director's assistant do? Fifteen years later, when I got glimpses of my mum's job, either through visits to Television Centre or from her constant stream of gossip about her colleagues which I tried to tune out, I thought I had a fair idea. It seemed to involve visits to the tea trolley which circled the Television Centre corridors at 11 and 3, a long gossipy lunch with her friends Mavis, Gwen and Betty in the waitress service restaurant in between, a few phone calls and then home at about 5.30. Every six weeks or so there would be a massive panic about 'my camera script' and then I would be packed off to Mrs Gregory's for the weekend of the studio recording and doubtless plenty of after-show drinks.

But that was unfair. By the late 1960s, she was assigned to the rather formulaic and unambitious '30 Minute Theatre' strand, one-off plays all confined to the studio with no location filming. That was my fault. My arrival and the need to arrange childcare had severely curbed her ambitions, making her job less interesting. As an older mother she was not going to make me a latchkey kid as she had done with eight-year-old Stephen when she started in television.

Over the years she did still work with some great directors – James MacTaggart, Ken Loach, the *Quatermass* man Rudolph Cartier (who once sent her some commemorative stamps from the 1972 Munich Olympics for me, somehow convinced that I was a dedicated philatelist). But as she aged, she became more conservative, sniffy about kitchen-sink dramas, bemoaning the fact that plays were no longer broadcast live and nostalgic for the 1950s 'when it was all so much more fun'. She may have been right – certainly that had been a time when talented young people could rise fast in television drama.

In 2021, I discovered that one of the few survivors of that era, a great director who had known both my mother and my father in the 1950s, lived not far from me. I called Alvin Rakoff, by then 94, and he invited me over to his Chiswick home for a chat. He remembered meeting Sylvia – 'she was Michael Barry's right-hand woman' – and it was Barry, as head of drama, who had given him his big break.

Rakoff had arrived from his native Canada in 1952 with a letter of introduction to the BBC and within four days had sold the drama department a script. 'Then I was given a big adaptation to do, a novel the BBC wanted adapted for a Sunday night play. Then from the end of 1953 they let me join the producers/directors course as a guest because, supposedly, I'm still going back to Canada.'

By 1954 he was a fully fledged producer/director, along with Rudolph Cartier, one of the few younger men in a department then dominated by theatre veterans. His first play was called *The Emperor Jones*: 'Michael Barry said he had £750 he could give me to do a production, which was low cost even then. The play was an hour and a half and live. And I did it and it was very successful and from then it exploded and Michael kept giving me a play every six or eight weeks.'

Meanwhile, Sylvia had been moving up the ladder, which went from assistant floor manager to floor manager and on to production assistant – and in 1956 came her big break, a chance to act up as a production assistant.

This was a vital role, effectively the director's operations manager, and it could be the springboard for a career in management or as a producer. That is what it was for Verity Lambert, who, in 1963, was BBC Drama's youngest producer and the only woman when she was given the job of launching a new sci-fi drama called *Doctor Who*.

Lambert had left school at 16 and started at the new ITV station ABC Weekend TV as secretary to the head of drama – sound familiar? She then moved into production and was a production assistant on *Armchair Theatre* in the late 1950s. One evening, there was an incident which illustrates the hair-raising nature of live television. Midway through a production called *Underground*, one of the actors collapsed and died. The show went on, with the director hurrying down to the studio floor to allocate the actor's remaining lines among the rest of the cast. Meanwhile, Verity Lambert rushed to the gallery and directed the cameras until he returned.

A couple of years earlier, Sylvia was bracing herself for her first production as PA, one which also promised a few challenges, though perhaps not on the same scale. She described them in a long and hilarious letter to her sister Bunty:

They told me they were giving me an easy half hour play to start with, but I find it has seven sets, instead of the usual full length play's two or three – which really means from my point of view tripling the complications and concertinaing an hour and a half's action or more into half an hour, which is much more difficult than doing a full length play on one or two sets.

Everything at the double, or rather the double-double, so to speak, with me dashing around the studio cueing madly (not my thing at all!). There are times when I am responsible for double-cueing at each end of the studio, which is physically impossible, then I have to relay cues to my stage manager and also to arrange that he will be on the right spot to be relayed to, apart from being responsible for organising the actors, the scene staff, the scenery, etc, and with a possible strike pending!

But that is just the beginning of her problems:

Added to all this they have thought up a really good one for me – I have to have an elephant in the studio too here, at our new Riverside studios which are a shade smaller than here.

I have the plan in which all the sets are drawn in

(including the elephant) and as far as I can see we shall have to get him in first and build the sets round him, and how he is to spend a penny I can't think – even then we have to have one set on trucks so that we can strike it to make room for setting a later one, and if I push one set forward to allow a passage to the door for the elephant it will throw all the other sets out of position.

And there is even a plan for a role for the 14-year-old child actor in the family:

The story is of a magician, so there are also magic tricks to be performed (which indeed there will be) and the latest is that Stephen in an Indian costume shall ride the elephant in (we have to make them both disappear!).

It is only a small part and she thinks Stephen will be sniffy about it, having done much bigger roles at the Old Vic. But he says he'd love to do it, even though it will be Corps night at his new school, Alleyn's, and he'll have to rush over to Hammersmith in his army kit to make it in time for the rehearsal before the live transmission later that night:

Anyway I said I'd warn the producer of the difficulties, and then he'd have to decide whether to take the risk of his not being there in time for rehearsal – but I expect they'd want to just see him do it once on rehearsal in costume, before actual transmission, and school won't give him an inch of time off and I've undertaken not to even ask.
I am told with great glee by all my friends (?) that

the last time they had an elephant (it happens rarely and obviously they saved it up for me) it was taken for a walk outside A.P. for hours and refused to co-operate, and then went back to the studio and did the lot – so I visualise a floating set.

I did my best yesterday by ordering a small baby elephant (female, because naturally they're reputed to behave better – except when 'in season', but I imagine that wouldn't count for a baby anyway), white or light for superimposition. But since the boy idea was added I shall have to check again, because I have a feeling they might not like to be ridden on, the older ones are trained to it, and I don't want to have to worry about S having trouble with his mount as well as all my other problems.

Beneath the relentlessly jolly tone of this letter I can detect real anxieties. By now, Sylvia was in her early forties, twice the age of Verity Lambert as she forged a similar path. TV drama was still very much a man's world, with very few women rising even as far as production assistant. And those that did faced other challenges:

On top of all this, as if it weren't enough, it will be bang in the midst of 'women's trying days', and also a new producer's first production with us. Norman [a drama department administrator] *and I had a long discussion yesterday as to what I was going to wear. Sheelagh, the only other girl doing this job, did the first show in skirts, and thereafter took to slacks, as she says when you're dashing around if your skirt catches on a cable it's apt to be left behind or is up over your head (and she's not a girl who usually would wear slacks, but says one is forced into it). I said to N. that too, perhaps I'd look tougher in slacks, and be less likely to be tolerated as a silly woman trying to do a man's job, but he said that he thought it was a mistake to think that discarding one's femininity would necessarily help, and it might indeed be an asset, as long as one knew one's job and didn't try to trade on it. And I haven't got any slacks fit to wear at the moment, and don't want to buy any specially – after all this may be my swan song!*

I always feel so awful at these times anyway that I mark little Xs in my diary as times to avoid doing anything at all if possible, social or too much work. Let alone strenuous physical exercise which this will be. And looking at the schedule I see that my next one is due to be the same dammit. Anyway everyone is calling this one my Baptism of Fire, so if I get through it I shall feel I can cope with the job in general.

So – what happened next? Did the elephant behave itself in the studio? Was Stephen chosen for the role and did he arrive in time from school? There was no further talk of the elephant play in Sylvia's letters. She had mentioned to Bunty that the play was on Friday 13th July – 'and you know how superstitious I am' – so I searched the *Radio Times* online archive for that evening's television listings. But the evening started with a western, followed by *The Lost World of the Kalahari* presented by Laurens van der Post and then *Joyce Grenfell Requests the Pleasure*. No sign of a 30-minute play involving a disappearing elephant. I even visited Riverside Studios in Hammersmith and spoke to their very helpful archivist but I could find no trace of the production.

Then, one evening, as I was trying to bring some order to my file marked 'Mum at the BBC', I came across a sheaf of job applications for permanent production assistant jobs. In one form in July 1956 she wrote this:

Since my last application for this post I have been working as holiday relief floor manager, and during the planning and production of Nom de Plume: 'Elephants Don't Disappear' I carried out the full duties of production assistant. I was told afterwards by the producer that I had done well and that I took control of the studio floor 'as if I had been doing so all my life', so I now feel confident about this side of the work, which I had not undertaken before.

Armed with the title, I went back to the *Radio Times* archive and found 'Elephants Don't Disappear' on Friday 31st August listed as 'a BBC telerecording' – one of the early productions to be recorded 'live' and then broadcast later. And running my finger down the cast, there among 'other parts played by' was Stephen Rich.

What I also found in the *Radio Times* archive was a reference to Sylvia's next play, *Who Goes There!*, a *Sunday Night Theatre* production, broadcast live this time on 5th August. It is a 90-minute comedy featuring an aristocratic family living in a grace-and-favour apartment in St James's Palace and an Irish chambermaid who comes to visit her fiancé Arthur, a Guardsman mounting sentry outside the palace. According to the *Radio Times*, the writer takes the 'hilarious clash of these two worlds … an intrinsically funny situation, stirred it into near-farce, and tempered it with wit and authenticity'. So authentic, in fact, that 'six real Guardsmen will be taking part in tonight's production and Bernard Breslaw [*sic*], who plays the part of Arthur, has been undergoing coaching by a Sergeant of the Irish Guards to bring him up to the impeccable standards required.'

Radio Times does not list the members of the production team but I know that it included both Sylvia Rich and James Cellan Jones. How? Because among her vast, messy collection of just about every document from her BBC career, I found this memo from Sylvia to a drama department administrator:

I feel I must write to say that James Cellan-Jones was invaluable as A.F.M. for 'Who Goes There'. It was hard to believe that this was his first full-length play. He was absolutely reliable at rehearsals, filming, and in the studio and showed willingness to undertake any task and to act on his own initiative.

His pleasant manner in dealing with artists and staff did much to keep our sometimes difficult rehearsals running smoothly and I was most grateful for his firm support.
(Sylvia Rich)

CHAPTER 7

A PLEASANT YOUNG MAN

Now, for the first time, I knew how my mother and father had met. They were on the crew of a BBC drama production in the summer of 1956 – Sylvia an acting floor manager in her early forties, Jim her assistant in his mid-twenties. Perhaps I could find out more in the dusty files of the BBC Written Archives at Caversham.

It was when I got back to August 1956 in Jim's files, just a year into his career, that I struck gold with the first and only mention of Sylvia. It came in a memo from a drama department administrator which had obviously been sparked by Sylvia's note about the pleasant young man who had been so helpful on *Who Goes There!*:

> *It was nice of Mrs Rich to think of writing the attached note about Cellan-Jones but we do not think it would be proper to put it on his personal file as she requests. Mrs. Rich is, after all, only a grade D Assistant herself and her commendation could carry no serious weight. If, however, the Producer or Production Assistant shares*

her view, a similar note from him would certainly be an
appropriate document for insertion in his personal file.

I nearly shouted out in triumph at my find, and then anger at the tone of the note, but, mindful of my two companions in the silent reading room, restricted myself to taking a few shots on my smartphone and whispering under my breath, 'You patronising bastard!' The memo reminded me of the *New Yorker* cartoon set in a boardroom, where the chairman is saying, 'That's an excellent suggestion, Miss Triggs. Perhaps one of the men would like to make it.' Sylvia may have been 'only a grade D assistant' but she was acting up as a production assistant, effectively Jim's boss on the play, and probably in the best place to judge his work.

Of course, what Mr Budd the administrator almost certainly did not know when he wrote the memo was that by then Mrs Rich and Mr Cellan Jones were in a relationship that went beyond the purely professional.

Then again, Mr Budd did not have access to the red Kayser stocking box I had discovered at Ruskin Park House. While it had offered no insights into their initial meetings at work, it did contain a seaside hotel receipt for two nights' bed and breakfast in April 1957, a clutch of love letters from Jim to Sylvia along with some poetry, and some long, intimate letters from Sylvia to her sister Joan and to a couple of old friends describing the progress of the affair.

The first of the love letters comes in an envelope postmarked Castle Douglas, 28th August 1956. Jim, who had just turned 25, presumably knew this was Sylvia's birthday but at that stage, I learned later, would have been unaware it was her 42nd.

'*Chere* Sylvie,' he begins. 'Here I am in fog-bound Celtic twilight and what an amusing household it is too.' He has driven up to the Scottish borders for what sounds like a rather posh house party and the coming out dance of someone called Sue, who appears to be an old family friend.

> *She has grown quite a lot since I saw her last and is madly in love with a Frenchman who is fighting in Algeria much to the disappointment of everybody ... I'm hoping to do some shooting at the end of the week but the grouse haven't been rising much.*

It all feels like a very different world from Sylvia's but it is clear that just three weeks after the transmission of *Who Goes There!* things have moved on rapidly between the two.

It was hell seeing you on Thursday and not being able to sweep you off into a corner and neck furiously – v. frustrating indeed. I am in an almost continuous state of breathless excitement which is very bad for the nerves. When the hell are you going to send me a picture of yourself – I don't want to forget what you look like – as if I could.

No child really wants to have to imagine their parents' sex life. And given my mother's prudishness about the whole subject of sex when I was a teenager, I found myself blushing scarlet when I first read this. And then it got worse:

I dread to think what will happen when I come back to London with all this load of piled-up frustration. As the soldier said, don't bother to paper the bedroom walls before I come over because all you'll be seeing is the ceiling.

Reading this made me not just embarrassed for me but for my father – what was he doing sharing this barrack room crudity with my mother? Then I reflected that he was very young, 25, and maybe after growing up as an only child and then spending years in an all-male boarding school, he was still learning to talk to women.

Then, perhaps aware that Sylvia is working and looking after her son in their small flat in London while he is hanging out with Scottish high society, he attempts to reassure her that he really isn't having a lot of fun without her:

Social life is a bit gay here – we're going to a v. respectable cocktail party on Wednesday and a v.v. respectable dance on Friday. I'm sorely afraid the shooting will be rather respectable too – not the rough sort I'm interested in.

This is where I finish and crawl off to eversoearlybed (unaccompanied)

You wait till I get home,

Luv,

Jim

Hardly the most tender or romantic of letters – at this early stage, the affair between the young man and older woman seems like a lusty summertime fling. Ten days later, he is away on duty as a military reservist with the Parachute Regiment and again feeling frustrated. Though getting up at five to do repeated parachute jumps seems to be proving a distraction.

I've done three today: we were just going up for a fourth when they said there was a lightning warning and made us come down again. We're going again tomorrow and I've got through it so far without taking any Oblivon. ˙ *We had a horrid Sergeant-Major despatching us who refused to shout GO! to Officers and said 'Any time you're ready, Sir, when you like', which threw me sideways. I trickled out of the balloon like half an oz. of saliva. There was a bit of a wind so we were jumping*

˙ Oblivon, a sedative available only on prescription and withdrawn in 1967, features several times in their letters, with Jim giving Sylvia a couple to take before her driving test.

rather low and as we were carrying equipment we came down rather fast. Still, at a quid a time, it's the fastest money I've ever earned.

Reading this, I remembered the photo of Jim landing in his parachute which appeared on our mantelpiece at Ruskin Park House when I was in my teens. Sylvia must have wanted to start sketching in a picture of my father for me, and a flattering one as an action man. It then becomes clear that Jim must have already been introduced to Stephen, then appearing on stage at the Old Vic – perhaps things had been going on even before *Who Goes There!.*

I've just read in the paper that tonight is Stephen's first night. It's too late to wish him luck but I do hope it goes well.

We are going on an airborne exercise for three days next week with an unpleasant drop somewhere and a lot of odd sleeping in ditches and things.

Sylvia for heaven's sake I shall be in such a locked up state by the end of this camp that you had better shake the mothballs out of your chastity belt even though parachuting is a celebrated anaphrodisiac.

See you in a fortnight you delicious creature.

Luv

Jim

Again, I felt embarrassed reading this but perhaps I was being a prude? After all, she had left these letters for me to read, knowing their contents. They were two grown-ups and while they might have faced disapproval from some quarters in those socially conservative times, it seems that her family and her colleagues were more sympathetic.

After all, it was nine years since she had left Richie and while it seems there had been a couple of male friends in the intervening years, none appeared to have lasted long. It was in letters to her sister Joan that she shared her most intimate secrets. The 'Aunty Joan' I knew was the very picture of respectability, but her romantic life had been anything but tranquil. After her husband had set off to work one morning and never come home, leaving her with her two young daughters, there followed a series of tempestuous relationships, notably with a Bill Bardsley, a drunk to whom she was briefly married and who was at one stage threatened with jail after their divorce because he'd fallen so far behind with his maintenance payments. In a 1953 letter to Sylvia – three years before Jim came on the scene – there's some prescient advice for my mother, who has apparently written about some fling:

> I am glad you enjoyed your few days of voluptuous ......
> I can only surmise the meaning of the six dots. You be
> careful, my girl – husband not available to blame for any
> 'mistake' now! (I gather he is fairly prolific too!) I have
> no lover in any sense of the word, married or single,
> at present, except of course Bill who remains in the
> background and is likely to stay there. He says he will
> always hope for a reconciliation – but I am merely sorry
> for him – no other feelings.

But a few years on, Sylvia was ready for a new romance. The early years in London had been full of worries – about money, about Stephen's schooling and about finding somewhere decent for them to live. Now things were looking up, mainly because after a five year wait for a council flat, they had finally moved into Ruskin Park House in the spring of 1955.

'Our great news this year is that we have at last found a home,' she wrote to her old Warwickshire friend Ethel later that year. 'We have been on various Council and agents' lists for years, and suddenly one of them bore fruit. It's one of the unsubsidised Council flats (they call them flats for "higher income groups" much to our amusement!).'

I struggle to recognise either the 'delightful' Ruskin Park on the doorstep or the idyllic picture she paints of the cramped flat, but it seems both she and Stephen found life in south London a vast improvement on Maida Vale:

So we wake in the morning to sunshine and birds singing and trees outside the window, and really feel quite poetic about it, it's such a contrast to our former dark and dreary place. The rent is high, but not more than we paid before for our so-called furnished flatlet, and I can manage it quite comfortably.

Furnishing it has been great fun, with Stephen using his Old Vic earnings to fit out his room, the one bedroom:

There's still a lot to do, but it's already very comfortable and looks quite gay and cheerful, and we shall add things bit by bit. It doesn't need a lot as it's quite small, labour saving and easy to run, big windows and a balcony and plenty of cupboards, and built in fires etc – and gardens, which are well kept, and a laundry downstairs which is bliss.

Buried deep in the letters I found under the dressing table at Ruskin Park House, though not in the collection preserved for me in the red box, was another clue to the change in her circumstances and mood brought about by the move to the flat, her own place without a prying landlady.

It is a letter dated 23rd June 1955 to Messrs Lambert Prorace, a company supplying contraceptive equipment whose products I can now find only in the Science Museum. She asks them to send her 'one latex cap pessary, size 75' and a tube of what she describes as 'contraceptaline jelly'. She encloses a postal order for 11 shillings 'which was the previous cost. But that was some time ago, so if the price has changed no doubt you will let me know.' Perhaps she is referring to a similar order I found from October 1945, when Richie was just home from the war.

But she is concerned that this parcel should not fall into the hands of 13-year-old Stephen: 'I should be grateful if you would post this on a Saturday as my son gets home from school before I return from work and may find it hard to resist a nice parcel! I am at home on Saturday mornings.'

Now, June 1955 was several months before Jim even joined the BBC, so either she had another lover or she was hoping that one would hove into view soon. Later, she will declare herself unimpressed by the quality of Messrs Lamberts Prorace's products …

In November 1956, a long gossipy letter to Joan gives the first detailed picture of the relationship with Jim from Sylvia's point of view. I say long – I've just done a count and it's over

3,500 words, and none of them dull, a series of vignettes of her work, her social life with Jim, her musings on whether there is a future in their relationship and her concerns about Stephen's jealousy.

She's just finished a difficult six weeks working on a production of *The Marie Celeste* with the same producer as on *Who Goes There!*, a tricky customer who found fault with everything she did:

> *I wasn't positive enough, had no grip on things, didn't fight for facilities with admin. And all I wanted was a nice soft job, with everyone happy and no battles, not strong enough in support, wanted to finish at 5.30 and go home, and so on.*

That was unfair – she was always prepared to work late. She says she had been growing in confidence in the new job but now feels completely undermined, just as there is an advertisement for a permanent promotion to production assistant:

> *I can't decide whether it's worth my applying for it or not in the circs. but probably shall, though without much hope as on the whole I think the bias is in favour of the men and perhaps rightly. Sheelagh is still the only woman appointed – though I and one other have been actually doing the job, on an acting basis, since last June.*

But fortunately, things are going much better in another area of her life: 'Have been seeing a lot of Jim, which is very good for me as he won't let me take all this too seriously.'

He had even come along on a day's location filming for *The Marie Celeste* out in the English Channel. The scene, which appears to break all modern health and safety rules, involves a lifeboat capsizing and pitching three actors who are non-swimmers into the sea: 'J, being a Cambridge swimming Blue, offered to come as life-saver, and had to dive in and rescue them.'

Apart from a little accident where one man got concussed – 'not too badly' – all apparently went well. But as Jim had driven Sylvia down from London to meet the crew one imagines that tongues were soon wagging about the relationship. Sylvia's letter goes on to paint a picture of a whole series of outings with her sociable young man about town:

Jim took me to see Under Milk Wood *which we thoroughly enjoyed, and went backstage to see an actress he knew afterwards, and have seen several good films, and been to one rather interesting bottle-party – at which I nearly lost him (though he says not). But it's bound to happen soon. There is a crooner, one Edna Savage, who keeps ringing him up trying to make a come-back.*

I've just looked up Edna Savage, a pop singer who had her only hit in 1956 with 'Arrivederci Darling', which made it to number 19 in the singles chart. She would have been 20 that year, while Jim was under the impression that Sylvia was in her mid-thirties. Small wonder, perhaps, that she was resigned to losing him.

There is then a very racy description of a dinner party at the Mayfair flat of Jim's cousin Pixie, who as far as I can work out is Pamela, the 22-year-old daughter of Cecil's brother Alan, a prosperous dentist.

She is fascinating, a nurse, and keeps up an endless and very entertaining flow of conversation. I just sat quietly and listened, as indeed we all did. I love hearing about J's family – they all seem to be the kind of characters one finds in Nancy Mitford novels.

It turns out to be 'a very amusing evening' but the chatter is 'very low at times' – by which she means plain smutty. One man's girlfriend hasn't come after a quarrel 'because he didn't leave it in for long enough' and there's much hilarity over a double entendre involving the word 'come'. Sylvia then reflects on Jim's attitude to sex:

Very extrovert is J – discusses all subjects, and chiefly this one, with absolutely no inhibitions, but at the same time with a lot of sensitivity and somehow it's never blush-making, but either amusing, or interesting. I've learnt far more from him, than in all the rest of my life in this context. And I thought I was the woman of the world who'd do any teaching – but far from it.

J says there ought to be a degree for outstanding merit and proficiency in sex relations and 'bags I practical examiner'. What it is to be young and enthusiastic!!

At some stages, she appears to be falling for him hard; at others, she seems resigned to the fact that sooner or later, when Jim finds someone closer to his age, it will all be over:

He's such a joy in all sorts of ways, mostly in taking my mind off my worries and letting me let off steam, always available when I want him, and does more or less anything I want to – so different from his predecessors, who were very casual, always late for appointments and did what they wanted to mostly! A great pity about all those years between us! But there's nothing I can do about it so must make hay while the sun shines.

But there was a more immediate problem at home in Ruskin Park House. Stephen, now 14, was extremely close to his mother and while in some ways independent for his age – after all, he'd travelled four years earlier alone to the lying in state of George VI – he was childishly possessive about Sylvia. One incident she describes to Joan reflects these two sides of his character. With his earnings from the Old Vic, he takes her out to a smart restaurant in Kensington:

I think the chicken must have been cooked in wine or something because he was very gay afterwards and said he felt as he imagined people would feel who'd had just enough drinks to be happy but not too many – usually he's very tired after evening outings. I'd had a sherry and later a glass of wine but he'd only had a sip of that. Then he said very wistfully, 'Mummy I do love taking you out, just us, and I know I'm not as entertaining as Jim, but I do hope you enjoyed it.' So I hastened to assure him that he was just as entertaining and so forth – because he's a bit sort of jealous, though he tried not to be, and says I know it's very nice for you having Jim around and of course you must go out sometimes I know, but I hope you won't too often.

Sylvia reassures herself that Stephen and Jim get on pretty well, that the couple don't go out on the town that often and spend several evenings a week at home at Ruskin Park House. She also thinks it is nice for Stephen to have a man about the place but admits that he is far too emotional and hopes he'll grow out of it soon.

The epic letter to her sister, probably typed at Lime Grove one evening, ends with an insight into her attitude to letter writing.

The building is being locked up around me so I'd better go. Told Stephen I'd be a bit late, as it's so difficult to write personal letters in the day time and I did want to write to you. (Have not much to do yet on this play but people keep coming and talking and I always write scandalous bits, or feel I might have, that might catch their eye, apart from it looking bad.)

But it's no use me trying to write letters by hand as I can't say all I want to and it takes ages and degenerates into a worse and worse scribble as time goes on and nobody can read it.

At this stage of my progress through the red box, I had reached some fairly settled conclusions about the relationship between my mother and father. She was the one who was bound to end up getting hurt; he was having a good time and liked her, but would not feel much compunction in ending it after a few more months. The next letter I found changed all that.

It was a note from Jim, scrawled on scraps of lined paper, undated apart from '9'o'clock on Monday' but almost certainly written in December 1956 as there is some mention of Christmas. They appear to have had some sort of row and Jim embarks on an emotional assessment of their relationship:

When I met you I thought you were pleasant and gentle, sweet and attractive and I liked you more than anyone I had met for a very long time. But I didn't fall in love with you for some time. Now, at this moment, it seems devastating that I can think of nothing else.

If this evening means that things have begun to come to an end, as I feel it does, then I am going to be very unhappy for a long time. The most stupid little things hurt me dreadfully. When you walked out this evening I was dreadfully hurt because you didn't turn and say goodbye to me. I can hear you saying, 'Well if you're as stupid and neurotic as that, it would be much better to pack the whole thing up' and that's why I shall have to try and hide what I feel.

He says this love affair has been a slow burner, in contrast to previous short-lived infatuations.

With you it happened differently – I know you, I know you quite well, I even know a little about you and of what goes on inside of you. I have no illusions. And that's why

127

it's going to hurt so much more when it finishes. Women are much tougher than men (than me, anyway) and you could break it off and then carry on and converse with me as though nothing had happened. I would show to everybody what I felt and give everything away.

You said something last night which showed how contemptuous you really feel for my rather morbid and self-pitying habit of analyzing everything and expressing everything I feel and why I feel it, so I shall do my best not to in future, whatever happens. I got hurt again when you said you wouldn't be able to see me at all during the week. I know you thought I only wanted to make love to you. But even driving you home occasionally – just catching a glimpse of you – does something for me.

He admits that he has been infuriatingly inquisitive about her past, asking endless questions about Desmond Hawkins – a Bristol producer and broadcaster who started the natural history unit – among a string of other BBC names – 'I feel jealous as hell every time you mention him or Grigson.'

He signs off, 'I love you most tenderly, Jim. Quarter to ten on Monday.'

But then there is another sheet marked '1.20 am Tuesday' and he seems to have pulled himself together: 'I'm really in a much more sensible frame of mind altogether now.' He has written some poetry to go with her Christmas presents – some of these verses are in the red box later – and that seems to have calmed him down. But he is still sending her both versions – neurotic Jim and tranquil Jim.

I didn't look through the letter again – if I did, I know it would so disgust me that I would tear it up. So I'm writing this in a rational state of mind and you can probably see the two sides of me in these two parts.

I'd always thought my mother was the neurotic one, moody and difficult, apt to burst into tears at the slightest excuse. But Jim's letter speaks of an almost adolescent fragility when it comes to matters of the heart. Or perhaps, like his father Cecil, he's just an emotional Welshman.

The next letter, dated 30th December, is from his parents' house in Swansea, where he'd spent Christmas, and he's mostly back to his cheerful, flirtatious self. He starts 'Angel', recounts his dreadful journey there in his rickety old car – 'the garage bloke said all four shock absorbers were nearly falling off' – and mentions Joan, who has apparently been very kind, giving him dinner and putting him up for the night (I'd love to know what my aunt, who could be waspish, thought of young Jim). But he is clearly missing Sylvia:

Life is a bit drab here without you. I am coming up on Thursday the 3rd & will be with you on Thursday night if that is all right. Will you write me a tiny note & say if it is. (That's just an excuse because I want a letter from you.) I have got a new rather sensitive film in my camera (the sort Butch described as 'good for bedroom stuff' in his inimitable way) and I am going to take masses and masses of pictures of you and have the good ones enlarged to enormous size. I am looking forward to seeing you again.

Then there's just a hint of the neurotic tone of his last letter:

I hope I'm not too bloody in the next few weeks when I come back: I really have been rather tiresome rather often recently. I've been reading DH Lawrence's poems these last two nights and I will bring them back as there are lots I want to read to you.

Lucky Sylvia ...

He ends by giving us a glimpse of high society Swansea social life in a household ruled by the formidable Lavinia:

My mum is having a thrash of some description tomorrow at lunchtime. As far as I can judge it seems to be 3 bottles of gin between 50 people so I don't suppose it will be what you might call madly gay. She expects everybody to be away by 1 o'clock so we can have lunch but I think that's a bit optimistic even on 1/17 2/3 of a bottle of gin per person.

It's very nice to see the old folks at home and all the rest of it but I am looking forward to seeing you again. It won't be long but I can only exist till then with superhuman patience.

Twelve 'loves' then snake their way back and forth across the page in rather charmingly teenage fashion, and all seems well again.

But then I find another letter from Sylvia to Joan in late January and it is clear there is tension at Ruskin Park House, not between Sylvia and Jim but between the couple and

Stephen, who had just turned 15. He made them promise not
to be away for more than two hours when they leave the flat to
pop over to the pub, but when they return late he's furious: '…
he stormed into his room and started to undress and refused
supper, and Jim said he gave him a murderous look when he
went in there and didn't speak.'

There is more drama in the morning when he awakes
weeping from a bad dream and doesn't want Sylvia to go to
work. Sylvia and Jim agree a strategy of keeping calm and
carrying on: '… the line is to be more casual and offhand and
not let him take things to heart so. Jim says he goes on at me
till I find myself apologising almost for no reason.'

But in the confined space of the one-bedroom flat it can't
have been easy to keep a lid on the tensions. And then another
character arrived on the scene, just to keep the pot boiling.
Stephen's father often drops by to take his son out, and this
time he finds Jim visiting too.

*Richie came over and met Jim for the first time – they
seemed to get on quite well together, though Jim found
it quite a strain I think. Was rather taken aback when R.
came into the kitchen (I'd left them having a drink and
talking) and said, 'You're not having an affair with that
young man are you?' Almost said Yes, and then thought
it would be unwise perhaps, so passed it off with a gay
laugh and 'Really, he's just a colleague', or words to that
effect, to which R. replied, 'Well, you'd be very silly if
you did' and left it at that.*

It is hard to believe that Jim, at 25, had much in common
with Richie, by now in his late fifties and hostile to the BBC

and anyone who worked for it. I imagine Jim brought up his status as a reservist with the Parachute Regiment as a better avenue for conversation than the latest goings-on in the drama department.

But Sylvia's attempt to convince Richie that there was nothing going on was never going to wash, as becomes clear when he leaves:

Richie came over and put his arm round me and whispered 'Don't go and make a fool of yourself over that young man!!' and I gave a gay laugh again and said 'I can't think what you mean', and he said 'I know you – and I'm not blind' – so then I decided that while he was on the way out I'd continue the discussion on another tack, so just said 'I want to talk to you, I'll walk downstairs with you'.

She had decided beforehand to ask him for a divorce – despite being separated for ten years they were still married. She had even taken an Oblivon to stiffen her resolve.

… on the way downstairs I asked him if he ever intended to divorce me, and he said he's never thought about it, and why, and who did I want to marry, and did I want to marry Jim, and I said of course not I just thought it would be a good thing to clear the situation up, and that I might want to marry again some day, though for years I thought I never would, but when Stephen was 'fledged' I might feel lonely and want some companionship – all of this is true, but he said I never know whether to

believe you or not (and went on to imply that I could lie with an innocent air, or dissemble if I preferred the word!).

She points out that he too might want to marry someone else, which turns out to be the wrong approach. This 'sent him up like a firecracker' – he says never, and he'd be as likely to go upstairs and shoot Stephen as to marry again. She tells Joan that she suspects that Richie thinks that she may go back to him, even just for companionship, once Stephen has left home. She is relieved that she has at least raised the question of divorce even though she does not feel optimistic that Richie will agree:

Jim and I talked about it that night, and wondered if I might be able to get a divorce in America, but it's all

too involved, and one would need lots of money, and anyway it'd probably only be valid there.

When I first read this it came as a surprise to me that Jim was discussing with Sylvia the possibility of her getting a divorce – which must have meant he was actively considering marrying her, and this was well before she revealed she was pregnant.

In his next letter, from Renfrewshire on 10th February, Jim appears both upbeat and very much in love. He has hidden her Valentine's card in his car which she is driving while he's away and wants to make sure first that she has found it, second that she hasn't smashed up the car yet. He is at work on a production in Scotland and paints a lively if not always flattering picture:

Glasgow is the ugliest town I have ever seen – it is almost unbelievably and frighteningly ugly.

Tenements are not just confined to the Gorbals. Almost the whole town is composed of them, and horribly sordid they are, too.

I went to Edinburgh yesterday – we are doing the transmission from the Gymnasium of a boys' club there – and what a contrast!

In Edinburgh, which is much more to his liking, he visits the flat of someone he describes as the youngest millionaire in Scotland:

It was laid out expressly and solely for the purpose of seduction as he carefully explained: 'This is where the damage is done.' We drank the finest whisky I have ever tasted out of the most beautiful Georgian rummers I have ever seen and he showed us his concealed lighting (3 circuits in different muted shades with a switchboard) – but no dimmers. Following my advice he is having a dimmer board installed next to the primary seduction couch (there is a secondary one with amber lighting next to the fumed oak bar for heavy drinking customers). He is having the plans drawn up for me and I am putting them by until I win the Pools.

His letter charges on into page five with news that he has bought a new suit made of Terylene: 'normally when buying clothes I don't give a damn for anyone's opinion least of all a woman's. But when buying this I kept wondering "Will Sylvia like it?"'

And after such a long letter, he demands something similar from her:

I shall expect reams of uninhibited prose back, not like your last letter, which read as if you had the Lord Chamberlain and the British Board of Film Censors looking over your left and right shoulders respectively.

He ends with some verse he has composed. What woman can resist poetry in a love letter, especially when he includes some reviews?

'Mr Cellan-Jones is a young man with an excess of emotion and an unhappy dearth of talent. He would do well to leave poetry to those intellectually fitted for it' – Geoffrey Grigson, 'New Verse'

'No true poet, who draws his inspiration from the birds and beasts and the wonderful activities of Nature around us can fail to be depressed at this young man's stark and unfeeling style' – Desmond Hawkins

'Mr Cellan-Jones tells me that this poem was written in ten minutes without a fair copy and with no corrections or crossings out. This I do not find difficult to believe' – Sylvia Rich

And he signs off:

Your faithful (so far)
adoring
heart-contracted
Sylvia-missing
humbly respectful
Jim
P.S. I love you and I miss you very much. Angel. Jim

A week later, he writes again from Edinburgh, thanking Sylvia for her 'divine' letter, so presumably her response to his demand for less inhibited prose has been met. There is, however, a hint of that moody Jim we saw before Christmas, coupled with an obsessive interest in her past love life:

If I'm in a gay mood when I come back I won't give a damn, but if I'm in one of those ghastly depressions I'll be probing and prying ... Also and I am sorry to introduce what you doubtless feel to be a sordid note, but I am suffering acutely from frustration.

Within the battered red box, the various items weren't perfectly ordered and I had to shuffle them around and try to work out the chronology. Suddenly the pieces of the puzzle began to fall into place. After that letter from Jim came the April receipt for two nights' bed and breakfast in Angmering-on-Sea, nine months before my birth.

First, I found a short note in a BBC internal envelope marked for Mrs S. Rich, 'to be called for at reception'. Sylvia has written on the envelope, obviously at a later date, 'June/July 57'. It is as if, years after the love affair which determined her future, if not my father's, she has a picture of me in her head as an adult, bent over the contents of the box, and wants to give me a helping hand as I try to make sense of it.

The note inside has a new urgency:

Dear S,
Thanks for the crinkle. Here's the car key. Take care and drive slowly + carefully + don't run out of petrol! Use my name as much as you like in the letter to R. Je t'aime et je suis toujours avec toi. *Ring me tomorrow.*
Love, Jimmy

This obviously needs decoding. Crinkle appears to be slang for money but what does he mean by the letter to R.? The R., I decide, can only mean Richie and the urgent tone of the note signals that some kind of crisis is under way.

All becomes clear in the next two documents in the box. First comes a copy of what feels like a hastily typed will dated 13th July 1957, Jim's twenty-sixth birthday.

This is the Last Will and Testament of me, Alan James Gwynne Cellan-Jones of The Knoll, Uplands Swansea. I hereby revoke all other wills or statements relating thereto and desire that after payment of my just debts all moneys owing to me, all moneys held in account in my name and all my personal chattels and possessions including my car (Reg. No. NWN 584) should be given without let or restraint to Alsie Margaret Sylvia Rich.

Then, dated 18th July, is a handwritten letter to Sylvia's solicitors in Bristol.

Dear Sir,
Mrs Rich has informed me that you are advising her on the conduct of a possible suit for divorce.
 This letter is to inform you that I have committed misconduct with Mrs Rich on a number of occasions and that I am the father of the child she expects.
 I admit full liability in both matters.
Yours faithfully,
AJ Cellan-Jones

So a huge moment for me – my first appearance in the letters. Sylvia is expecting a child and now has good grounds to seek a divorce from the husband she left back in 1947. It is a crisis but one which seems to have a resolution in sight. Jim is doing the decent thing – gladly, it seems – and sticking by her. Indeed, by coming forward as the father of her child and agreeing to be cited in a divorce he must be intending to marry her. This is no brief affair; my parents have been together for a year and they are obviously in love. Everything is going to turn out just fine.

CHAPTER 8

LAWYERS

Somehow, despite decades of silence between them, both of my parents reached the same conclusion about who was to blame for things going so badly wrong between them – and it wasn't either of them. When, during my teenage years, she began to open up a little about their relationship, Sylvia would sit with a glass of whisky, a slight smile playing across her lips, then say with a sigh, 'But for the lawyers, it might have all worked out OK.' As for my father, in the short couple of paragraphs about the affair in his memoir *Forsyte and Hindsight* – which he sent me for my approval – Jim said, 'The lawyers behaved badly, as they will, and made unpleasant threats.'

That had always sounded a little too convenient to me but yes, the sheer number and size of the bundles of legal documents Sylvia left behind suggests the lawyers had feasted on the misery behind the breakup and perhaps contributed to it. Then, 26 years after I had first found them, I sat down to actually read one particular set of papers and everything changed. They were in a BBC ring binder, on which Sylvia had written LEGAL – WILL, C-J AGREEMENT, DIVORCE.

When I first opened it back in 1996 I found on the top some dull correspondence from the mid-1960s about changes in the law on maintenance payments and closed it quickly. But when I returned to the file I realised it was in reverse chronological order and I needed to start from the back.

The first item, dated 25th June 1957, was a copy of a typed letter from Sylvia to Cecil Parker, the Bristol solicitor who had helped her in her various custody battles with Richie. This was the first in a correspondence stretching over seven months to January 1958, and far from being a dry procession of legal to-ings and fro-ings, it told a compelling tale of hope and despair, love and betrayal, which kept me absorbed for the rest of the afternoon. It felt like a novel – except that it was the real story of the bitter dispute surrounding my arrival in this world and who would take responsibility for my upbringing.

That first letter, written three months after Jim and Sylvia had spent the weekend in Angmering-on-Sea, is remarkably light-hearted – and frank – as if she is writing to a wise old friend rather than her lawyer.

'Here I am flying to you for help again!' she begins. She reminds Cecil Parker that she told him some time ago she might want to get married again and had asked whether he thought Richie might finally agree to a divorce:

> *Well I did ask him about it, but he didn't seem to intend to take any steps and getting tired of my prolonged chastity I fell from grace! So for the past year I have been having what I suppose is known as an 'affair' – a very discreet one, and very circumspect; as far as Stephen is concerned a 'friend of the family' relationship.*

140

She then goes into some detail about Stephen's resentment of the affair, and her concern that at 15 he is still fixated on his mother:

Another snag is that the man in question is a good many years younger than I am and I think Stephen almost feels it is like another son competing for my affection.

There is more about Stephen and his moods and you can almost hear Cecil asking what on earth this has to do with any legal advice. But then she drops her bombshell:

But, to come to the point, it seems that Fate has caught up with me, and either, without wishing to seem irreverent, there is such a thing as an immaculate conception, or the Family Planning Association is talking through its cap! Because I very much fear I'm pregnant.

Telling your lawyer about the failure of your contraceptive arrangements seems unconventional today, let alone in the 1950s. But finally she gets round to asking him for some professional advice:

If this is really so, though it is not confirmed by the doctor yet, and seems unbelievable, and in fact scientifically impossible, and I may just be worrying about a freak of nature. But if it is, and continues, Richie might then agree to divorce me, though I'm not sure, and presumably there would be no disputing the 'grounds'. And what I want to ask you is, if he does, how long would it take, and could it be got through in time for me to be made an honest woman of!! I know that's ungrammatical but you know what I mean. I don't specially mind for myself, but it would seem the best thing to do for the child, and for Stephen too really. I don't know how I shall be able to tell him, and if he really set his face against the idea of my marrying again I wouldn't, but I think perhaps it might be the best thing to appeal to his better nature on behalf of the child, and say it was fairest from that point of view.

However, it's all still a question of lots of 'ifs'. And I wanted to write to you to find out what the position would be about time taken and so on 'if'. And would it cost an awful lot. We would I suppose be eligible for some legal aid, as neither of us have any income to speak of. However, it may be that I'm crossing bridges before I come to them, and it's all nothing. But I would like to hear from you.

Having got to the point you might think she would stop there but not a bit of it. There is another page of quite entertaining meanderings – about Stephen's theatrical activities and her hopes he won't have to do National Service, about her adventures learning to drive and how nice and empty London's roads were during petrol rationing – before she returns to the matter in hand. After the earlier light-hearted tone, a darker note begins to intrude.

If I hadn't been so ultra careful I'd have felt I deserved this. But really I don't – and I had so many gorgeous plans for the future when Stephen was properly launched, and at last I might have some money to

*spare – holidays abroad, perhaps a little car – all sorts
of pipe dreams, and now I see them all disappearing ...
and the thought of all those nappies again, at my age!
Really it's most unfair.*

She is beginning to realise that having a baby at 43 will
almost certainly mean an end to her hopes of promotion, and
with it any prospect of an improvement in her finances:

*I'm due to start a holiday relief attachment too – as
studio manager. I did it last year for six months till
Christmas when they decided the holiday period must
be considered up! But it's a job that's usually done by
men, involving control on the studio floor, acting on
instructions from the control gallery through one's
walkie-talkie – in charge of scene hands, actors and
actresses, in fact the whole of the production in the
studio ... I got a nice fat sum of 'Acting Pay' for it last
year but 'If' this happens, I shall no doubt be retired
to the desk, probably by September at the latest – and
as the attachment doesn't start till mid-August I shan't
make anything like as much as last year. But I suppose
it's no use railing against fate.*

Will stop now. Write to me soon – and reassuringly.

It seems clear by the end of the letter that she is far more
worried than she first appears. Yes, Jim is sticking by her, but
she must get that divorce from Richie and then make sure her
child is not born out of wedlock.

Once again, I am being forced to reassess my mother,
abandoning my teenage assumptions that she was a tiresome

neurotic woman, always playing the victim, never shaping her own destiny. Here, while there is plenty of anguish beneath the surface of the letter, she appears determined to get on the front foot, taking action to get her legal position secured.

The next letter is a reply from Cecil Parker, though it appears only page two has made it into the binder because it begins in the middle of some advice about Stephen:

Adolescents are always inclined to view everything from their own point of view and they do not always appreciate what is for the best. He cannot expect you to put him first in everything when, before very long, he may desire to lead a more independent existence and may perhaps marry and have a family of his own.

He offers to put Sylvia in touch with a London solicitor, as both she and Richie are now living in the capital. Then he concludes with some news about his own family and a wistful thought about the passing of the years: 'I feel older every day. One thing about your present situation is that it brings home to you that you are still young!'

By now, we're well into July and a couple of weeks are wasted with an exchange of letters with the London solicitor Cecil has recommended. One letter confirms that an important document has arrived:

I duly received a letter from Mr. A.J. Cellan-Jones confirming he was the father of the expected child and that adultery had taken place on a number of occasions.

But on 25th July, Sylvia writes again to Cecil to say she is back in his hands because Richie's solicitor turns out to be in Bristol. Her anxiety levels about the speed and the cost of the divorce are clearly rising. She says she thinks Richie will also want to expedite matters and may even be reasonable in his demands:

About costs – though James has said that he accepts liability and would be willing to meet costs, I do feel, for his sake, that we should make no voluntary offer unless we are asked to do so. I get the feeling, when I talked to my husband, that he might not press for costs, and if he does not intend to do so, I would rather we did not make the offer first, as perhaps it might then be accepted. Can we not wait, and see if they ask for a prior arrangement, before making a definite commitment? The difficulty of making an immediate arrangement is that it would mean cashing James's Insurance Policy, or selling the car, and we do not want to do either of these things until they are inevitable.

Both her estranged husband and the father of her baby seem to be behaving well, but by now Sylvia is sinking into depression.

I am taking Stephen away this weekend for about ten days holiday, to get away from it all (as if I could!). I have been so depressed lately he has been affected by it too, and I hope it will do us both good to have a break.

Cecil replies to say he is happy to take over again, but he too is starting his holidays and will be away for three weeks, leaving her in the capable hands of his colleague, a Mr Burland. This gentleman gets straight down to business, writing to Sylvia – or rather Mrs Rich – in August about the meeting he has had with Richie's solicitor:

He said that provided you and Mr. Cellan-Jones will agree to give signed confession statements, admitting adultery, to their London Enquiry Agent and deposit with us £84 to cover all the costs, court fees, Enquiry Agents fees etc. incurred, Mr. Rich will give instructions for his Solicitors to proceed with the Divorce proceedings without any delay.

But she will have to give more details about the affair:

Can you please send us your Marriage Certificate and a photograph of yourself – the latter for identification purposes when the Enquiry Agent interviews you?

Where did the adultery take place and when do you expect the birth of your child?

But with the clock ticking and the baby due in mid-January he has some distressing news about the timetable for the divorce:

It seems quite certain that this case will have to be heard in London and, that being so, the Petition will be filed there and, if the case can be heard in November, as Mr. Mayes has said, then the decree should be made absolute in February 1958. If this date is not likely to be early enough to enable you and Mr. Cellan-Jones to be wed, then it will be necessary for Mr. Rich (as he is the only person who can do so) to be persuaded to apply to the Court, by separate Summons after the case has been heard, to shorten the time between the hearing and the making of the decree absolute.

So to get divorced before her child is born, marry Jim and remove the stain of illegitimacy from the baby, she is dependent on the goodwill of her estranged husband, who has never given up on the hope of a reconciliation with the woman who deserted him ten years earlier. But incredibly, a few days later, on 7th August, there is some good news. Mr Burland has had another meeting with Richie's solicitor:

We think, provided that you place us in funds without delay, that there is a chance of getting the case heard in Bristol if you and Mr. Cellan-Jones can come to Bristol one day very soon so that someone in the office of the solicitors for Mr. Rich can take confession statements from you both in these offices.

The next day he writes again, stressing the importance of getting the money sorted so that things can move swiftly. It is essential, he says, that she sends them £84 so that the case can be heard in Bristol in September or October. Sylvia replies the next day from Ruskin Park House, agreeing to come to Bristol on 13th August and supplying answers to his questions:

The adultery took place at the above address (in my son's absence) and also at the Three Crowns Hotel, Angmering on Sea in Sussex.

I expect the birth of my child about mid to end of January 1958.

On 13th August, Sylvia travels alone to the Bristol offices of Wansbroughs, her solicitors, for a meeting where Richie's legal team is also present. There, in what I imagine was a room full of pinstriped men, she has to make a confession statement, once again describing where the adultery took place. The following day, Mr Burland sends her a document to sign and has an enquiry about Jim:

Please return it to us by return of post and send us the cheques as arranged if you have not already done so.

You will remember that we are waiting to hear from you the present address of Mr. Cellan-Jones because he will have to sign a similar form. If you will let us know his address we will write to him with the form and explain the whole position.

We cannot impress upon you too much that it is essential that all these things should be done at the earliest possible moment to ensure that the case will be heard in September.

By now, a big question is looming in my mind and presumably in that of her solicitor. Where is Jim and why has he not been there to support her in what sounds to have been a pretty grim ordeal? We know that in mid-July he signed a confession of adultery and wrote a will leaving all his worldly goods to Sylvia. So, four weeks later what has changed?

Sylvia's reply to Mr Burland – when is Cecil Parker getting back from his holiday? – indicates for the first time what may have gone wrong. She has been unable to contact Jim and it looks as though the Cellan-Jones family has stepped in:

> *I went to see his cousin last night and she thought he might ring while I was there, but he did not. I gather from her that there is considerable opposition from his family to this divorce and to the idea of his marrying me under such circumstances. I do not know how much he may be swayed by this.*

The cousin was of course Pixie, fascinating hostess of that riotous dinner party at which Sylvia was entertained by her descriptions of the Cellan-Joneses, drawn like characters out of a Nancy Mitford novel. Soon it will become clear that her sympathies lie with the family rather than the older woman left pregnant by her cousin. But Sylvia is not ready to give up on Jim quite yet:

> *As I believe I told you, it was his suggestion in the first place that we should marry, not mine, and until his family were told he was steadfastly with me, and we made plans in detail, and it never occurred to me to have any doubts about it. Though, since I saw you and his cousin, I have had moments of uncertainty. I know him very well, and have great faith in his integrity, and I cannot feel that in the end he will retract his promise, even though he may have been led to feel doubts about the success of such a marriage.*
>
> *Normally of course we should be writing to each other at this time and I should have been sent his address, but when he went away we had both been through so much*

emotional stress about all this that I said I would not write, but would keep in touch with his cousin – I did not then know of her opposition to the divorce, and he looked so ill and distraught that I thought it might be a good thing for us to be away from each other for a time, until we felt calmer. I did not realise that his signature would be needed to the petition so immediately and he said he would come down to Bristol and see you on his return if all went well.

Now we find out where Jim has gone – he is away somewhere with the Parachute Regiment, jumping out of planes, which only adds to Sylvia's anxiety:

I do not feel it would be right to ring the War Office to get his address and perhaps cause further difficulties for him, while he is flying and parachuting, which as I told you I am very nervous about in any event.

She says she realises the delay in contacting Jim may mean pushing the divorce hearing back from September to October, but feels she has to risk it:

If of course I hear that Mr. Cellan-Jones is returning to Moor Street this weekend I will get in touch with him and will ring you immediately. Otherwise it will I fear have to wait until he gets back on Saturday 24th. I do appreciate how much you have done to expedite the hearing, and that it will be entirely my own fault if, in consequence of this delay, the case cannot get through in time. But I did not feel, when Mr. Cellan-Jones went,

that he was in a fit state to be doing anything which
seemed to me so dangerous and nerve-wracking, and
I feel that it would be wrong to add to his worries at
this stage, until he is safely back, even though it adds to
mine.

She appears to be walking on eggshells, desperate not to do anything which might scare off the apparently neurotic Jim. But she is beginning to see that Pixie may not be a friend to her:

It occurred to me at one stage that his cousin might be
willing to forward the petition on, but now that I have
seen her I do not think she would do that, and perhaps
it is as well.

Please do not mention to 'the other side' that I have
even a glimmer of doubt as to Mr. Cellan-Jones' ultimate
intentions. I haven't really, but if my husband thought I
had he might withdraw the petition, and now that it has
started I am most anxious it should go through as soon
as possible whatever the outcome. I think that what the
family are most anxious about is the possible publicity
attached to their name – but I feel that as the case is
undefended there should not be any at all. What do you
think?

Now things are becoming clearer – Cecil and Lavinia Cellan-Jones are concerned that there will be a public scandal. Mr Burland replies to Sylvia on 27th August, enclosing a copy of a letter that has been sent to Jim at his London flat. It informs him of the steps taken so far by Mrs Rich to formally admit to adultery and tells him that he will need to come to Bristol to make a similar confession statement. Then there is the small matter of money, the deal on costs agreed with Richie's solicitors:

Mrs. Rich will have told you that we have agreed the Costs at £84, which is a reasonable amount, and that Mrs. Rich has already sent us a cheque for £20 and is arranging to send us a further cheque for £64 by the end of this month. No doubt you will be making arrangements to reimburse Mrs. Rich.

It might not sound like a lot today, but in 1957, £84 was a sizeable amount to find in a hurry, over two months of Jim's pay. (In October, Jim was to apply for a £48 loan from the BBC – ostensibly for a Murphy television but I like to think it might have been a way to cover some of the costs of a divorce.)

In the last days of August, though, things take a turn for the worse. On the twenty-ninth, Sylvia writes a desperately sad letter to Mr Burland. Jim's couple of weeks with the Parachute Regiment are over, he must be back in London, but she has heard nothing from him:

I have not seen Mr. Cellan-Jones since his return last weekend, and am very anxious about messages I have received via a friend indicating that something has happened to change his intentions, and that he does not at the moment wish to see me. He is apparently very upset about the divorce, though I do not understand this since I consulted him before taking any steps and have indeed a note from him telling me to use his name in any statement I make to my husband.

Is she fooling herself here, I ask myself? No – I remember that note from Jim in the box of love letters: 'Use my name as much as you like in the letter to R. *Je t'aime et je suis toujours avec toi.*' I love you and I am always with you.

She continues:

I wish I could talk to him because I cannot understand what I have done to suddenly antagonise him, and I have always had complete trust in his loyalty, and indeed still have. I hope this is not wishful thinking, but I have never had cause to doubt him before. I have been asked by friends if I have any enemies who may have turned him against me during his absence, but I cannot think that I have, or what anyone could have said.

Before he went away I knew he was upset at the trouble he thought this was causing to his parents, but I understood him to agree that he would come down to see you and make a statement on his return.

Do please let me know as soon as you hear from him because I am desperately worried about things – even if he has changed his mind about marrying me, I take it this would not affect the divorce going through, since the evidence you already have seems conclusive.

And I do want it to go through as quickly as possible whatever happens, because I cannot believe that he himself really intends to leave me to face this ordeal alone. It would be quite contrary to all I believe I know about his character and integrity.

I hope to let you have the other cheque this weekend,
and shall wait anxiously to hear from you.

She still has faith in Jim, though it is fraying at the edges.
But her letter has crossed with one from Wansbroughs with
some disturbing news. There has still been no word from Jim,
but they have been 'rather surprised to receive a letter from
Messrs. Borm-Reid & Co., Solicitors of Lincoln's Inn, London,
W.C.2., who inform us that they have been instructed to act on
behalf of Mr. Cellan-Jones.' By hiring his own lawyers, Jim is
not only signalling that he is going to let her 'face this ordeal
alone', he is saying he is not on her side any more in the pursuit
of a divorce and is going to look after his own interests.

Reading this legal drama is an unsettling experience. Part of
me is gripped by scenes which could have been from a BBC
classic serial – *The Forsyte Saga* perhaps – but then I lose that
detachment and am overwhelmed by sadness. Two people who
just a couple of months earlier had seemed to be deeply in love
are now making each other thoroughly miserable.

As September dawned, Cecil Parker was finally back from
holiday and the clock was ticking, with a court hearing on
the divorce petition scheduled in Bristol in the middle of the
month, but Jim's intentions remained far from clear. Sylvia
sent a cheque for £64 to her solicitors. They replied that if Jim
did not reimburse her in full then they may encourage Richie's
solicitors to go after him.

On 4th September, Sylvia writes to Mr Burland a letter so
full of pain that over 60 years on I find it difficult to read:

I feel so distressed at the recent turn of events that I

find it hard to write or think clearly. From a message I have had I gather now that the costs are not disputed but they want to get the petition reduced to desertion only to keep Mr. Cellan-Jones' name out of it, in which case they would be willing to pay the costs and perhaps more. But I am not at all clear if this is really what they intend to ask, and I do not like the sound of it at all – it savours too much of being 'bought off'. I have thought about it, and feel that I would far rather give evidence.

Such has been the breakdown of trust that she fears that Jim may not even accept his financial responsibilities as the father of her child:

I do not feel I can trust Mr. Cellan-Jones any more, he seems to have changed completely and I think perhaps that unless there is some legal indication which would be evident if the divorce goes through as it stands, that he is responsible for my child, he may later deny any liability for helping me with its support, which at present he is admitting he will be responsible for. But he has said so many things and obviously not meant them, that I cannot any longer feel any faith in him at all – and though I suppose, when this is over, if he does still want to marry me, I might agree, I don't know now how it would work, though before I thought it could be very happy. But he seems now such a changed person.

And sadness has turned to anger – if Jim and his family want a fight, she is prepared to give them one:

I do not wish to be vindictive, but I do not really see that it will do him any harm to be named in the divorce, or indeed that there should be any publicity – we are not people of any importance, or 'news' value.

She retains some faint hope, however, that he will do the right thing.

I feel very hurt and sad about it all but hope at least that he will help me to support and care for the baby, as otherwise I cannot see daylight at all, and do not know how I shall manage.

She is looking over a cliff here, knowing that her situation is far more precarious than when she came to London with Stephen in 1950. Then at least she could go out to work, leaving her son under the not so watchful eye of the landlady. But without some money from Jim how would she afford the childcare she would need for the baby if she was to return to work?

But on 7th September there is finally some good news from her lawyers. Jim's solicitors have written to Wansbroughs to say that he is prepared to come to Bristol on Saturday 14th September to make a confession statement. His solicitors do suggest that, since Mr Rich is also alleging desertion by Sylvia, the confession of adultery may not be necessary. But Wansbroughs stand firm. If he does make his statement that means Sylvia will not need to come to the court hearing a few days later – 'But,' the solicitor warns her, 'you must hold yourself in readiness to attend on the 18th September on short notice, in case he does not keep his promise.'

A few days before the day on which so much hung, Parker writes again, this time in the tone of a wise uncle rather than a lawyer, concluding:

Needless to say, I am very sorry indeed that things have taken such an unhappy turn from your point of view. You have been badly let down, but perhaps it is better that the man in question should show his true colours now rather than after a marriage of necessity.

That Saturday in September 1957 must have been a day of extraordinary tension for my mother. Would Jim turn up in Bristol and make the confession that would allow her divorce from Richie to go ahead? Or would he go back on his word again? I can imagine her pacing up and down the narrow hallway in the Ruskin Park House flat, listening for any footstep that might signal the arrival of news from Bristol.

The next item in the folder shows that news did indeed come that afternoon in the form of a telegram from Wansbroughs: 'STATEMENT MADE NOT NECESSARY YOU ATTEND COURT WEDNESDAY'.

So Jim confessed and the threat that she would have to appear in court was lifted. But, as she writes to 'my dear Cecil' on the following Tuesday, the version of events Mr Cellan-Jones gave in Bristol does not match hers:

I heard from Mr. Burland yesterday, and I expect he will have told you what was said on Saturday, and of J's complete denial of any promise or intention to marry me. But of course he did make such a promise, and he himself knows quite well that he did. However, it seems obvious that he now has no such intention, and I certainly would not wish to marry him now – not as a proper marriage – though I think it would be only fair to the child to go through a formal ceremony to legitimise it. However, I don't suppose he will agree now even to do that.

I hope I shall not need to take affiliation proceedings [establishing Jim is the father of her child and so liable to maintenance payments] *as you mentioned. I feel it would be the final indignity and disillusionment. Richie said years ago that one day God would make me pay for having left him – so I suppose this is it!*

The following day, the court in Bristol granted Sylvia's estranged husband a decree nisi and her marriage to Richie was effectively over. But, as the letter from Wansbroughs containing this news explains, attention now turns to another legal battle: 'We are writing to Mr. Cellan-Jones's solicitors today informing them and enquiring what he proposes to do with regard to the costs and your expected child.'

Over the coming weeks, Sylvia would turn away from any thought of marriage and concentrate on getting the best deal for her baby. But from now on it would not be James Cellan-Jones but his parents, Cecil and Lavinia, who would be at the centre of that battle.

CHAPTER 9

MEET THE PARENTS

One day, as I sat at home in Ealing, surrounded by these letters from the 1950s, my Parkinson's stiffened fingers ever so slowly tapping out this tale, a news item came on the radio. In 2021, for the first time since records began, the majority of babies in England and Wales had been born out of wedlock. The Office for National Statistics said there had been 624,828 live births that year, 320,713 of them, or 51.3 per cent, to women who were not married or in a civil partnership when they were delivered. There was some speculation that the figures had been distorted by the lockdowns associated with the Covid pandemic, which had made it much harder to stage a wedding, but the trend was clear and had been for decades. Indeed, terms such as illegitimacy and 'born out of wedlock' now seem hopelessly quaint and old-fashioned – except to the person who has inserted into my Wikipedia page the fact that I was 'born out of wedlock'. A friend who is a volunteer editor for the online encyclopaedia keeps removing the term on the grounds that it is archaic but within hours it is back again.

How different things were in the late 1950s, before the dawning of the sexual revolution and the arrival of the oral contraceptive pill. After soaring during the Second World War, peaking in 1945 at nearly 9 per cent of births to women aged 15 to 44, the illegitimacy rate had fallen back to around 5 per cent in the 1950s, but were just beginning to nudge up as the decade ended. While the data on the social class of the mothers of illegitimate children is scant, it is still pretty clear that poorer working-class girls and women were more likely to have children born out of wedlock, and illegitimacy rates for middle-class women in their forties were extremely low.

So in the eminently respectable and socially conservative district of Uplands in Swansea news of such an event must have come as a dreadful shock. I never met my grandparents but it is clear from the letters Sylvia collected that they feared that the liaison between her and their son would scandalise their friends, colleagues and neighbours, and were determined to stop that happening. Unusually, it was Cecil who acted first, writing to Sylvia a week after Jim had travelled to Bristol:

21st September 1957

Dear Sybil [sic]

You may remember meeting me when I was staying with my niece. Needless to say, my wife and I are desperately worried on your behalf as well as Jimmie's and we would like to do what we can to help.

I have written to your lawyer suggesting that we meet and that he might like to be present.

Could you manage to come down to Bristol for a Friday afternoon or Saturday morning meeting – the sooner the better.

Yours sincerely,

CJ Cellan-Jones

I don't know her feelings about him mangling her name, but it seems Sylvia had previously formed a favourable impression of Cecil when she had met him at the home of Jim's cousin Pixie – 'gentle and kindly' is how she described him in a letter to Geoffrey Grigson, whereas Lavinia was 'from all accounts a tartar who not only rules them but the outlying branches of the family as well'.

The surgeon's letter to Cecil Parker on the same date begins:

As the parents of the person presumably responsible for Mrs Rich's condition we feel a certain amount of responsibility and wonder where we could help in this unhappy state of affairs.

This must have seemed to the lawyer a promising move and he was quick to advise Sylvia that a conference with the Cellan-Joneses could be the beginning of a solution to her problems:

I personally think that a meeting could do no harm – and might do a lot of good. Mr & Mrs Cellan-Jones might be prepared to make some secure provision for the child if a marriage is out of the question, and that would at least be something saved from the wreck.

He ends with another unlawyerly instruction – 'Keep your chin up.'

A few days later, on 26th September, Cecil Parker writes to say the plan is for her and the Cellan-Jones parents to meet in his office on Saturday 12th October. He wants Sylvia to arrive early so that they can talk tactics. Then he mentions an idea that she has apparently come up with – that if there is to be no marriage she should change her name by deed poll from Rich to Cellan-Jones. He isn't sure the surgeon will like this:

The concurrence of Cellan-Jones is not necessary, but any help which might be forthcoming from Dr Cellan-Jones might be conditional upon your not taking such a course. The trouble is that 'Cellan-Jones' is not a very common name. We will discuss this matter when we meet and before we see Dr Cellan-Jones.

On 5th October, Cecil Cellan-Jones writes to Sylvia again – getting her name right this time. He tells her that he and Lavinia will be spending the night before their meeting at a Bristol hotel and suggests that she might like to have dinner with them. It sounds like the dinner from hell – having small talk over the brown Windsor soup with the parents of your now estranged lover – and I can't imagine that Cecil Parker would have thought it a good idea.

Would she have gone? Would she have thought it was a good idea? It's not clear, and the next item in the file is a letter from the Swansea surgeon to Cecil Parker four days after the Bristol meeting. He says he is grateful to him for Saturday's 'courteous and helpful interview' and asks him to send details of his fee.

Obviously, as you suggested, we must wait until some date in January or February next before continuing our discussions [...] In the meantime, however, you have noted my agreement to guarantee future legal payments. Moreover, when the position is clearer, I will consider whether I can help further.

After a long discussion with my son, I find that, because the risk of damaging publicity might prejudice his present employment, he still talks of going abroad.

He asks that all future correspondence be directed to him, rather than his son. Now, however courteous and helpful his tone, it seems to me that there are several worrying things about my grandfather's letter. He may have agreed to cover 'future legal payments' – presumably the minimum maintenance rate under the law – but any further help with the cost of raising a child is left very vague. And then there is the question of Jim possibly going abroad for fear of 'damaging publicity' affecting his BBC career. What's that about – and why would leaving the country solve it? Once he's gone, what's to stop his parents saying it's nothing to do with them?

When Cecil Parker writes to Sylvia about this letter he seems to be of the same mind.

Now that James Cellan-Jones seems to have it firmly fixed in his mind to go abroad, I feel that affiliation proceedings (which could be commenced now) or an Affiliation Agreement, should be dealt with as soon as possible – otherwise we shall not be able to serve the Summons upon him abroad, or he may not be inclined to sign an agreement once he is out of the country. After all, he has broken one promise to you and could break another.

In the circumstances, I am all for having an Agreement drawn up and signed by him, and Dr Cellan-Jones as guarantor, now.

He warns her that under the present law she won't get more than 30 shillings (£1.50) a week, and that only until the child is 16, although from April 1958 a magistrate can extend that to 18 or even 21. He then moves on to the plan to change her name by deed poll, designed, it seems, to remove the stain of illegitimacy from the child. He has spotted a snag:

When you go to register the birth in London, or elsewhere, you will, I am told, almost certainly be asked to give the name of 'your husband', and unless you give the name of Cellan-Jones as your husband (which, of course, would not be a true declaration), no particulars will be inserted in the column in the Certificate provided for the name of the father, and anyone seeing such a certificate will immediately conclude the circumstances surrounding the birth.

He then asks, rather unhelpfully, 'What are you going to do about this?'

His letter crosses one from Sylvia asking whether he has heard from Dr Cellan-Jones and making similar points to his about the need to nail down an agreement. It is clear that with three months to go before the baby is due, two subjects are preying on her mind – the precarious state of her finances and the status of her child.

She asks Parker to find out whether any maintenance deal can start before the birth:

I find that things are going to be much more difficult than I thought. When Stephen was born I was given three months leave on full pay, but I now understand that was purely a war time regulation and now I have to take unpaid leave though I believe there is a grant of about six weeks' pay provided I return to work for not less than three months – payable later on. It may be too that I shall have to go on to part time work after the child is born, in order to be able to care for it, in which case my salary will be much reduced, but I hope to be able to find a way to avoid this. In these circumstances I shall have to continue working as long as possible because every penny will count – but I do not think it can be much beyond the end of this year.

Reading this over 60 years on made me stop and catch my breath. Looking back from the twenty-first century, when mothers get statutory maternity pay for 39 weeks and big employers like the BBC are obliged to offer flexible working conditions when they return, Sylvia's plight seems shocking. But back then, women were still not expected to return to work after having children and if they did so, then it was assumed that their husbands would still be the main provider.

So how was Sylvia assessing her future that October? Had she given up all hope that Jim would do the decent thing and marry her? And what was my father's state of mind?

Having immersed myself in the legal drama, I put down the file of correspondence with Wansbroughs and returned to the red box which my mother had said would help me understand how it was.

I picked up that letter to Geoffrey Grigson where she describes Jim's parents and read it more thoroughly. It is a reply to a letter in which Geoffrey and his new wife Jane have given her what looks like eminently sensible advice about her situation, including urging her not to rush into a marriage with Jim which will probably end in misery a few years later. Sylvia says it is good to have both a man and a woman's perspective and their letter has cheered her up:

Before, I was fast sinking into that awful emotional morass I'm prone to, going round in circles, and every way I turned seemed blocked by mountains of difficulties – and dissolving into tears all too easily which is no fun for Stephen or me, and no help to anyone.

She tells them her divorce from Richie is going ahead but there is a startling revelation which does not appear anywhere in the legal letters:

There was a moment when I thought I might have to try and call it off, because Richie hinted darkly that he might also name an earlier co-respondent – Sir Blank from Bristol, and my only other love during the last 12 years. Round about 1951, when Stephen was getting more independent and the stresses of home and work less all absorbing, I started to come out of my disinterested hibernation and to think that six years of chastity was long enough and I'd better love again before taking to the shawl and bath-chair. This lasted about three years, though intermittently because of the distance between Bristol and London and other pressures, and settled down into calm affection very soon, ending with pleasant recollection on Jimmy's advent. I won't mention his name, since you know him well ...

Who was Sir Blank from Bristol? Sir George Barnes seemed a possible candidate – except I was not aware of any connection he had with Bristol. More likely perhaps was Desmond Hawkins, a great BBC figure who overlapped with Sylvia in Bristol during the war and went on to found the natural history unit. Certainly there's a jealous hint in one of Jim's letters that Hawkins may have been one of her former lovers. Whoever it was, Sylvia decided that Richie had no evidence beyond a few mentions from Stephen of a man coming to dinner and it was all an attempt by her estranged husband to rattle her.

She then turns to a lengthy analysis of Jim's character and their relationship. She reckons he has been shaped by his forceful mother:

He was born, an only son, when she was a little younger than me, and slapped down regularly throughout childhood – so though now very mature in some ways, is very over-emotional and immature and dependent on others. He has a cousin here who tells me that she has always defended him against Mum, and he has always gone to her and said 'What shall I do' about all his problems – till recently when he came to me instead, which I don't think she liked very much. But I have made most of the decisions during the last year or so.

She says a relative hit the nail on the head when he said the reason Jim and Stephen did not get on was that they were too alike:

Both dependent, highly emotional, inclined to self-

dramatisation (me too, I know!) – both with a strong streak of feminine in them. Jimmy's volunteering for a parachute regiment was really like me at school, jumping in at the deep end when I couldn't swim – an attempt to prove to oneself that one isn't afraid – as one is.

He has said from time to time that he'll try and be stronger, and not lean on me so much – because I ought to be the one to do the leaning – and indeed now rather need to. But again like Stephen in lots of ways he is very young even for his age, though much older in others.

Jim had just turned 26; Stephen was still only 15, so this comparison is far from flattering for the man she had been so keen to marry. And in the next sentence comes what feels to me something crucial, a reason a young man could pin his cowardice on, the reason he has cooled on the idea of marrying her, although she doesn't see it:

And he still doesn't know how old I am. At first he thought I was about 25, then when he knew Stephen was 15 he worked out that I must be about 35, but he's never got beyond that. And of course I'll have to tell him if we do marry, which I should think will shatter him completely. I think really you and Jane are right, and we'd better not marry.

The fact that, over a year into their love affair, she still hadn't been honest about her age, I find shocking, but not altogether surprising. 'A gentleman never asks a lady her age,' she used to say to me, 'and as far as the lady is concerned, a little white lie never hurt anyone.' Well, it did this time. I think that she must have been fooling herself if she thought Jim had not worked out her age yet – after all, he had appointed his own lawyers six weeks earlier and they would presumably have checked out her marriage and possibly birth certificates. Knowing her true age – and realising he had been deceived about it – must have been a factor in changing Jim's mind about marrying her. Or maybe two weeks away from Sylvia on the parachute course had given him time to think about whether he really wanted to burden himself with a wife and a child at this stage of his career – and now he had an excuse to extricate himself.

In the rest of her letter to the Grigsons Sylvia veers between anguish about how she will combine her job with childcare when the baby comes and she is coping alone, and musings about Jim, which suggest she still thinks they have a future together.

'Jimmy writes me wonderful poems, sonnets, verses – which I think are quite good,' she tells the poet Grigson. 'When I've got over being sentimental about them I shall publish them and make a lot of money.' Then she says that their relationship and her pregnancy is yet to become the subject of common gossip at the BBC and implies they are still together:

Because of the constant interchanging of staff only a few close friends really know about Jimmy and me, though others may surmise. He says if we do decide to marry we can say that we did it on purpose as the only way to get R. to divorce me …

But she knows this is not a true picture. Two days before writing this somewhat delusional letter she had received a note in the BBC internal post from Jim:

Dear Sylvia,

Please ring me at GER 4903 tomorrow (Sat) morning as
early as possible. If you don't get this in time please ring
Sunday morn – very early.

He signs off with a chilly and businesslike 'JCJ'. Nothing poetic or even mildly affectionate there. From now on, what happened between them was no longer about a love affair, even a fading one. It was all about doing a business deal.

In 1957, 15-year-old Paul McCartney had just met John Lennon for the first time in Liverpool, and that October, as the Soviet Union sent a Sputnik satellite into orbit, the space race began. Change was also afoot at my parents' employer. Radio could hardly be argued to be the 'senior service' now. Two years after ITV started broadcasting, bringing commercial television to the UK, nearly half of all households owned a TV set. For the first time, the BBC faced competition and soon found that viewers preferred the more light-hearted fare provided by its boisterous new rival. As if to demonstrate that the BBC had no intention of losing this battle, a grand new headquarters for its television service was taking shape at White City in west London – Television Centre.

The previous year, Sylvia had written to Bunty enclosing pages from the staff magazine showing her future office and described walking to work at her present office at Lime Grove past the building site with 'steaming black tar and bare-topped workmen steaming by it'. The building was due to open in 1960 – 'It's progressing quite fast, and fascinating to watch it grow' – and she had put an 'x' on a chart of the complex to show where her office would be. The impression is of a woman who loved her work and was confident that she would play a part in the future of the BBC at its exciting new television factory. But now, in the autumn of 1957, her mood was much darker. She would have been taking the same route to work – two buses from Ruskin Park House then a tube to White City. It was a long journey at the best of times, but by now she was six months pregnant, tired and frantic with worry.

The legal battle with her former lover over her child's future was intensifying and must have been all-consuming. Throughout October and November, letters winged their way between Ruskin Park House and Wansbroughs' Bristol office, as Cecil Parker tried to nail down two things: a maintenance agreement to give his client at least some financial security as she brings up a child on her own and a manoeuvre which will see Sylvia acquire Jim's surname even if she can't marry him. Cecil fears that her attempt to acquire his name could make Dr Cellan-Jones less willing to play ball – for it is his parents, not Jim, who are taking the lead in these negotiations.

Parker reminds Sylvia that even if they go to court, the maximum they could win as a weekly maintenance payment would be 30 shillings – and this is what he is proposing to Dr Cellan-Jones. The payments would only start once the baby was born but Sylvia thought they could push for a bit more financial help with all the costs before the birth and also hope for an uplift.

Leafing back and forth through the letters from October and November, trying to understand Sylvia's state of mind, I noticed that she seems to feel she has established some kind of relationship with Jim's parents. Then one sentence makes it clear that she did have dinner with them the night before the Bristol meeting after all:

*I understood from what they said to me on the Friday
that they thought Jimmy should pay the standard legal
amount and they would be prepared to supplement it,
though they did not say to what degree.*

Sylvia's response to this appears to show that, for her,
giving me my father's name and so disguising my illegitimacy is
even more important than securing my financial future: 'About
the name change, what I'm terribly afraid of is that I may be
leaving this too late. I'd rather lose Dr C-J's surety than risk
not doing it in time.'

The negotiations with the Cellan-Joneses seem to be moving
painfully slowly. With barely two months to go before the
baby is due, and Sylvia getting ever more anxious about how
she will cope when she has to stop work and has no money
coming in, Parker decides to get tough. On 8th November he
writes to Dr Cellan-Jones with an ultimatum:

*As there is the possibility that your son might leave
the country, which he is free to do at any time, I really
should advise Mrs. Rich to issue a Summons against him
in order to protect her interests.*

He says she will shortly have to give up work as she is
finding the one-and-a-half-hour journey from Ruskin Park
House to Lime Grove a great strain. He continues:

*We all realise that 30/- per week does not go very far
towards the maintenance of a child and it goes a very
little way as the child's age increases and clothes and
education have to be paid for. It is my duty to point*

*out that unless we can agree Terms reasonably soon I
shall be bound to advise Mrs. Rich to issue a Summons
against your son.*

All of this legal toing and froing is costing money. Cecil
Parker and his colleagues at Wansbroughs are putting plenty
of hours into Sylvia's case and while they hope and expect
that Dr Cellan-Jones will meet the costs associated with the
maintenance agreement, they still have not been paid for their
now completed work on the divorce from Richie. On 11th
November Parker writes to Sylvia to say the total bill works
out at £30 10s but he has decided the firm will accept £20
'and I hope that you will be able to manage this'. She writes
back to say she will have to pay in instalments. While I suspect
that Cecil was a good deal more generous than he would have
been to other clients, £20 still amounts to about three months
of the maintenance payments she can expect. I can picture my
mother doing frantic sums on the back of her cheque book as
she tries to work out what she can afford to pay.

But what is happening between Jim and his parents, and
what is his state of mind? His BBC annual review reports,
'He has established himself as a most reliable Assistant Floor
Manager,' and from October until just before Christmas
1957 was working on a major production, a serialisation of
Nicholas Nickleby. He had also secured that £48 loan from
the Corporation towards the cost of a television and would be
paying it off at a rate of £3 a month for the next 19 months.
In the detailed account of his monthly income and expenditure
he supplied to the BBC in order to get the loan, he makes no
mention of the £6 a month he will soon be paying in child
maintenance.

By now, Sylvia has not seen Jim since early August but on 14th November he makes a sudden reappearance in her latest letter to Cecil Parker. She begins by explaining that she is keen to win the trust of Dr Cellan-Jones:

I liked him very much, and one of the things that has saddened me most is that I think James has, perhaps not intentionally, misrepresented me or denied our earlier plans to his parents, so they found it difficult to know who was telling the truth and were naturally inclined to believe his version rather than mine.

Then, out of the blue, in walks Jim to the flat at Ruskin Park House:

He came to see me a week or so ago, to collect some of his things and to ask for the return of his letters – he said that he had not lied before, but freely admitted to me that he had lied about our marriage plans both to his parents and to Mr. Burland. I asked him at least to admit the truth to them now – it can do no harm, except perhaps to his pride, and no one can force him to legitimise the child if he doesn't want to – but he said he intended to stick to what he had said to them, and that they believed him and not me. It's a great pity, because they seemed at our first meeting quite well-disposed towards me, though naturally thinking first of James' interests, and if we could establish mutual trust I had hoped that they might take a natural grandparents' interest in their son's child, and not just a financial one. But if they are going to mistrust me always that probably won't be possible.

There is so much to unpack here. She obviously did not return his letters, at least not all of them, or I wouldn't have found them under the dressing table nearly 40 years later. So can I trust her account of who was lying about their marriage plans? But this is where it becomes clear why I never met my grandparents. She goes on:

> *I don't know why he won't admit the truth – which is of course simply that something or someone caused him to change his mind. I don't know what. I thought perhaps another woman might have come into the picture, but he says that there is no one else and that he sits at home in the evenings drinking – which is very silly and morbid of him. He says that I was wrong not to tell him my age, though admits that it wouldn't have made any difference at the time. He said something about my suing him for breach of promise if he admitted the truth, but I told him that, as far as I know, I couldn't do that anyway (even if I'd for a moment thought of it, which of course I haven't) because as I understand it while one is married to someone else no promise of marriage can be considered binding. So he needn't have worried on that score anyway.*

Again, we only have Sylvia's version of this conversation. Did Jim really say the age difference would have made no difference if he'd known it earlier? Perhaps, but then he may have not been entirely honest to Sylvia, or to himself. The picture she paints of him sitting at home drinking alone – 'silly and morbid' – certainly sounds convincing. She ends her letter to Cecil Parker with the hope that the negotiations with Dr Cellan-Jones can be settled without much further discussion. But two weeks later, on 28th November, there is devastating news in a letter from the doctor to Parker:

Further to my last letter telling you that the agreement had been sent to my son, I am sorry to say that we have heard nothing from him – excepting that he keenly resented our 'interference' in his affairs.

I feel that the only result of our attempt to help has been to alienate him.

He seems to have no intention to return to Swansea and in these distressing circumstances there is nothing we can do, at the moment.

His permanent address – so far as I know – is 16A, Moor Street, London W1 and I suggest that you communicate with him directly.

There has clearly been a huge bust-up between Jimmy and his parents. One can imagine him sitting at home in his Soho flat, drinking himself into a state of misery and fury about his circumstances and then lashing out at his father and mother. And perhaps at Sylvia too because when Cecil Parker writes to Sylvia a week later on 4th December, he refers to a letter she has received from Jim:

Thank you for your letter of yesterday's date which Mr Burland has shown to me.

It appears that Mr James Cellan-Jones is now displaying his true colours, and his letter to you merely confirms my view that you would be wise to take

*proceedings against him as soon as your change of name
has been effected.*

This letter from Jim was nowhere to be found among
Sylvia's papers, neither in the legal file nor in the red box
containing his love letters. Perhaps it was so hurtful that she
did not want me to see it, however keen she was that I should
understand 'how it really was'. Cecil Parker obviously saw it
as a declaration of war and he warned Sylvia against assuming
that his mother and father will ride to the rescue.

*I know you are hoping that his parents will give some
voluntary help after the child is born, but, frankly, I
hesitate to view the prospects with much confidence,
as they are under no legal liability and they do not
seem to have been of any practical assistance so far.
That may not be their fault, but the fact remains
that they have given no definite undertaking – and
as time goes on, their feelings of responsibility may
diminish.*

*You will appreciate that your change of name will
be unlikely to improve relations – and may well have
a deleterious effect. Nevertheless, that position must
be faced because Cellan-Jones has not been willing
to enter into the Agreement which we prepared at his
father's suggestion, and he refuses to negotiate with us
and says that unless he can settle with you direct, he
will leave the whole matter to the Court. He is talking
nonsense when he says that he is fed up with receiving
threatening communications from lawyers. He has
had no communications from us since the divorce*

proceedings. His father will have to pay the costs relating to the proposed Agreement, and I propose sending him my firm's bill in that respect very shortly, telling him of the letter you have received from his son – which has left us with no alternative but to advise you to take proceedings.

He tells her she can issue a summons right now for the maximum amount of child maintenance which the law allows, though the first payment will not be made until the child is born: 'I know that 30/- per week is very little, but "a bird in the hand is worth two in the bush".' And as a postscript, he tells her no, this isn't a matter where you can get legal aid.

This must have been the lowest point for Sylvia. She is 43, nearly eight months pregnant, and it is three weeks to Christmas, with all the expense that entails. She is feeling ill and would like to stop work early but with no prospect of help from Jim or his parents she has to carry on, and even getting the minimal support the law allows will involve racking up further legal bills. Stephen, already highly strung, is presumably even angrier with Jim than he was before. With his sixteenth birthday just around the corner there were important decisions to be made about his future, but he insisted that his priority was looking after his mother and the baby. He was both on the verge of adulthood and still very much a child, excited about Christmas. One can imagine the atmosphere in the flat was tense in the extreme.

But on 6th December Sylvia receives better news from Mr Burland at Wansbroughs:

Dr. Cellan-Jones telephoned us this afternoon and said that his son will be coming home to Swansea tomorrow, Saturday, and it appears that he is now anxious to adopt quite a different attitude, so that Dr. Cellan-Jones hopes to be able to write to us favourably in the early part of next week. I hope, therefore, to be able to report more favourably to you one day next week.

Peace, it seems, may be about to break out, and the following day a letter from Dr Cellan-Jones to Cecil Parker appears to confirm this:

My son travelled down to Swansea overnight and, after a long discussion with him, I am glad to tell you that the position as regards the proposed agreement is now much more favourable.

But not so fast. The letter raises a whole series of issues about the maintenance agreement which will keep the lawyers busy for weeks. First, there is a complex problem about tax being deducted from the monthly maintenance payments, which would reduce the amount Sylvia receives. Her lawyer has suggested Jim tops up the payment to cover the tax but he isn't keen. Also, according to his father, Jim is unwilling to sign up to continue the payments after the child has reached the age of 16, suggesting instead that when that time comes, a further agreement should be concluded. Finally, he does not see why the payments should start before the child is born.

The reason that Jim has come back to the negotiating table at all is explained in a letter from Sylvia to Parker on 10th December. The BBC had intervened:

I've just had an interview with one of the administrators of our Department (James' and mine). He says that he saw J. last week and suggested that it was time he got this allowance question settled – which presumably, together with my letter saying that if I was asked to suggest what I needed, it was considerably more than 30/-, caused him to decide to consider the Agreement after all.

Whatever Sylvia may have said a few weeks earlier about the affair being unknown to most of her colleagues, it is clear that the drama department's bosses have been told about the baby and the argument over maintenance. Jim's interview with the administrator must have come before the call to Bristol from his father detailing his change of heart. In his memoir, he suggests that the 'scandal' over the affair damaged his career at the BBC, delaying by some years his progress towards a director's job. That was one thing I wanted to find on the day I scoured the Caversham archives but everything I read from this period was very positive about his talents and his progress.

As I read about his behaviour at this point, my sympathies were with my mother. While Sylvia is not exactly a reliable witness – she could be economical with the truth, and not just regarding her age – Jim, at 26, sometimes seems like a panicky teenager, unwilling to face up to his responsibilities. And while he may have resented the way his private affairs intruded on his work, this is the point where Sylvia's career stalled while his advanced, albeit slowly.

But still the legal letters flew between Bristol, Swansea and Ruskin Park House as the negotiations inched their way forward in the run-up to Christmas. Unbeknown to the Cellan-Joneses, plans for Mrs Rich to change her name by deed poll were also advancing.

Cecil Parker remains anxious that Dr Cellan-Jones may be so angry if he hears of the move that he will walk away. But for Sylvia, it remains the ever more pressing priority, 'desperately urgent' as she writes to Parker on 21st December. She even thinks of cancelling the trip to Bunty and Bill's home in Birmingham for Christmas but her doctor says she must get away for the sake of Stephen as well as herself:

We are both rapidly cracking up under the strain of all this. I am still working, or trying to, as of course now I must go on to the bitter end, but when I get home I can only just collapse into bed and this means that he has to cope with all the household end of things, and trying to soothe my ever-growing anxiety and he is getting tense and taut and fearful and tearful like me under the strain. I suggested he might go down and have a cheerful Christmas with his cousins without me, but he will not leave me, and the doctor says in any case I cannot stay alone.

The difficulty is that I hardly dare move, or undertake the journey, in case this birth is precipitated (and the doctor says it well might be in my present state of health) before the Deed Poll is settled. It is terribly important to get the change of name legally settled before the baby is born.

In the end, Sylvia and Stephen did go to Birmingham for Christmas with her sister Bunty and her family, rather than sit stewing anxiously in the cramped confines of the flat. But even as they set off on the train she was feeling desperately ill, as she describes to Cecil Parker in a letter on 2nd January:

We travelled down on Christmas Eve and I was put to bed forthwith and the doctor came and said I had bronchitis of all things! So there I stayed, but with batteries of sisters and nieces and doctors as well as Stephen to look after me, so it was much better that we were at that end, and Stephen was able to go to the children's parties and enjoy his Christmas and get a little relief from domestic stress without having to worry about me too much. We were finally able to come home on Tuesday, and I am back now doing light work here.

More than 60 years later, I talked to my cousins, Bunty's daughters, Susan, Christine and Jane, about that Christmas when their aunt came to stay. Susan, the oldest, remembered coming home a little later than expected. 'I was told off for making too much noise because Aunty Sylvia wasn't very well and she was in bed, I think, in Mum and Dad's room.' Jane, just seven then, remembered, 'Aunty Sylvia wearing a pretty nightie,' and all three recalled what a beauty she was, looking much younger than her age.

But when she returned home and wrote that letter to Cecil Parker, there were just two weeks to go until the baby was due, and still nothing was settled. She does now have the deed poll in her hands but the ever cautious Cecil is advising her not to sign it until the last moment possible. Sylvia thinks it is only Lavinia who might possibly object to her becoming Mrs Cellan-Jones:

I think it is Mamma who is not keen on the idea, and of course it's pretty obvious that she's the boss – but, though I may be wrong, it didn't seem to me that Dr. C-J or James minded my doing this.

By now, the tension of the long months spent trying to negotiate a deal seems to be getting to Cecil Parker too. On 6th January he reacts testily to Sylvia's enquiries about why tax may end up being deducted from her maintenance payments:

I have already explained the income tax position to you – and if you do not understand it now, I am afraid you never will! Income Tax is a very difficult subject. I am incapable of mastering it myself, and I can only pass on to you the views of the experts [...] I know that this seems hard from your point of view, but so long as the attitude of the Law continues as at present towards the responsibilities of the fathers of illegitimate children, the mothers will have the worse end of the stick.

In Britain in the late 1950s, the birth of an illegitimate child was still regarded as something shameful, with most of the blame attached to the mother, not the father. But as her struggle continues to secure a decent level of support for herself and her child in a legal system weighted against her, Sylvia seems to achieve a measure of calm in the final days of her pregnancy. On 9th January, she sits down to write a long letter to Edna, an older friend she has known since the early days of her marriage to Richie. 'I don't know if you've heard anything of our disastrous problem of the past year,' she begins, and then recounts the details of her affair with Jim. She describes how they had discussed marriage long before she fell pregnant, then the complete shock of finding she was expecting a baby at 43 which seemed 'scientifically impossible', and the mounting tensions as they tried to secure a divorce from Richie, while getting round to the realisation that a marriage between them would never work.

At this point, she appears to accept that a big issue was that she had not been honest about one matter: 'Then of course, wrongly I suppose, I'd never told J. my real age.' For Jim, she wrote, finding out that she was 43 had been 'a great shock – according to his parents.'

It is as if she wants to get her side of the story out there before the dangerous moment of childbirth. Although the death of mothers in childbirth had become far less common by the late 1950s, it was still a much greater danger, particularly for a woman in her forties, than it is today.

On 16th January, she writes to her sister Joan to tell her that she had sat Stephen down to prepare him for just such an eventuality. By now, Stephen, who had turned 16 the week before, had become her most steadfast support, 'completely loyal, and encouraging, and certain that he can help' as she had written to Edna, 'in fact if such a little boy can be called a tower of strength, he has been.'

She told Joan that she felt the boy needed to know what he should do if anything was to go wrong:

I am not being morbid, but reading about this unknown germ that is affecting maternity hospitals finally decided me that I ought to cover all eventualities and prepare him. So on Sunday morning I got us both some elevenses and then sat him down with me and talked quite calmly to him.

If she dies, she wants him to know that he can rely on her family for help and will be able to draw on her savings and a small BBC pension. She tells Joan she is particularly worried that Richie will try to take over, occupying the flat and directing Stephen into 'some dreary but safe job' whereas she wants him to at least have a chance of a career in the theatre or BBC Drama.

Instead, she wants Stephen to ring Joan or Bunty if there is an emergency so that one of them can come straight to Ruskin Park House. Once at the flat, they have a vital task:

Whoever did, I would particularly like to go through every drawer, cupboard and wardrobe in the flat and extract all the masses of documents that, in accordance with my cautious feeling that everything should not be kept in one place, inhabit all sorts of curious hiding places, the kitchen, my room and his. Lots of them unimportant [...] but wills, custody agreements, legal letters by the hundred now I should think – and last but not least my love letters! Albeit few but cherished – which I should not want Richie to read.

She also brings Joan up to date on the latest dispute over the agreement with the Cellan-Jones family. Jim has now refused to sign up to continuing the payments after the child is 16.

His reason, according to his father, now being that I have talked freely about this affair to members of the Corporation so that there is now no question of avoiding publicity. I don't think he was really – I think it's just bloody-mindedness. The letter said 'in spite of my assurances', which seems ironical since he has not kept a single one of his assurances so far. In any case the allegation is quite untrue – I've only talked about it, when his name has been mentioned, to one girl, who in fact told me, not I her.

She says she became furious about this and decided to go and confront Jim – remarkably, they were still working along the corridor from each other in Lime Grove:

I went to see him in his office to ask him to substantiate his statement, to find he'd gone on a parachute course and then on leave to Swansea. The solicitors advised me to take out a summons forthwith and not carry on any further trying peaceful negotiation and I decided they were right. But the parents would I know go sky high at the thought of a summons being served on him in Swansea, where papa is a magistrate and everyone from the policeman upwards would know all about it – and I don't want to upset them, though in some ways I think it would serve J. right.

She must have put this letter in the post and then decided it was time to act – whatever the consequences for the maintenance agreement, she needed to change her name before the baby was born. The deed poll was included in Sylvia's paperwork, a very formal document on what feels like parchment. It begins:

I absolutely and entirely renounce relinquish and abandon the use of my former surname of Rich and assume adopt and determine to take and use from the date hereof the surname of Cellan-Jones in substitution of my former surname of Rich.

After a good deal more legal flummery, it says at the bottom 'SIGNED, SEALED AND DELIVERED by the aforementioned Alsie Margaret Sylvia Cellan-Jones.'

The document is dated 16th January 1958. The following day, Sylvia gave birth to a healthy baby boy at Queen Charlotte's Hospital in Hammersmith, west London, almost as if she and I had been waiting for the matter to be resolved.

Why she chose to travel all the way across London to Queen Charlotte's when King's College Hospital was a few hundred yards away is a mystery. The hospital, where my two children were born, is handy for Ealing or Television Centre but certainly not for Ruskin Park House. Perhaps she had chosen it in case the baby arrived prematurely when she was at work. In fact, there is no detail in Sylvia's letters about the birth – was it sudden, did Stephen come with her, did it all go smoothly? What I do know is that she was admitted as Mrs Cellan-Jones and appears to have had quite a sociable time during her stay. For several years afterwards she received letters from a Claire Vecsey, a woman she had befriended on the labour ward, inviting her to reunions with the other mothers. She did not attend, and later Mrs Vecsey would send photos of the mothers and babies, telling her how much she had been missed.

In 1962, a chatty letter arrived from an address in

prosperous Barnes. It begins, 'Dear Mrs. Cellan-Jones, It just does not seem possible that such a long time has passed since we were together at Charlotte's.' Then, in between describing her daughter's fourth birthday party and some grumbles about her troubles with au pairs, she drops in this startling paragraph, presumably in reply to a letter from Sylvia:

> *I was very sorry to hear about your separation. Of course, your husband was a terribly handsome man and I suppose the women just would not leave him alone. As they say, a god's gift to women.*

It appears that Sylvia had let it be understood on the ward that she was married, and perhaps kept a photo of Jim on her bedside table because I'm as certain as I can be that he never visited. Four years on, far better to claim a separation than admit the truth about a child born out of wedlock.

My grandmother Lavinia Cellan-Jones did send flowers to Sylvia at Queen Charlotte's. But the note she wrote her on 20th January is far from joyful at the arrival of her first grandchild. 'We have heard of the birth of your son with very mixed feelings – as you can imagine,' it begins. It goes on to say that she and her husband agree this is no time for Sylvia to be worrying about money so she is sending the £30 'mentioned in the agreement'. She is sorry about the delay in completing that agreement but promises that they will sign for whatever is the law and 'my husband and I will also help separately'.

But Sylvia comes home to Ruskin Park House to find a letter from Cecil Parker posted on the twentieth when he was still unaware of my birth. He informs her that he has issued Dr Cellan-Jones with a final ultimatum – sign up to the agreement or we will see you in court. He also warns Sylvia that her decision to sign the deed poll could have consequences:

This means that the agreement will show your name as 'Cellan-Jones' whether the other parties like it or not. It should not make any material difference to them as if there is an agreement there will be no publicity; but it might cause them to decline to complete – at the last moment.

Then a few days later comes the news that must have been a huge relief to Sylvia as she and Stephen got to grips with looking after the baby. The ultimatum had worked: Jimmy and his father had backed down and agreed to sign. 'It would seem obvious,' writes Cecil Parker, 'that they realise that in order to avoid Magistrates' Court Proceedings, they are going to have to meet us on reasonable grounds – which is all we have wanted throughout.'

On 25th January, Dr Cellan-Jones sends Cecil a cheque for £158 with a document stating, 'I direct that this money shall be placed on deposit at the Bank in a special account for the maintenance of the child of Mrs Sylvia Cellan-Jones (born on 17.1.58) between the ages of sixteen and eighteen years.' Once Jim arrives in Swansea, he explains, they will both sign the maintenance agreement which will see Sylvia receive £6 10s per month for the first 16 years of the child's life. And after all of Parker's concerns, he turns out to be quite wrong about Cecil Cellan-Jones's attitude to Sylvia's name change:

Because of your promise that no publicity will arise I do not object to the description of Mrs Rich as 'Mrs Sylvia

*Cellan-Jones' in the agreement – in fact I sympathise
with her desire to disguise illegitimacy.*

The deed of arrangement, another ornate legal document I
have in my possession, was signed on 3rd February. It begins:
'The Mother has given birth to an illegitimate male child and
the Father agrees that he is the father of that child.' That
father, described as an assistant floor manager, agrees to pay
a monthly sum to 'Alsie Margaret Sylvia Cellan-Jones' for
the maintenance of that child as long as she agrees to drop
any other claims against him. Cecil Cellan-Jones, consultant
surgeon, agrees to act as surety. Jim and his father's signatures
are witnessed by James Strutton and E.H. Robertson, possibly
medical colleagues of Cecil's who could be relied upon to keep
their mouths shut.

Finally, the battle was over but before Sylvia and Jimmy
could go their separate ways one last matter had to be sorted
out – the baby's birth had to be registered in a way that would,
in Dr Cellan-Jones's words, 'disguise illegitimacy'. That meant
that Jim had to be present and at the bottom of the red box
of love letters I found this brief note from him: 'Anytime on
Saturday morning at Chelsea any time you like. Please let me
know time, and I will meet you there. JCJ'

They met at Chelsea register office on Saturday 22nd
February. I presume Sylvia left me at home with Stephen and a
bottle and headed off on the bus, tense and miserable, having
agonised for ages over what to wear. A few days after what
was to be her last encounter with Jim for many years, Sylvia
wrote to Lavinia Cellan-Jones. Of all the thousands of letters
I found when I cleared out the flat, this is the one I find most
heartbreaking.

25th February 1958

Dear Mrs Cellan-Jones,

Thank you for your card. Jimmy met me in Chelsea on Saturday and we completed the registration. We have called the baby Nicholas Rory – I had wanted to call him Nicholas James but Jimmy said not. So Rory was decided rather on the spur of the moment with the Registrar waiting. I'm not very sure about it but Stephen had liked it and I couldn't think of anything better.

I'm glad that the legal business is now settled. I never thought it would be so protracted – and it has not been pleasant for any of us. I hope we can now forget it.

I asked Sir George Barnes to be a godfather but he says that he is now too far away to perform the obligations and to get to know the boy. I must think again.

Please will you come and see the baby when you are next in London. I would so much like you to. He is a lovely baby and making good progress now. My family say he is very like Jimmy, though it isn't so obvious to me.

Did any of his ancestors have red hair? Because the baby is distinctly chestnut.

Yours sincerely

Sylvia

Lavinia sent cards and a little money to Sylvia each Christmas until her death in 1962. But she never did come to see her grandson.

CHAPTER 10

EARLY YEARS

I'm looking at a photograph and trying to understand what it says, rather in the way my Cambridge supervisors wanted me to look beneath the surface of some twentieth-century modernist French novel and divine the subtext. It's the first of only half a dozen or so photos of me before the age of 10 – I am writing this just 24 hours after the birth of our first grandson and I already have on my phone more pictures of him than were taken of me in my childhood.

The photo I am studying is a rather beautifully composed black and white shot of my mother standing holding me wrapped in a white shawl by the window in the living room at Ruskin Park House. She is wearing a simple striped blouse, her face is beautiful but slightly drawn, her skin blemish-free and she is gazing down at me, while I look placidly into the camera.

You can see just behind me on the windowsill the small bookcase Stephen made in a school woodwork class. It was in the same place 38 years later when I cleared out the flat, with the same editions of *Reader's Digest* augmented by a few Dick Francis thrillers. It was Stephen behind the camera, one borrowed from a neighbour, and in a letter from Bunty to Sylvia he was rightly complimented on his skills as a photographer.

But as I look at my mother gazing rather solemnly down at me, I am aware now that this was a time when my future was in the balance, when I could have ended up in a different home with another surname and led another life, which did not lead to me cradling a beautiful grandson called David Cellan-Jones against my tatty old Welsh rugby shirt yesterday. For at the time the photo was taken, Sylvia was under overwhelming pressure from family, from friends and from BBC colleagues to give me up for adoption.

The pressure started before I was born. Replying to Sylvia's long letter recounting the story of her affair with Jim, her wise old friend Edna had some advice:

> *I have a suggestion to make which I hope you give very careful consideration. It is this – I have some very charming friends who are anxious to adopt a baby – they have applied to their local adoption society but*

these things take time. If you like I will write to them
telling something of the background and the whole thing
can be done legally and in the proper manner.

In March, two months after my birth, a BBC colleague
Betty writes with a similar idea. 'What I would say to you is
this – why don't you have Nicholas adopted?'

Now, Betty herself had just given birth to an illegitimate
child but says for her it's different – she has always wanted
a child and this may be her only chance, whereas Sylvia has
spent 16 years bringing up Stephen. And even now, when her
BBC colleagues all know about my existence, she reckons
something can be arranged with little fuss by the Church of
England Adoption Society which advertises in *The Times*:

Nobody at your work need know – you could say that
your sister was going to bring him up or something
like that ... If the baby is adopted there's a 90 per cent
chance of his being extremely happy in a well educated
home with a proper father and mother.

Despite some updating of the law, adoption in the late
1950s remained a largely informal affair. According to a study
by Dr Jenny Keating of the Institute of Historical Research,
only around a quarter of adoptions were arranged through
registered societies like the one Betty mentions – 'so all the
rest were mainly informal arrangements by friends and
acquaintances, or individual professionals like doctors and
matrons.'

That appears to be what Bunty has in mind when she too
writes in March, a time when Sylvia is at a low ebb:

I do hope you have cheered up a bit since you wrote and did so wish I could dash up to see you when I had your letter. I know we've been all over this before and how easy it is for me to talk but I do feel dear that you must accept the way things have turned out in this affair and for Stephen's sake and your own get on with life.

Then she returns to a theme she has obviously visited before: 'I still think for Stephen's sake, yours and the baby's, it would have been better to consider adoption.' She says she knows a local young couple with a thriving photography business 'and all they want is a baby boy'.

Now, my aunt went on to become the most wonderfully loving and supportive figure in my childhood. She and her husband Bill welcomed me to their home in Harborne for long stretches every school holiday and I adored her until the day she died at the age of 101. So at first, reading that she urged Sylvia to have me adopted was a bit of a shock. But both she and Mum's friends Edna and Betty had a good point – in the early months of 1958, it looked as though life would be better not just for Sylvia and Stephen but for me if we went our separate ways.

Betty puts it like this:

You must have already suffered and struggled to bring up Stephen almost by yourself. I feel you owe it to yourself to have as good a time as you can in the future, and not have to be bothered with a new child all over again.

She says she also feels for Stephen, who at 16 is just at the beginning of his adult life. It's not fair to tie him to home and a baby brother:

Then there's the sheer terrible physical struggle for you having the worry of coping with a baby in your private life, and the office for the rest of the day – I can imagine you being worn out for the next 15 years just existing. Lastly and perhaps the most important of all, is the baby. He won't have a father, and he won't really have a mother, since she won't be there for most of his life, and so he won't have the solid background which I feel is every baby's birthright.

Edna too says a baby will be bad news for both Sylvia and Stephen:

I am sure you do not want to start all over again with a young baby on your hands, just when you were getting your life more organised. Of course Stephen will be terribly jealous – he probably does not think so, but after being an only child for sixteen years he will not like the attention that will be lavished on a baby. He might think he will not mind but he does not realise what it will mean to him.

They were both wrong about Stephen. He wasn't jealous because he didn't see himself as a big brother, more as a substitute parent for me. He changed nappies, put me to bed in the cot in the corner of his bedroom and later delivered me to the childminder or nursery school in his unreliable old banger. In the process of taking on so much responsibility he found his feet and grew up – quite literally. A worrying growth deficiency which the doctors had puzzled over and which left him looking much younger and shorter than his age suddenly fixed itself. While he was away touring Scotland as one of the lost boys in *Peter Pan* his voice broke and soon he was transformed into a tall, thin adult, rather like his father.

But for my mother, it was a different story. A life and career that had been blossoming were suddenly plunged into the deep freeze. She faced what seemed an impossible dilemma – to carry on doing a job she loved, and which paid the bills, she would have to find childcare. A childminder or nursery was likely to be beyond her means and there was not room in the flat for a live-in nanny or an au pair.

There was some good news on the financial front. A BBC administrator wrote to congratulate her on my birth – 'I am so pleased to hear the long burdensome wait is over' – and with some practical help:

I am pleased, too, to be able to tell you it has been agreed that you may continue to be paid monthly during your thirteen weeks' Maternity Leave. This news will, I am sure, help to lighten your financial worries.

Well, up to a point. The clock was ticking and Sylvia would have to be back at work full-time in mid-April. The £6 10s monthly payments from my father began in February but she feared that at some stage it might arrive with the tax deducted. In July, her fears proved justified. Jim, playing by the book, had first paid the tax to the Inland Revenue before sending on a reduced payment of £3 14s 9d. From the correspondence with her lawyers, it looks as though she could claim the tax back but no doubt it was a lengthy and painful process.

So here she was, a single mother again at 43, trapped in a tiny flat with probably 20 years of struggling to make ends meet ahead of her. No wonder many of those close to her were urging her to break free by giving her baby away. Many – but not all. In April, Jane Grigson wrote her an immensely wise and kind letter with advice from her and Geoffrey: 'We're both very glad that you didn't marry Jimmy. And I expect you will be too when the nastiness fades off,' she wrote. And she continued with a shrewd analysis of my father:

Don't you think that if you and Jimmy had really been made for a happy marriage with each other, solicitors, parents, financial settlements, wouldn't have affected your relationship but strengthened it?

She and Geoffrey had been through some hard times when Geoffrey's wife – from whom he had been separated for some years – refused to divorce him. But she says they stuck together through thick and thin.

Jimmy doesn't sound mature enough to look after you properly; to say balls off to the solicitors and his mum, this is my life and my child and my happiness, and I and no one else am going to settle it?

Then she turns to adoption. Sylvia had written that Michael Barry, her former boss as BBC head of drama, is another voice advocating adoption on the grounds that the baby will damage Stephen's career in the theatre:

We see the point of all that Michael Barry says regarding Stephen and the stage, but surely having the baby adopted wouldn't really settle that one. Don't you think that Stephen would feel guilty and miserable, at any rate later on, if the baby was adopted on his account?

Was it Jane's letter that determined my future? Probably not, but I am still grateful to her – especially as if I had been adopted I would not have met the Grigsons and spent happy weeks at their Wiltshire farmhouse during my childhood.

But Sylvia, it seems, was determined to keep me, whatever anyone said. She had a stubborn streak and always resented being told how to live her life – whether by her parents, who didn't want her to leave home at 16; her husband, who did want her to leave the BBC; or later her sons, who suggested that buying the flat from the council might be a good idea. From the moment that she started telling family and close friends she was pregnant, she seems to have resisted any pressure to do anything but go ahead and become a mother again.

There are hints in a letter from Joan a year or so after I was born that Sylvia might have been under pressure to terminate the pregnancy. She writes, as the sisters often did then, about something she has seen on television the previous evening:

There was a very interesting programme on I.T.V. last night on Abortion. Apparently 160 are carried out each day and One in Four homes have experience of it. There are some dreadful dangers involved particularly with syringes creating air locks in the womb to say nothing of the shock factor which accounts for a number of deaths apparently.

Remember, at this time abortion was illegal and procuring one was a criminal act. Nevertheless, it seems the law was widely flouted:

There was one place operating on such a large scale in London that a secretarial staff was employed and taxis provided to fetch clients to and from the nearest station. Fees at 100 to 150 guineas a time.

Then she writes this: 'I think it would have done the C.J's good to have seen it.'

What is she hinting at? Does she mean that Cecil Cellan-Jones and his wife encouraged Sylvia to have an abortion, despite the fact that anyone in the medical profession would see their career end in disgrace if they were found to be involved in such lawbreaking? The next paragraph hints, however, that the surgeon may have suggested a legal route to ending the pregnancy:

Of course several gynaecologists said they practised it in hospitals in extenuating circumstances. For example where a mother-to-be catches German Measles in the first six weeks of pregnancy then more often than not the child would be born blind or malformed. But it seems that wherever it is practised under safe conditions there must be extenuating circumstances, much more extenuating than you could have proved.

Perhaps the suggestion came during the dinner in Bristol with Jim's parents the night before the September meeting, but by then she was around five months pregnant and thus any legal route to termination was almost certainly closed.

In any event, she sailed on and in the spring of 1958 set about the job of finding childcare so that she could pursue her career at the BBC. The answer to this conundrum came in the form of Louise Gregory, a childminder who lived a few hundred yards away on Champion Hill, now a fashionable address, then very much not. Mrs Gregory, or 'Auntie' as I learned to call her as soon as I could talk, was an emergency foster mother as well as taking in children like me for daycare. She was to become a major figure in my life, looking after me five days a week and overnight when Mum was working late at Television Centre. Even after I started coming home on my own in secondary school, I would still be despatched to stay overnight at Auntie's every six weeks when Mum's latest play was in studio, right up until I was 16.

By April, Sylvia was back at work and she had obviously been in touch with the drama department during her three months away because she was immediately called to an appointment board for a permanent job as a production assistant. She didn't get the job but seems to have quickly resumed her previous duties as a director's assistant, straight back into the old routine, building up to the weekends in studio, with no concession to her other life as the mother of a young baby.

And remarkably, it all seems to have worked. For the first couple of weeks of my life, Joan's daughter Anne came down from Birmingham to stay in the flat to help. How three people and a baby rubbed along in that tiny space heaven knows but Anne, one of my godparents, later told me it was a precious moment in her life and when she went home, after years of trying, she and her husband promptly produced three daughters in quick succession.

From then on, it was Stephen and Mrs Gregory who became my prime carers during the week.

When I search my earliest memories two hazy images come to mind. In the first, I am standing up in my cot in the bedroom I shared with Stephen, bawling my head off and demanding to be let out. From time to time, my brother appears, says some gentle words to soothe me but makes it clear I'm not getting out until I calm down, so I begin bawling again.

In the other image, I am sitting on a beach on a furiously hot day with Auntie and a clutch of other small but rambunctious kids. Somehow, we have come on a short holiday to the Isle of Sheppey, some 40 miles east of London. I know this is not a false memory because I have documentary evidence in the form of a postcard. It is postmarked 'Sheerness' and in strangely neat handwriting reads:

Dear Mummy, We got here safe on Friday about ten. All day today we have been on the beach. Auntie says I am a good boy. It has been very hot today and we all went in the sea. I hope you have a very happy holiday. Lots of love from Rory.

Obviously this had been written by Mrs Gregory – except for the name and address of the recipient which was in my mother's handwriting: 'Mrs A.M.S. CELLAN-JONES, ST TROPEZ, FRANCE'.

So, far from toiling away at work, Sylvia was on holiday in the South of France, in the village beloved by Brigitte Bardot and other celebrities, a byword for glamorous tourism in the early 1960s. I've also found from around the same period postcards addressed to me at Mrs Gregory's house from a holiday in the Swiss ski resort of Grindelwald. From the age of 20 when she took that day trip to Le Touquet, Sylvia had always valued her holidays and spent a good proportion of her income on them. And looking back, I don't begrudge her those weeks away from a squalling infant and what was probably an untidy and claustrophobic flat. After all, from the age of five, I was taken by her each August for a week in a hotel by the seaside – Bournemouth, Newquay, the Isle of Wight. By the time I was in my teens we even ventured abroad a couple of times on package holidays to Majorca and Sardinia, though her stress levels about everything from getting to the airport on time to whether she had packed her sleeping pills made these trips less fun. In any case, by then I was in that teenage state of perpetual resentment and embarrassment where you want to be as far away from your parents as possible.

Paradoxically it seems to have been in my first two years that Sylvia was at her most free, with Stephen and Mrs Gregory combining to allow her to hold down a demanding full-time job, have some kind of social life and even go abroad on holiday. Then in 1960, when I was two and he was eighteen, Stephen went away for three months on tour with *Peter Pan* in Scotland. In a newsy letter to her lawyer Cecil Parker, with whom she kept up a regular correspondence even when there were no legal matters to discuss, she says that while this will be good experience for him, she will be left 'holding the baby'.

My social life – not that it was very exciting anyway before – is now nil, as I have to rush home every night now to collect Rory from Mrs. Gregory and take him

*home and put him to bed. Stephen always did this
before – so that by the time I got home all was peace.
Luckily Mrs. Gregory has been wonderful and has
agreed to keep him for an extra hour every night, as I
can't get home from work until 7 p.m. at the earliest
– she will also keep him for weekends if I'm doing a
weekend play. But shall be delighted when Stephen
gets home again and I can come out of purdah
so to speak.*

She must have known that Stephen would not want to stick
around at Ruskin Park House for too much longer, as he set
about building a career in the theatre. But in the meantime,
Sylvia continued to try to climb the ladder in the BBC drama
department. She applied again in 1959 for promotion to
production assistant and was rebuffed once more. That
December, she received a letter from Kenneth Adam, the
director of television, telling her that she had been given
a special pay award 'because of the sustained outstanding
merit of your work'. Perhaps the BBC felt guilty about her
circumstances – or perhaps she really was doing outstanding
work. If so, you might have thought she would have been more
successful at promotion boards. Nevertheless, she persisted. In
1963, the BBC was preparing to launch its second television
channel the following year and she saw an opening, applying
for jobs either as a production or a research assistant. In her
application she stressed her experience:

*I have already had considerable experience of the work
of a Production Assistant, during 1956–60, when I
worked for some months each summer as Holiday Relief*

Floor Manager. Now that BBC2 is to start, I hope there
may be further opportunities for me to do this work.

Once again, she was rejected by the appointments board.
In 1965, at the age of 50, she had one last try at promotion.
By then, she had to admit that her last period acting as a
floor manager was some way in the past. On the application
form, she was in reflective mood about her experience back
in the 1950s:

I have always regretted, though, that there was no
Training Course for P.A.s at that time, as I feel sure that
this must be of immense value. As it was, one was just
tossed in at the deep end, no 'trailing' even.

I shall always remember my baptism of fire, as someone
called it, thirteen sets and an elephant in Riverside 1 –
live of course. But I enjoyed the work tremendously and
hope I may now be given the opportunity of a Training
Course and attachment.

Though I have not worked as P.A. for some time I have
been constantly in touch with the problems involved as
the duties of the P.A. and Assistant are bound to overlap
in many productions.

She was, of course, turned down. I imagine her bosses
shaking their heads and, with a wry smile, saying, 'Dear old
Sylvia, she's a trier but seriously, at her age, and with a young
child at home …'

So she resumed her old job as director's assistant at
Television Centre on the fifth floor where, strolling round
the circular corridor, she must have occasionally encountered

a familiar face. Jim had been away in Bristol for a few years from 1959, but by 1963 he was a director on attachment to BBC2 back in London. Now 32, he was one of a group of drama directors who would be given an assistant at the start of each new production and the administrator must have had to remember not to pair him up with Sylvia.

By now, it was just me and her alone at Ruskin Park House. In 1964, Stephen, now 22, had set off on the *Queen Mary* for New York to make his fortune on Broadway – or rather, for a short-term contract as an assistant stage manager on *Blitz!*, a musical set in wartime London. He was to be away for two years, returning eventually with the American actress he was going to marry.

We missed him dreadfully, though he was a good correspondent, keeping us abreast of his adventures in weekly blue airmail letters and postcards. But life seemed drab without Stephen, the brother who had taken me on adventures – racing across London in the front seat of his car, backstage at the Mermaid Theatre, where he was stage managing *Treasure Island* and mad Spike Milligan swept me up and capered with me on the revolving set where the action took place. Now my life revolved between Mrs Gregory's noisy flat where the television was always on, tuned to ITV, and the quieter Ruskin Park House, where Mum and I sat eating our fish fingers or cheese on toast while the Home Service or the Light Programme played on the radio.

But every holiday there was something to look forward to – escape from Champion Hill. Often that meant heading slowly across London and up the M1 in Mum's Mini to stay with Aunty Joan and Uncle Barry in Bedfordshire or being put on the Midland Red coach from Victoria to Birmingham to spend a fortnight with Bunty and Bill and my cousins. But the biggest adventure of all involved catching the train to Wootton Bassett in Wiltshire. There, I would be collected in a battered Volvo by a gruff elderly poet and transported to a draughty sixteenth-century farmhouse, where books filled every nook and cranny, where the kitchen was the laboratory of a kindly woman who was becoming Britain's best cookery writer, and where a long, straggly garden ending in a stream was the perfect playground for me and a characterful little girl called Sophie.

CHAPTER 11

THE GRIGSONS

One day in 1953, a young woman called Jane McIntire went for an interview for a job as a picture researcher at the publisher Thames & Hudson, which had commissioned an encyclopaedia called *People, Places, Things and Ideas*. She got the job and so began work with the book's editor, an irascible poet she had long admired, Geoffrey Grigson. Soon, they were in a relationship. Grigson's marriage to his second wife, Bertschy, was already in trouble and it was not long before Jane moved into the sixteenth-century Wiltshire farmhouse he had bought for a few hundred pounds in 1945.

Jane, who had studied English at Cambridge, worked with Geoffrey on several books for children but also had success as a translator from Italian. Bertschy refused point blank to grant her estranged husband a divorce, and so Jane decided to change her surname by deed poll to Grigson. Their own situation made the Grigsons all the more sympathetic to my mother in late 1957 when she told them of her predicament.

Sylvia had not worked with Geoffrey for over a decade but they had nevertheless remained in touch over that period. She always felt he had been a huge influence on her and when she said her early years at the BBC were the equivalent for her of a university education she made it clear that he was the inspirational tutor. The poet and critic could be difficult and cantankerous but never spoke down to her or treated her as a mere secretary, and it's evident from her Bristol friend Hilary's diaries that Sylvia could give as good as she got.

After he left the BBC in 1945, Grigson gave Sylvia a great reference and wrote often with career advice, encouraging her to spread her wings and leave Bristol: 'I couldn't bear to think of you wasting your efficient sarcasm (and other qualities) by ministering to the needs of Filbert Felps,' he wrote in October 1945, referring cattily to her new boss, Gilbert Phelps. 'I've learnt a lot from working with you for – how many years? – and it's been a good lesson. Even if you ought to have scratched my eyes out now and then.'

For her part, Sylvia wrote back offering gossip about former colleagues, requesting advice on her problems and even offering her own views of his output as a writer and broadcaster. When, in the summer of 1949, Gilbert Phelps went on holiday for a week, he left Sylvia in charge of producing two talks, one by Grigson. In advance of the recording, she wrote to him:

Me producing you, as I recollect, means me standing humbly by while you do precisely as you like. However, it would be a nice gesture if you would make this the best and liveliest talk in the series, when I should get the credit for ably producing 'one of our more difficult speakers'!

Amid the light-hearted banter, her admiration for him and

his work is clear. In 1950, she wrote to thank him for sending her his memoir, *The Crest on the Silver*:

This is the book I have wanted you to write for a long time (not just from idle curiosity, I knew the outline anyway).

But so many people should read it, your friends and your enemies and your victims, all parents, all schoolmasters, all big brothers of little boys.

I got half way through it over the weekend. Parts of it made me cry (for which you will call me a sentimental fool, which of course I am).

I thought the time was past when you could make me cry and never thought that one of your books would.

By the time I was born, Grigson was in his fifties and becoming a grand old man of English letters, with a prodigious output of reviews, anthologies, nature writing and poetry. But far more important, he was now settled in the Broad Town farmhouse with Jane, who would eventually take over the correspondence with Sylvia. It was Geoffrey, however, who wrote to my mother in the frantic months before my birth with wise advice about not marrying Jim, quoting the seventeenth-century poet Michael Drayton:

Since there's no help, come let us kiss and part.
Nay, I have done; you get no more of me,
And I am glad, yea, glad with all my heart
That thus so cleanly I myself can free

But he admitted that he had consulted Jane about the

situation and in the summer of 1958, it was she who wrote
to Sylvia accepting her request that Geoffrey should be a
godfather:

*Thank you SO much for your letter. We were pleased
to hear about the baby, and G will do his best in the
godfather line.*

*The names are nice we thought, particularly Rory
which is not the name of every child you come across
and doesn't sound arch or chelseaily affected. Very
difficult to avoid these pitfalls.*

She goes on to describe in a rather understated but heartfelt
manner how she has had a miscarriage – 'which was distressing
to put it mildly, as it was a nice compact little girl just what G
wanted.' But the following year, they did have a healthy baby
girl and called her Sophie.

In March 1960 Jane wrote apologising for not replying to
three letters from Sylvia, the last with 'the very adorable photo
of Rory'. She went on:

*He is a sweet child isn't he? He looks so happy which
must give you a great deal of quiet self-satisfaction!*

*When he is a little bit older, you must send him down
to stay. My sister, a few miles away, has a small son
much the same age; and I can see the two of them and
Sophie haring about the garden and getting filthy in the
sand pit and stream.*

It was in 1964 when I was six that I made my first visit
to Broad Town farmhouse. Among Sylvia's letters is a note

from Grigson in 1945 scrawled on the back of a letter from the water board arranging to have the water supply to the sixteenth-century house switched on. By all accounts it was in a primitive state and even when I first visited nearly 20 years later, it was chilly, the plumbing was rickety and a visit to the toilet meant a trip outside to a chemical loo in an outhouse.

But to me it was a magical place. Leaving the modern, centrally heated flat in Ruskin Park House and ending up in the Grigsons' house was like stepping into the wardrobe and ending up in the Narnia described in the C.S. Lewis boxed set of Puffin books Geoffrey and Jane bought me one Christmas. The house seemed vast, at its heart a spacious kitchen with a stone-flagged floor and a giant cooker called a Rayburn, many times the size of our gas stove at home and serving to supply warmth if you huddled near it.

The walls were lined with books and paintings, many, though I didn't know it at the time, by artists like John Piper, who were friends of Geoffrey and had been commissioned by him to do talks when my mother worked with him in Bristol. Upstairs, down a corridor lined with more towering bookshelves which looked ready to topple over and bury you under dusty volumes, were bedrooms for me and Sophie, a huge one for Geoffrey and Jane, and off it his study, mostly out of bounds to us children. From behind the door you could hear the constant clatter of Geoffrey's typewriter, interrupted by the occasional curse. On Tuesdays, we all tiptoed around and Jane took his lunch up on a tray – it was *Country Life* day, when he bashed out his review of notable new books for the magazine, which seemed to make him very grumpy.

While I look back on that house as a mansion, I've just found an estate agent's listing for it on the internet and realised that, before an extension built by subsequent owners, it was a perfectly standard four-bedroom home; it just seemed vast compared to our flat. But what was huge was the garden, winding down through apple trees to the stream, with a plank across it as a rudimentary bridge, then a hedge which failed to deter the pigs from the neighbouring farm from breaking through and tearing up the Grigsons' lawn.

As Jane had predicted, this became a perfect playground for me and Sophie and sometimes her cousin Matthew. We were free to run around, make some noise and even dam the stream. My memory is that we did not quite manage to flood the garden but it was a close run thing. For a city boy for whom the great outdoors meant a muddy patch of grass outside Mrs Gregory's council flat where rough boys played football while I looked on nervously, the Grigson garden was sheer delight. And beyond it there were long walks through the Wiltshire countryside and up onto the white horse etched onto the chalky hillside above Broad Town. We would return with wild flowers we had picked, then press them under weights and stick them into a scrapbook, with Geoffrey, the naturalist who was then at work on the *Shell Country Alphabet*, telling us their names.

While my godfather was a combative man known for his bitter feuds with other writers he was good with children – as long as they did not interrupt him while he was at his typewriter. Still, I was a little bit afraid of him, as I was of all men, apart from my uncles. Growing up without a father meant I did not know what was expected of me when talking to these giant creatures with their loud booming voices. Later, I learned that sport was always a good starting point, though not with Geoffrey. Once, he came into the sitting room on a

Saturday afternoon to find me watching the football results on television. He had no interest in football but stood there, transfixed by the sight of the teleprinter typing out 'Forfar 4 – East Fife 5' across the screen. 'There's a creature inside the television eating it up!' he declared. I laughed nervously, and then he was gone.

But if Geoffrey was slightly scary, I hit it off immediately with Jane, a warm and wise woman who was both very motherly and yet never talked down to children. And when I found her letter to Stephen after my first visit in 1964, I was gratified to find she had liked me too: 'He was here for four and a half weeks; he seemed to enjoy it and we certainly loved having him. I miss him very much, especially that lovely grin.' It seems Stephen, of all people, had worried that I was not tough enough, the kind of thing his father had said about him. Jane told him to pull himself together:

For heaven's sake don't worry about him not being a little tough. Any small boy can be that. Rory is something much more interesting. He has great reserves within himself and lives well with himself. This is a great strength for anyone to have. I don't think he is in the least a weak character, even if he sometimes appears to give in. He doesn't give in over things that he really wants to do I notice! Sophie is a bit bossy but if he wanted to read or not do something he wasn't dissuaded. But this never led to rows. I think he is a very mature character, and a very loving one as well.

And I had not realised that the wild flowers scrapbook was my idea:

I think he's very intelligent; he wanted to make a collection of pressed wild flowers, and we all worked with this and he kept it up with great persistence and concentration. He wanted to know about things round here, especially about the white horses carved in the Wiltshire hillsides. It became quite a mania with him. For this reason it was always a pleasure to tell him things.

In my memory, I was always cautious about other children, at least at first, but it seems not:

He met lots and lots of different children here and got on extremely well and easily with them all. I think that the moment he begins to show an interest in something, one must be ready to feed his interest and take a good deal of trouble over it because he obviously derives a great deal of pleasure from these interests, and it seems to me that this should always be cultivated to give him his own sort of strengths, rather than other people's more brutish kinds. We hope we'll be able to have him here many holidays, and look forward to watching him grow up and develop.

I did have many more holidays with the Grigsons and they helped me grow up and develop in a couple of ways. Their book-lined house helped turn me into a voracious reader – or at least saw me search out more challenging material. At home, it was the weekly arrival of the *Radio Times* and the *Sunday Express* which fed my habit, with each scoured from cover to cover once my mother had glanced at them. Otherwise, apart from the cricket books my brother had left behind, finding something new to read meant a walk up Denmark Hill to the tiny local library where, beyond the well-thumbed Mills & Boon romances, the choice was limited.

But at Broad Town, the sheer volume of books, from children's classics to contemporary novels, was almost dizzying. Without the modern distractions of smartphones and video games – though Sophie and I did watch quite a lot of telly, discovering an exciting new programme called *Star Trek* – I was able to bury myself in a book for hours at a time. Once, I discovered an early edition of Henry Fielding's *Tom Jones*, published in six little volumes. I knew nothing of this eighteenth-century novel – to me the name meant a curly headed Welshman singing 'Delilah' on a Saturday night variety show – but the bite-sized format was strangely compelling and I galloped through all six books in a couple of days, much as I might binge watch a Netflix series these days.

But when I think back to my visits to the Grigsons, it is images of food that come to mind. My mother's very limited cooking skills – eggs, beans on toast, a watery stew on a Sunday – might have made me an unadventurous eater. Instead, every time I left the flat I was eager to branch out. My Aunty Joan used to tell the story of how at the age of five, I chose rainbow trout for Sunday lunch at her local pub. The adults tried to change my mind but I insisted, and battled manfully with the bones.

Joan was a good solid English cook – cakes, roasts, pies – with ambitions to be a little more adventurous than her husband Barry, who was conservative in his tastes. Joan's pride and joy was a Kenwood mixer and she stood me on a stool to watch her feed it eggs, sugar and flour, which would be transformed magically into a cake an hour later. She subscribed to the *Cordon Bleu Cookery Course* partwork and one evening tried out something called ratatouille. We prodded at it for a few minutes until Barry pronounced it 'a bit rich' and it never made another appearance.

Jane Grigson, however, was to be a leader, not a follower, of the revolution in British attitudes to food in the 1960s and 70s. The Grigsons had an unusual home in the Loire Valley in France, a cave house where they spent months each summer, and the village pork butcher there was the inspiration for her first cookery book, *Charcuterie and French Pork Cookery*, in 1967. On the recommendation of Elizabeth David, the woman who had begun the job of convincing the British that olive oil was for more than treating earwax, Jane was then appointed cookery writer of the *Observer*.

That meant the kitchen at Broad Town farmhouse, long the centre of the home, became her laboratory as she tested recipes for her weekly columns or for the books that were to make her known as the most scholarly as well as enjoyable of English cookery writers. While French cuisine was obviously a major influence, she also did much to remind us of our own culinary heritage. I have in front of me a copy of her 1974 book *English Food*, with a note inside reminding me it was a present from Diane on our wedding day, which took place less than a month after Jane's death in 1990. Flicking through the book, dedicated to Geoffrey and Sophie, I come to a section on eighteenth- and nineteenth-century poultry recipes, which takes me back to a scene in the Broad Town kitchen in the early 1970s.

I'd arrived for a stay just after Christmas, fortified for the train journey by a tomato sandwich on white sliced bread, to find Jane at work on something called Yorkshire goose pie. In the book, Jane quotes a recipe from the eighteenth-century cookery writer Hannah Glasse, which instructs the reader to 'bone a Turkey, a Goose, a Fowl, a Partridge and a Pigeon'. The next step involves placing the pigeon inside the partridge inside the fowl inside the goose inside the turkey and then encasing this whole Russian doll construction in a thick layer of pastry with at least four pounds of butter and baking for many hours. I watched with bug-eyed wonder as Jane executed this utterly bonkers recipe, perhaps missing out one of the smaller birds. In *English Food*, Jane quotes the painter Turner thanking a friend from Otley for sending him down a 'Yorkshire Pie equal good to the Olden-time of Hannah's ... culinary exploits'.

I can't remember whether we ever got to eat the mammoth pie which eventually emerged from the Rayburn oven – I suspect it had to wait for a food photographer to capture it in all its glory for the *Observer*. But food at the Grigsons' wasn't about outlandish recipes or expensive ingredients, nor was there any great fuss about what we were eating. It was about learning that vegetables could actually taste of something if they weren't boiled to extinction; that a dash of oil and vinegar transformed a dull old lettuce – and no, the bottle of Heinz salad cream my mum brandished on the dreaded days when she decided lunch would be some iceberg lettuce and a hard-boiled egg was not an acceptable substitute.

On trips to Oxford, where Sophie was having Mandarin lessons from an early age, they took us to a Chinese restaurant, which seemed impossibly exotic, where I tried and failed to master chopsticks. Above all, food was both fun and a participatory sport. One summer, both Sophie and I, gently coached by Jane, made Victoria sponges and competed for prizes in the bakery tent at the Broad Town fete. You may not be surprised to hear that while my cake was criticised by the judges for its mottled appearance – 'take care not to curdle the mixture' – Sophie's was highly commended, an early portend of her own successful career as a cookery writer and broadcaster. (Mind you, I did win the fete's fancy dress competition, coming as an astronaut in white overalls with one of Jane's colanders as a helmet.)

It is clear from the correspondence between Jane and Sylvia that I was becoming something of a gourmet. In October 1967, when I was nine, Jane wrote describing the feast at the wedding of Geoffrey's daughter Anna: 'We had smoked salmon and duck and orange and cheese and ginger ice cream and strawberry ice cream, just the kind of food Rory would appreciate I think.'

Sylvia's reply showed Jane was spot on: 'The food sounded quite marvellous. Rory read it out slowly, with dramatic pauses like an incantation (if that's the word I mean?), I think he was imagining himself eating it.'

I visited Broad Town most years from the age of 6 to 16, sometimes twice a year, and the letters between the two women, as well as arranging those visits, give a constant commentary on how Sophie and I are developing, what's going on in their working lives, and chatter about the BBC.

In 1965, Sylvia writes that, 'Television goes on and on like a never-ending relay race – v exhausting.' Then she casually drops in: 'Jimmy is directing a new serial called *Enemy of the State* starting on Sunday which I'm told is good.' Once more, they were working on the same floor in Television Centre, brushing past each other in the corridor.

A couple of years later, it seems Geoffrey and Jane are unimpressed by what they see on their television. Jane writes:

Why don't you persuade your boneheaded bosses to do some plays by Ionesco or somebody interesting? Very bored with the run of Wednesday Plays. If they really think that Cathy Come Home *is a triumph for anyone they must be certifiable! The decline of the BBC TV is a really saddening spectacle …*

Again, in Sylvia's reply my father makes an appearance:

Sorry you hate our programmes so! Nothing new and exciting to report I'm afraid. Jim is directing some of The Forsyte Saga *– BBC2 is better by far than 1 I think now.*

Sylvia's letters paint a vivid picture of her hopes and anxieties about me as I grow older and she tries to juggle work and childcare as a single mother. In response comes calm reassurance from Jane. In 1969, when I was 11, Sylvia shows some awareness of how boring I was beginning to find life in the flat with her compared with a visit to Broad Town:

I'm so happy that Rory is with you – Sophie's company and yours will be so much more enlivening for him than having to listen to my dreary old television problems. Do let him help where you can – he is quite good at washing up, peeling potatoes etc and I don't want him to get out of practice.

When she reports my success in winning a scholarship to Dulwich College – a great relief as the fees were unaffordable – there is a lovely reply from Jane:

How splendidly unsurprising about his scholarship. Give him a hug and tell him how pleased we are. You know we have always thought him exceptional. And so nice as well.

It is only now, as I read these letters, that I realise what an important figure Jane was in my childhood, despite the fact that I saw her at most twice a year. She was an adult who clearly showed me both love and respect, and she was also a wise counsellor to my increasingly anxious mum, probably saying things my beloved aunts would be reluctant to express.

Sylvia seems to have used her as a sounding board, worrying in one letter about me doing my homework in Mrs Gregory's flat, surrounded by noisy children and with 'commercial television' always on. In another, she frets about my stay in hospital to have my tonsils out and how long it is taking me to recover. Jane writes back with a book recommendation for me, *The Lost Domain* by Alain-Fournier.

Even after I stopped visiting in my late teens, the letters continued, as did the Christmas presents, though a cheque replaced the books which had been such an important part of my education. But by then, the dynamic between the two women was changing. As I began to break free of home, Sylvia seemed ever more anxious about letting me escape into adulthood and the dangers out there in the wide world, while Jane, 14 years her junior, tried tactfully to suggest it was time to let go.

When in 1977 I headed to West Berlin on a six-month gap year programme, after winning a place at Cambridge the following October, Sylvia is worried that I may be led astray in that sinful city, but Jane is not.

I hardly think you need worry about Rory's exposure to vice in Berlin. He is an incredibly well-balanced person and will keep his head. In any case vice is always quite difficult to get into, unless one is absolutely determined on it, or dreadfully inadequate.

She then says that she does not think Geoffrey's 'aphrodisiac advice' to me would be quite what a mother would like: 'Probably along the lines of make the most of your opportunities and don't be nervous of the superior-looking girls!'

The sad truth is that, try as I might, I failed to find any vice, but when I mentioned in a letter home that my aged Berlin landlady had two rather attractive teenage granddaughters, alarm bells rang. Sylvia expressed her worries to Jane again but was not convinced by her reply. 'I've thought a lot about your letter,' she wrote back. 'No, I don't want Rory to marry the first girl he goes to bed with … But "sex just for fun"? – like fireworks. Aren't you undervaluing it a bit?' I suppose that, given her situation, she was bound to see sex outside marriage as a complicated matter.

I'm so glad I didn't know at the time that this dialogue about my non-existent teenage sex life was going on. But I am grateful to Jane, who continued to push back in the most gentle and tactful manner over the next few years as Sylvia provided further evidence of my reckless behaviour, whether that was splitting up with a girlfriend she liked or giving up my pension to move jobs.

My final visit to Broad Town farmhouse came in 1985 when I accompanied my mum to Geoffrey's funeral. He had been ill for a while but even in his eightieth year had continued to be incredibly productive, with five books – poetry, anthologies, nature writing – published in 1984.

The funeral service was held in the village church just a short walk from Broad Town farmhouse and afterwards Geoffrey was buried in the churchyard. As the mourners turned away from the graveside and followed Jane and Sophie back to the house, Sylvia held back for a moment and then blew a kiss in the direction of the grave. At the time, I was impatient and – as ever – embarrassed by what I saw as yet another attention-seeking gesture by my increasingly annoying old mum.

Now I see it differently. She was saying goodbye to the man who had set her life on a different course, given her wise and honest advice in difficult times, and, as a fond and generous godparent, had had considerable influence on my childhood and future too.

CHAPTER 12

SCHOOL, MONEY, CLASS

One day in 2019, after I had described a right-wing newspaper columnist in a tweet as a racist, he sent me the following message:

I do hope you've got a decent lawyer, Rory. As yet another flatulent and talentless BBC public schoolboy you probably do. But I do too, believe me. I've been waiting for this sort of thing from a serving BBC idiot for quite a while.

A threat then, but one whose impact was diminished by the fact that it was sent via Facebook Messenger, a service I rarely used. As the writer was not a Facebook friend I did not get a notification about the message, and I only saw it about a month later when I was clearing the spam from my inbox.

As a matter of fact I did not have a lawyer, but as there had been no formal complaint to me or the BBC in the last four weeks, it felt as though the writer was all mouth and no trousers. But while I was not going to rush out and seek blue-chip legal advice, the message set me thinking about his description of me. Flatulent? A little unfair. Talentless? Well, everyone's entitled to their opinion. But 'BBC public schoolboy'? Bang to rights. I had been educated at Dulwich College from nine and before that had attended its prep school from the age of five. From Dulwich, I went on to Cambridge and a degree in modern and medieval languages, and, after just a couple of months of work in a bank, to a career in the BBC. A privileged start in life then, and one which, in the extraordinarily ornate English class system, placed me in the upper strata of the middle classes, indeed even on the fringes of upper-middle class. A typical BBC public schoolboy.

Yet growing up, it certainly did not feel like that. Another take is that I was an illegitimate child with no contact with his father, brought up in a one-bedroom council flat by a serial single mother who farmed me out for much of my childhood to a cockney childminder in another council flat packed with too many foster kids. That is also accurate, and sends me hurtling down the social ladder to the lower-middle, bordering on working, classes but again, that does not feel quite right.

The truth is, as ever, far more nuanced and complicated. By one definition, I was the first in my family to go to university and get a degree, if by family you meant my mother's side, though my Aunt Bunty spent a term as a Birmingham student when she thought of becoming a teacher. The Parishes, after a bit of a helter-skelter ride down the social scale – from gentleman farmers to pub managers and B&B hosts – had settled comfortably bang in the middle of the Midlands middle classes. But on the Cellan-Jones side – a mystery to me until my mid-twenties – it was a tale of rapid upward mobility, albeit with a distinctive Welsh flavour. It culminated in a house in the best part of Swansea, a Rolls-Royce and a son James despatched over the border to the Dragon School in Oxford, Charterhouse and Cambridge.

It is clear what my mother thought – education was the key to advancing up the social ladder. She had left school at 14 and felt her education only really began in Geoffrey Grigson's BBC office in the war. He and the other producers in the talks department had been to public schools so that was what she wanted for her sons – but the problem was money.

Searching back through the Sylvia files, there are huge volumes of letters and documents relating to my schooling, and that of Stephen before me. Stephen started at an ordinary Bristol state primary school and Sylvia, as I had found out, had even contemplated leaving her job at the BBC and becoming secretary to the headmaster of Dartington, a progressive school in Devon. She did all the sums, met the headmaster for tea at a London hotel and was lobbied hard by Geoffrey Grigson to take the job. 'He says I'm shutting my eyes to its virtues simply because I don't want to leave the BBC,' she wrote to her sister Joan.

As I sit now reading the letter where she confirms she won't be taking the job, I realise it was another sliding doors moment. If she'd gone to Devon, she would never have met my father and I would not be writing this.

But Sylvia did not give up on her belief that if you wanted to make your way in life a good education was the key and that almost certainly meant paying for it. In 1951, with Stephen aged nine and decisions about a secondary school imminent, she outlined her worries and her philosophy on this matter in several long letters to Richie. (Despite their estrangement, she kept up a constant lengthy and quite frank correspondence with him throughout the 1950s.) In one letter, she reminds him that she needs the 18 shillings for Stephen's train fare to stay with Richie because her finances are stretched and a big expense is imminent:

I believe I told you I shall work I think now on Good Friday and Easter Monday, thereby I hope earning myself two guineas overtime to pay Jo's registration fee at Westminster where I'm thinking of letting him sit for the junior scholarship exam.

Stephen – or Jo as they still called him – didn't get that scholarship, so that two guineas was kissed goodbye. But later, in another letter to Richie, she summarises her ambitions for him (and later for me) while doubting they are achievable:

I would still like a public school and Oxford or Cambridge education for Jo – more than anything in the world. The point is that having searched all round for ways to give it him I have come to the conclusion that nothing but plenty of hard cash will do it – and that that kind of education is only for the well to do, especially now that fees have increased still further.

Then she reflects on her own education:

Most mothers want as I do the best education for their sons – it is really only since I have been in the B.B.C. that it has meant so much to me and that I've realised how much the public school and University background can do to give a boy a wider and fuller life when he becomes an adult. But there are exceptions, either way.

Plenty of people without it still become happy and successful adults and plenty with it turn out 'proper drear'. One of the things it does is to give them social confidence! but Jo has plenty of that anyway! I hated school myself and left thankfully when I was fourteen with no education to speak of. All I have I have acquired since I've been here, and it has made me wish that I'd stayed at school longer.

All the same I have progressed further here than some women I know with Roedean, Girton, B.As and so forth as a background.

All this is really to say that I haven't changed my ideas of what I want in the least, but have been forced to realise that I was flying too high for our station in life, and that I must make the best of what is available, which I have always thought was pretty good anyway. But one always wants better, and if possible the best. There's no crime in that.

Stephen never did make it into the kind of school Sylvia aspired to, though after they moved to Ruskin Park House in 1955 he did get a place at Alleyn's, which back then was a grammar school free to those who passed the 11-plus. Like his mother, though, his real education came elsewhere, as a child actor at the Old Vic, something which the headmaster at Alleyn's made clear had to stop once he was at a serious school. But Stephen left Alleyn's at 17 with few qualifications to pursue a career in the theatre, first as an assistant stage manager, later as a director and playwright. He was still sharing the one-bedroom flat with Sylvia – and now with me, a noisy one-year-old in the cot in the corner. As the nearest thing

I had to a father he must have felt some responsibility to bring home a bit of cash.

But if Stephen didn't get the chance of a public school and Oxbridge education, when I came along Sylvia was all the more determined that things would be different. Among the biggest, bulkiest folders of letters that I retrieved from under the dressing table in the flat in 1996 was one marked 'Education File'. It contained every single one of my school reports – 'a cheerful soul ... but academically he is letting things slip, and cheerfulness is not enough on its own'. But far more surprising – and disturbing when I looked back from my late thirties – was the evidence of her desperate quest to get me into a top school, probably as a boarder.

From 1961, when I was three, there is correspondence with a clutch of public schools. She wrote to Westminster, to St George's Windsor, even to Eton. There is a letter from Colonel H. St J. Carruthers, bursar of Westminster, thanking her for sending a cheque to register me as a candidate for a boarding vacancy ten years hence in 1971. (My half-brothers, Simon and Din, did end up at Westminster in the 1970s and did not know of my existence – so finding an older boy sharing their name would have been a shock.)

St George's Windsor writes back to say the only way I could get a place would be by winning a choristership when I was eight – all non-chorister places were booked until 1969. Trying for a place as a chorister would involve singing a set piece as well as something of my own choice – growing up in a flat where music was limited to *Sing Something Simple* on the radio on a Sunday evening, that was not going to happen.

Then there is a letter from the headmaster of Eton. 'Dear Miss Rich,' he begins – somehow she must have forgotten to use the Cellan-Jones name she adopted generally for any communications with schools.

Entry at Eton is not made on a central school list, but on one of the lists made up by masters, who will be in charge of houses when the boy is due to come. Boys come at the age of twelve or thirteen, so masters are now making up their lists for 1974, as it is very rare indeed to find a place left on a master's list if a boy is entered when over a year old.

So his message is you're too late, Miss Rich, you should have applied the moment he was born. He does mention that the occasional place falls vacant when a boy who has been accepted by the school fails the Common Entrance exam, but that it is then left to the 25 housemasters to decide who to take in his place. Hopeless, then – but in any case, it is hard to imagine how Sylvia thought she would pay Eton's school fees.

But the most prolonged correspondence is with the rather less grand Monkton Combe School in Bath. Sylvia was interested in this option because her sister, my beloved Aunt Joan, was living near Bath at the time. She arranged for Joan and her husband Barry, a solid, patient and amiable man who Joan met while trying to decide on the purchase of a lawnmower, to visit the school. Joan writes approvingly of Monkton Combe – 'good dormitory accommodation, a bit crowded perhaps, but very bright and clean (a teddy bear on one bed!)'. She also encourages Sylvia to consult my Cellan-Jones grandparents about her plans for my public school education 'without asking for help, unless offered of course'.

It sounds as though she did write to Lavinia Cellan-Jones,

who wasn't at all happy about this news. When his mother passed away in 1962, Jim wrote to Sylvia saying he'd spoken to her shortly before she died 'and she was terribly upset and worried that you were thinking of sending him [me] to Monkton Combe.' Jim says, 'She thought it would worry me' – presumably because he and his new wife Maggie were then living in the West Country while he worked for BBC Bristol's drama department and somehow there was the threat of scandal if a boy named Cellan-Jones turned up at a nearby school. He insists he is not worried and Sylvia should send me wherever she wants, but he goes on to ask her not to send a letter of condolence to his father. He'd apparently not known that his wife had been corresponding with Sylvia since shortly after my birth and had become very upset when he had found their letters.

That letter also talks of Lavinia having left some savings certificates that might have been intended to pay for my education, with Jim promising to send them on. But on the back of the envelope my mother has written this: 'Later – nothing actually developed from these suggestions – no additional savings certifs – or school fees, expenses.'

This does not endear me to the grandparents who I never met and who had greeted news of my birth 'with very mixed feelings'. And yet, while she complained about a lot of things and worried constantly about money, Mum did not seek to make me resentful of the Cellan-Joneses, which makes me think better of her.

In the file is also a typed note about various obscure educational establishments that might take me on as a boarder. 'Oak Lodge – a home for children, parents abroad etc. 5 guineas a week.'

'Sherrardswood School Welwyn Garden City – 75 guineas a term boarders.' 'Leeson House, Swanage, pre-prep: 5–10. Fees: £80 per term.'

Somehow, when I first skimmed this file shortly after Mum died, I didn't really take in the truly frightening thing about it. Coming back to it now on a hot summer's day a shiver runs down my spine as I realise something terrifying – she wanted to send me away to boarding school, perhaps even from the age of just five! So much has emerged in the last two decades about the abuse that was rife in English boarding schools in the 1960s, and maybe I've read too many first-hand accounts of the misery that scarred some of the victims for life, but I can't help but feel horrified that she would have contemplated sending me away. Joan's description of the teddy bear on the bed in the Monkton Combe dorm is obviously meant to be reassuringly cosy to Sylvia – but to my twenty-first-century eyes it's downright sinister.

Thankfully it never happened, I wasn't sent away.

I think it was advice from an old BBC colleague that saved me. Eileen Moloney had been a producer in the BBC Bristol talks department in 1941, sharing an office with Sylvia's boss Geoffrey Grigson. In a letter from a Bath address dated 23rd August – no year but I'm assuming it's 1961 – she starts by saying, 'From what I can make out Monkton Combe is a very good school, the children seem happy and it is certainly beautifully situated.' But, she goes on, 'Sylvia dear I don't think you ought to contemplate sending Rory away to school at five.'

She proceeds in wonderfully BBC producer style (she says she learned about child development while running a series called *Parents and Children*) to set out six points reinforcing her argument against boarding schools for young children. The really formative years, she explains, 'are from babyhood through the early years when he is forming a relationship of love and affection with one or two people'. The lack of this relationship is a factor in delinquency and 'in all the child's relationships in adult life, friendship, marriage, his own children, his relationships in his job – the lot'.

Studies have shown, she goes on, 'better a bad home with drunken or even criminal parents than an "Institution" where little children are looked after by busy teachers working on a shift system where the child is unable to feel it belongs.'

But Eileen has a solution – 'Supposing on the other hand Rory went to Mrs G as a weekly boarder he would maintain continuity in his relationship with her and with you. It is so important that he shouldn't feel subconsciously that you or she or both are "rejecting" him.'

And so here's who really saved me from being sent with my teddy bear to that terrifying dorm at Monkton Combe – Mrs G, Louise Gregory, the childminder my mother had found when I was just three months old. I did not become a weekly boarder but it seems that this was how the arrangement was made that I would stay for a night or over a weekend when Mum had to work late when her production was in the studio. The three-bedroom flat always seemed packed with foster children, many from an Afro-Caribbean background. Social workers would arrive in the evening with another child who was an emergency case – it seemed no questions were asked about whether four or five children to a bedroom might be too many.

The crisis that came when Auntie moved three miles away to Pearson House, a council block at the foot of Sydenham

Hill, was partly solved by Stephen and his ancient Riley delivering me to her – after all, working in the theatre as a stage manager meant a late start most days. But after a while, Mum bought her first car, the pale yellow Mini, and she began the routine of dropping me at Pearson House at nine, then driving to Television Centre for a day at work, picking me up again just before 7pm.

Mrs Gregory was a cheerful soul with quite a robust attitude to childcare – step out of line and the foster children could expect a thwack, though I was treated a little more gently. She was her family's sole breadwinner – as she used to regularly remind her husband George, or 'Uncle'. He had been a hospital cook but contracted multiple sclerosis and by the time I arrived in their house spent his day in his chair in front of the TV, reading the *Daily Mirror* and deciding where to place his bets before the racing came on.

That television was always on and nearly always tuned to ITV, which is the reason I have an allergic reaction to the dreary sound of the *Coronation Street* theme tune. Hearing it at 7pm meant my mum was late to pick me up. Mind you, one of my earliest memories is of *Coronation Street* being interrupted just as she'd arrived by a newsflash about the shooting of President Kennedy in November 1963.

By then, I had just started at the nursery class at Dulwich College Preparatory School, not as a boarder but as a day boy. At first, Mrs Gregory would pick me up at 3.30pm; later, I would walk the half mile to Pearson House, passing Kingsdale, the terrifying comprehensive which my mother was determined would not be my destination at 11. Later, it was good enough for the two Gregory children – Barbara, four years older than me, and Paul, a year or so younger, and a gentle soul whose room I shared when I came to stay.

But throughout my time at prep school and later at Dulwich College, Kingsdale was held up by my mum as the epitome of the kind of rough school you would want to avoid. And some of it was true – in the 1970s it had terrible exam results and its boys had a reputation for violence, beating up the despised college boys and chucking their ridiculous boaters onto the railway line.

So to keep me out of the south London state school system, Sylvia bit the bullet and paid the fees at Dulwich Prep, hoping to set me on the path to a state-funded public school scholarship. In 1965, a bill for the spring term shows she was paying £46 9s 6d, which, when you add on whatever she was paying Mrs Gregory for my care, must have taken a healthy chunk out of her BBC salary.

Then she decided on a bigger gamble. While most boys started at Dulwich College at 11, there was one junior form for entrants at 9. But that would mean paying full fees because any assistance from the state only started at 11. Nevertheless, Sylvia decided to enter me in the exam for junior school entrance, reasoning that this would give me two bites of the cherry – if I failed now I could have another go in two years.

I can remember quite clearly the tension before the exam and interview which were going to decide my fate. We had decided that one question was going to be about my favourite television programme. Discussing this at Mrs Gregory's flat one evening as she arrived to pick me up, Mum discouraged me from choosing *Batman*, which I loved. Mrs G disagreed – 'Tell the truth and shame the devil!' she declared. I can't remember what I said when I sat in front of some scary Dulwich master but it must have worked because I passed.

Then the bills started coming in – not just the fees, but for the rather archaic uniform. Dulwich considered itself quite modern for a public school but still we had to wear ridiculous shirts with separate stiff collars fixed on with studs and a tiny cap which perched precariously on the top of my head – 'like a tom tit on a roundabout' as Auntie sardonically described it.

In the summer of 1967, just before I started at Dulwich College, Mum and I went on holiday to Bournemouth. Whatever her financial circumstances, holidays were always important to her – and to me. I used to love every bit of it: the bus to Waterloo station, the long train journey, perhaps the unimaginable luxury of a taxi to the seaside hotel where she and I would share a twin room. Every morning, I would rush down to read the menu for that night's dinner – then discuss over breakfast my choices: 'Mum, shall I have the tomato juice or the grapefruit segments, the chicken curry or the gammon with pineapple?'

The day was spent on the beach building sandcastles and tentatively watching families playing cricket in the hope that I might be asked to join in. Mum would drowse in her swimsuit, perhaps browsing through a copy of the *Daily Mail* she had snaffled from the hotel lounge. In the evening, we would dress for dinner, she in one of her two 'best' dresses, my favourite being a Mary Quant number she'd got in a sale on one of our Saturday trips to the West End, me in school shorts and shirt and tie. Perhaps before dinner a nice man would buy her a gin and tonic and me a Coca-Cola in the bar.

That particular holiday was one of our best – almost

unbroken sunshine, a wide, sandy beach a short walk from our hotel and, on the last day, the huge excitement of a powerboat race across the bay with Mum giving me a sixpence to put in the slot of a telescope for a closer view of the action. But what I didn't realise at the time was the shadow cast over that week by Sylvia's worries about how expensive Dulwich College was going to be. In a letter to her sister Bunty it all comes pouring out:

Just received the first term's bill for the College £84 which was a lot more than I expected. I understood it was much the same as the Prep or a little more, that was £63 including dinners – with this there's an extra £10 on top for dinners.

This has made her reconsider her gamble in sending me early to the college:

I really felt I'd bitten off more than I could manage and that I ought to have left him at the Prep till 11 Plus and seen what the 11+ decided then, when it might have been easier to make a change if he didn't reach a scholarship standard.

The idea of his taking the college entrance at the early age was that it might make it easier for him to get a free place at the 11 stage and this is what I hope for – but they are V competitive and if not I should have to rethink.

She is not going to disappoint me by changing her mind but we are both going to have to draw in our horns:

But he is so thrilled at the prospect and tried so hard for the exam that I wouldn't have the heart to change now even if I could at this late stage. However I've told him we shall just have to be terribly careful with everything else, and he goes around switching off all the lights which may save us an odd halfpenny or so but not more. He said just now we have to buy a Radio Times *this week and I said well I get my free one Monday – but he says he's got plenty of money, he would buy it, he liked to know his programmes at weekends.*

And as for that stupid, expensive uniform:

We have just been to the college shop to get the final items, and on return had a dressing speed test to see how long it took him to cope with those stupid studs. Can't think why they insist when it's now possible to buy those very good drip dry school shirts with semi stiff collars attached, however they do. He looks so grown up in the full outfit, I shall long to have him back in shorts at the weekend. It's funny again how some schools won't let them wear long until they're 12 and this one insists.

While I was nervous and excited about going to 'the College', as everyone at the prep school called it, getting into the uniform made me hot and bothered. I was all fingers and thumbs trying to get the collar studs in, and then there was the prospect of getting on the bus with rough kids who would instantly spot that I was a college boy and try to steal my cap.

*

Dulwich College was big – some 1,400 pupils – and scary. It was situated quite close to the centre of swinging London and had ambitions to give boys a modern scientific education but was still hanging on to plenty of the weird, ancient rituals typical of an English public school. We had to learn the school song in Latin, '*Detur Soli Deo Gloria*', and we gathered for an address by the school captain, who taught us how to pray 'the Dulwich way', cupping an elbow in a palm and covering your eyes with the other hand. The masters too were far more frightening than the mild-mannered men and women who had taught me at the prep school, with one gruff Latin teacher reducing me to tears, to our mutual embarrassment.

The first rugby lesson was taught by the head of the lower school, a giant of a man. He told us that he was going to explain the principle of tackling, which involved aiming at your opponents' legs just around the knees. 'You, step forward!' he shouted. I looked around, then realised he was pointing at me. The next thing I knew I was face down in the mud, having been flattened by what felt like a piece of heavy furniture.

But overall, I coped well enough. I joined the choir, did woodwork lessons and discovered that the junior library stocked *Look and Learn*, an educational magazine with a gripping weekly serial called 'The Rise of The Trigan Empire', competing with other nerdy boys to be the first to grab it each week. I assumed that I would now spend the rest of my school career at Dulwich.

It's probably a good thing that I did not know that my mother was not at all sure of that – the fees were stretching her finances to the limit and everything depended on me getting some kind of scholarship at 11. In the spring of 1969, she had to fill in a form declaring whether or not she wanted me to remain at Dulwich come the autumn or transfer to another school.

'I hope very much that my son will be able to remain at the College,' she wrote in a covering letter in March. 'I think though that I shall have difficulty in paying the full fees in the future, so that if he is not awarded an I.L.E.A. assisted place, or one of the Governors' Scholarships for which he sat on 27th February, my second choice would be Alleyn's.' Going to Alleyn's, the school my brother had attended, emerging with few academic achievements, would have been fine but there was no guarantee that I would be accepted there and in any case I'm sure I would have felt I had failed my mother.

I didn't get one of those governors' scholarships, so everything depended on the exam for the ILEA assisted place. In the 1960s the Inner London Education Authority put a lot of money into funding places at independent schools for children from poorer backgrounds. That policy was already coming under question as the debate intensified about the 11-plus exam which sorted children into two tribes: the bright ones heading to grammar schools, the rest doomed to secondary moderns which had few ambitions for their pupils. Now the comprehensive revolution was starting and the ILEA, which had offered completely free places, pared back its offering from September 1969 to a means-tested assisted place.

But that was still a valuable prize and in May came the news in a letter from the headmaster of Dulwich College that I had been successful. That letter was with a bundle of papers in which Sylvia has to give a detailed rundown of her financial situation to officials at the ILEA so that the assistance with fees could be calculated.

Under parents' income she describes herself as 'assistant to producer, BBC plays department with a gross annual salary of £1,629 and overtime of £140 2s 3d'. Expenses include rent and rates of £24 a month, weekly travel expenses of £2 and payment to 'the lady who looks after my son after school, until I collect him on my return from work, overnight on occasions when I work late – and during the school holidays.' This varies, she says, but averages 30 shillings a week.

But what is fascinating about this document is that 'Mrs Cellan-Jones' – a name she only used in connection with my education – is obliged, possibly for the first time, to explain my illegitimate status. Under 'other income' is 'voluntary contribution towards son's care: Father £10 monthly'.

In a covering letter she says this: 'I must explain that my son's father and I separated before he was born and that we were never married. He therefore has no legal responsibility and I am my son's sole guardian – though he makes a voluntary payment towards his care, via his bankers. This money is largely used in payment of the lady mentioned on p.6.'

The lady is of course Mrs Gregory. The ILEA officer did all the sums, worked out where we sat on the sliding scale and informed Sylvia Cellan-Jones that she would have to pay £32 per term for my education – quite a decent result as she had paid £94 for the last term's fees.

I never realised this at the time – and I don't think she did – but this was quite a moment. For 22 years, ever since she left Richie, Sylvia had been struggling to keep her head above water financially while giving first Stephen then me the education she thought we deserved. It had meant hardship and constant worry. Three years earlier, in a 1966 letter to Stephen, then in the United States trying to make a career in the theatre,

242

she reminded him of how hard things had been when they first came to London:

Perhaps you were too young to know about it at the time but when we came to London my salary was £5.15.6 a week, out of which we paid rent £3.5.0 plus extras. Looking back I really can't think how we managed – but we did, and though things gradually got better, we were always very careful, had to be.

Now things were much better – the school fees would increase, but so would her salary and the contribution from the ILEA. And even the 'voluntary' sum paid by my father was set to rise. By 1973, when I was 15, Jim was writing to Sylvia apologising for the delay in replying to her letter – 'my accountant has left the firm and my affairs in a muddle' – and proposing to increase the amount payable from £5.50 to £8 (per week, I assume). Having up until then seen little evidence of my father going beyond the bare legal minimum in financial support for me, it is a relief to come across this apparently generous upgrade. Sylvia's financial worries were largely over, I was growing more independent and she should have been able to enjoy life a little more.

But she never became more relaxed about money. In February 1977, having won a place at Cambridge starting in October, and desperate not to spend the intervening months at Ruskin Park House, I set off for West Berlin to spend six months living and working there on a scheme for pre-university students. I took with me a £100 cheque from Mum but she made clear this was a loan, not a gift, and when I returned home in August she wanted that money back.

She wasn't well off – I was about to start at Cambridge on a full grant in those far off days when tuition was free and students assessed as coming from low income households received up to £1,500, which was enough to cover their living expenses. But by then she was beginning to save assiduously, investing in shares and gilts and building up a portfolio that would be worth £140,000 when she died in 1996.

I did discover recently that in her final years she became positively open-handed. 'We called it Aunty Sylvia's family lottery,' my cousin Christine told me when I met her and her sisters Susan and Jane, daughters of Bunty and Bill, in Birmingham to talk about our family memories. She pulled out a letter from Sylvia dated 1995 in which she had enclosed a cheque for £250. 'I called her and said I couldn't accept it – but she insisted.' Her brother Frank, the one Parish that stayed connected to farming as a salesman for a fertiliser company, was another recipient of Sylvia's lottery. Having been for so long the poor relation, it must have been hugely gratifying for Mum to be able to show her family that she could be generous.

At that same meeting, my cousins and I reminisced about my many long visits to their home as a child. Their rented house in Harborne was my image of what a cosy family home should be, with Aunty Bunty serving up substantial meals of the kind that were not available at Ruskin Park House and Uncle Bill mowing the lawn on a Saturday before driving off for a pre-lunch pint, bringing me along to sit in the car with a Coca-Cola and a bag of crisps.

When I was five the Harlow girls were already in their teens and treated me as a slightly pesky kid brother, taking me to see a Beatles film, buying me sweets and warning me 'don't you dare tell Aunty Bunty' when I found them sharing a crafty cigarette by the fire in the sitting room. The cousins remembered their eccentric Aunty Sylvia with affection but recalled how I'd always arrive to stay without any pocket money. 'It was sad really – I suppose Chris and I did get a bit fed up,' said Jane. 'Your mother never gave Mum any money for you. We used to go and buy sweets down the road and you didn't have anything, and your Aunty Bunty would give us some money for you.'

That sense that money was tight and could run out at any minute was passed on to me. As a child I saved carefully and as a young adult I never dreamed of going overdrawn. I remember watching with amazement on a skiing holiday as friends from more prosperous backgrounds ordered a steak and then a pudding at a mountain restaurant, while I made do with a bowl of pasta, Sylvia's voice in my ear whispering '£10 for lunch? Are you mad?!' By then I was probably on as good a salary as most of them – apart from those who worked in the City – but I struggled to see myself as financially secure.

Then again, to my mother, I was dangerously irresponsible when it came to money. A few months into my first job at the BBC in Leeds, I realised I needed a car. I was being sent out across Yorkshire and Lincolnshire on stories and couldn't always hitch a lift with the reporter and camera crew. What's more, the old hands were explaining to me that the 22p a mile you could claim when driving your car on Corporation business was a nice little earner.

I had just passed my test at the second attempt and after looking around for a cheap motor, settled on a quite elderly red Ford Escort, priced at £900. I could just about scrape together £300; the remaining £600 would have to come in the form of a bank loan. Sylvia, in a letter to Bunty, made it clear she was not impressed:

I find it hard to accept this 'live now pay later' attitude, don't like him getting into the hands of usurers and money lenders (I know a bank loan sounds more respectable but there's not a lot of difference really). He gets a very good salary now and I'd have preferred him to save up and pay cash. Still, not much I can do about it now.

If Sylvia had tried to instil in me a degree of paranoia about money, she was far more relaxed about class. She may have wanted a public school education for me, and sometimes recited from Nancy Mitford's lexicon of U and non-U terms – lavatory, not toilet, dear, and it's a sofa not a settee – but she was far from a snob. While the BBC was and remains a very Oxbridge institution, the drama department, which back then recruited many of its staff from the theatre, was more bohemian and she had little time for people who put on airs.

She admired Mrs Gregory – certainly a toilet and settee woman – and wrote long letters to her addressed to 'Dear Louise' for years after I was no longer in her care. Of course, I was going to Dulwich College, one of the 7 per cent of children to enjoy a private education. But for a while in the 1960s and 1970s, the school was educating boys from a far wider social spectrum than today because of that ILEA assisted place scheme from which I benefitted. When I arrived, while some of the trappings of a public school education felt intimidatingly posh, I soon found friends who were little different from me – Tony, who lived with his divorced mum in East Dulwich;

Chris, whose dad was in the Salvation Army, and who used to walk home with me to his family's flat in the William Booth Memorial College, the vast forbidding Soviet-style building just below Ruskin Park House where the army housed its staff.

Which is not to say I always felt comfortable in my social status at school. My school days were far from a horror story of abuse or bullying, but my memories of Dulwich are certainly a mixture of boredom – I have never understood why anyone looks back on those long hours trapped in double maths with affection – and total, excruciating embarrassment. It was the growing realisation that the story I told myself and my friends about my origins was deeply unconvincing which made me stutter and burble whenever anyone asked me about my father.

Although my mother had never explicitly said so, I had somehow got it into my head that my parents were divorced. After all, that must be why I had this difficult surname, which everyone struggled to pronounce – including me. But I couldn't help noticing that there were no photos of their wedding and Mum only used her Cellan-Jones name in her dealings with school – the rest of the time she was Mrs Rich. Maybe when in a lunchtime kickaround my schoolmates called me a 'stupid bastard' as I let another goal in through my legs (I was a keen but hopeless goalkeeper) there was a certain edge to the banter?

On the few occasions I visited friends' houses – nothing grand, just comfortable suburban semis – I began to realise what 'normal' family life looked like. Mums would dish out exotic food like pizza or cola floats – a scoop of ice cream in a glass of Coca-Cola – while dads would tinker with miraculous model railway layouts in the attic or start a game of French cricket in the garden. If that was normal, I wanted it, not the suffocating tedium of Ruskin Park House, a home to which

I would never dream of inviting friends. At school, I did my best not to talk about my parents or my home and discouraged Mum from turning up at school events – fortunately her busy work schedule made that difficult.

Perhaps it was not the fault of the school that I look back on it with no great affection. After all, term time meant being trapped at home in the flat, and it was only in the holidays that life burst into technicolour when I would be away with my aunts in Birmingham or Bedfordshire or at the Grigsons' Wiltshire garden.

What Dulwich College did for me was get me into Cambridge – it was an extremely efficient exam factory sending something like 70 pupils to Oxbridge each year. I left in December 1976 after taking the Cambridge entrance exam in the winter after my A levels and gaining a place at Jesus College to read French and German. That anachronistic seventh term entrance system was of huge benefit to independent schools which, in any case, knew all the tricks of teaching to the exams and pleasing the dons. What is more, the majority of Cambridge colleges were only just beginning to accept women. A decade or so on, with seventh term entry scrapped and places to read languages mostly going to smarter female applicants, I doubt I'd have made the grade. But was I grateful? Of course not. While there had been a clutch of excellent teachers, and a group of friends mainly centred around a shared love of Crystal Palace Football Club, I left with a spring in my step and without a trace of nostalgia.

Over the ensuing years, I lost touch with most of my school friends, ignored the letters appealing for contributions to the scholarship fund and sent my own kids to a very good and socially diverse state school. I did return once to a dinner where old men, who turned out to be my contemporaries, brayed their support for UKIP and its leader Nigel Farage, who had arrived at Dulwich some six years after me. Not going to make that mistake again, I said to myself grumpily.

But ten years later, in the summer of 2022, an email arrived from the old boys' club, which by then was being run by Nick, who had been in my class – a quiet boy who was a solid cricketer and sat in the common room doing *The Times* crossword each lunchtime. There was to be a reunion on a July evening – all welcome. Oh, go on, one more go …

I walked from West Dulwich station and, arriving at the college gates, marvelled at the grandeur of the buildings, the vast acres of playing fields. In front of the pavilion, the first XI was playing a team of recent leavers and apart from the greater diversity and athleticism of the players, it could have been a scene from any time in the last 50 years.

We stood around by the brand new science and tech building clutching bottles of beer and glasses of wine, some in groups of old friends, others like me trying to make conversation with strangers. I met one of my teachers, Mr Tumber, who had taught me in my worst subject, physics (grade 5 at O level), and he told me he had been surprised but impressed to hear me talking about technology on the radio.

A man in his eighties told me he'd been one of three brothers at the school – and only realised later that he'd been the only one who hadn't got a scholarship, which left his parents struggling to pay the fees. A middle-aged man of Asian origin came rushing up and said he'd always wanted to meet me – he'd worked abroad in technology and had been a fan of my reports. He too had a tale of financial hardship for his parents and was still angry about it. 'I was second in the whole year and they still wouldn't give me a scholarship. So when they write asking me for donations I tear it up,' he said. 'Fuck 'em!'

He bought me a beer, there were a couple of speeches and then, grasping for the words, laughing at ourselves, we sang the school song, '*Pueri Alleynienses* ...' Talk turned to Kingsdale, once the sink school next door, now rated outstanding, one of London's best. Someone who still lived nearby told the possibly apocryphal tale of a boy who had failed to get a place at Kingsdale and whose parents were now applying for him to go to Dulwich, as second best.

Fees for day boys at the college are now over £7,000 a term and the days of state assistance are long gone, though the school offers a bursary scheme. As I waited for an Uber to take me home, I wondered what my mother would have done under those circumstances – and whether I would still have ended up as a typical BBC public school boy.

CHAPTER 13

MEETING JIM

It was in the spring of 1981 that I decided it was time that I met my father. I was 23 and preparing to take my finals at Cambridge while looking to start a career in journalism. I had returned to Jesus College the previous October after spending a year in Paris as an English assistant at a lycée. At that time, Cambridge did not require language students to do a year abroad and, to my astonishment, many chose not to take up this opportunity. So I returned for my final year to find that most of my friends – in languages as well as other subjects – had departed and a lot had gone to train as chartered accountants.

To me, this was a horrible prospect, even though with no likelihood of financial support from Mum, and Britain entering a deep recession, I would need to find a job fast – especially if I wanted to avoid returning to Ruskin Park House. But the grim thought of ending up as a chartered accountant emboldened me – I decided I must now take seriously my long-held ambition to become a journalist. When I had arrived at Cambridge in 1977, I had been intimidated by the thought of writing for the student newspaper, convinced that everyone involved would be a lot more sophisticated and smarter than me. But now, older and more confident after my year in Paris, I turned up at the weekly editorial meeting of *Stop Press*, as the venerable *Varsity* was briefly titled, and discovered an eternal truth about journalism and most other careers. Talent certainly helps but far more important is a determination to keep on hammering at the door until you are let in.

Soon, I was writing weekly news articles on everything from a court appearance by members of The Specials after a riot at their Cambridge gig to a demo at the union over a visit by the Chilean ambassador of the Pinochet regime. Quickly, I was elected joint features editor along with a friend who was studying Chinese (and went on to become a distinguished foreign correspondent). That meant I was free to write double-page spreads on the doomed battle to save the Kite district of Cambridge from redevelopment and visit local celebrity Clive James for a lengthy interview.

It was an intense period – long days in the library reading Rabelais and Ionesco, Goethe and Kafka for my finals in French and German literature, and a weekly all-nighter when we put the newspaper together, then strolled down King's Parade at dawn, swigging from a shared bottle of whisky, foolishly convinced that we'd soon be doing the same on Fleet Street.

Perhaps not so foolish. For back then, there were plenty of journalism training schemes offering a quick route into national newspapers or broadcasting, and they looked kindly on Oxbridge graduates. I applied for them all – the Mirror Group, Thomson Newspapers, Reuters, ITN and no fewer than three BBC training schemes. I was reasonably confident at first – my German supervisor wrote on one of my Kafka essays

'Well written but wrong, you'll make a good journalist' – and got invited to a number of interviews.

But by the spring, I still had not got a job lined up; I'd just broken up with my first serious girlfriend and finals were approaching fast. It was in this period of anxiety about my future that I began to want to know more about my past. I'm not sure what made me want to meet my father but it may have been an incident at one of those job interviews. I had got through to the final stages of the selection process for one of the BBC's prestigious training schemes and been summoned to a building across the road from Broadcasting House. There, I found an intimidating interview board, including the editor of the evening magazine programme *Nationwide* and the former head of television news, who I later learned had been kicked upstairs after one too many drunken incidents at work.

After a rigorous interrogation by the *Nationwide* editor about my ideas for his programme, and some babbling from me about my extensive journalism experience at Cambridge, the former TV news boss suddenly barked, 'Why no drama – given your father?' He had obviously looked at my distinctive surname and assumed that Jim, now a freelance drama director having recently left his job as head of plays at the BBC, had been a major influence on my life. Blushing and stuttering, I explained that I had never met my father. The BBC executive, appearing almost embarrassed as I was, changed the subject. I did not get selected for the training scheme.

It was not the first incident of this kind. Five years earlier, my mum had written to Jane Grigson seeking advice on which Oxbridge colleges I should apply to, and she mentioned a conversation with one of my teachers at Dulwich College:

The head of Modern Languages – Rory's form master last year – suggested diffidently that Jim might help to get Rory into his old college at Cambridge as his name is now widely known but we wouldn't be happy with this bit of nepotism – I think he must get in on his own merits if at all.

To say I would not have been happy with this bit of nepotism is an understatement – I would have been mortified at the age of 17 at any suggestion that the father who had played no role in my life should be asked to intervene now. In any case, St John's College, Cambridge, where young James Cellan-Jones barely scraped a third in 1950, would surely not have been swayed by such an intervention.

In spring 1981, I still didn't want anything from my father – certainly not a leg up the career ladder. But I did want to know more about his side of the story of my birth and, above all, I wanted him to stop being the subject of embarrassing questions to me. So I sat down and wrote him a letter.

At that time, Jim was about to turn 50 and was at the peak of his career. After making his name with *The Forsyte Saga* in the late 1960s, he had gone on to make *The Roads to Freedom*, a 13-part dramatisation of the trilogy of novels by Jean-Paul Sartre. This groundbreaking drama about French intellectuals on the eve of the Second World War with scenes of nudity pushing the boundaries of what was acceptable on television was certainly not regarded by Mum as suitable fare for me. But plenty of more conventional material followed – *Jennie*, a series about Lady Randolph Churchill for Thames TV; Henry James's *The Golden Bowl*; and a spell in the United States making *The Adams Chronicles* about founding father

John Adams. He was about to embark on his first sitcom, *A Fine Romance* with Judi Dench and her husband Michael Williams.

His children too popped up from time to time in his plays. 'Did you see Jim's play with Rory's half-brother and sister in it?' Sylvia had written to Joan in November 1980. It had been 'an awful play' about an alcoholic, but, she writes:

> *I was interested to see the children and told Rory it was on so that he'd be prepared for any comments – he thought Din (short version of the boy's Welsh name) looked rather like himself ... I thought the girl looked like her mother a bit, and had one glimpse of a likeness to Jim when the boy ran up the street, half-smiling, at the end.*
>
> *Rory has met several people at Cambridge who know, or whose parents know, Jim, but this doesn't bother him – in fact he retails to me any interesting comments.*

I'm not sure she was right to say it didn't bother me. Certainly, I was less embarrassed than I had been as a teenager when the Cellan-Jones connection was brought up. I was also both curious and not a little envious about the life being led by my father and his family. It seemed to me they lived in a different and more glamorous world from me and Mum, who had been retired for some years and was growing painfully eccentric. What I didn't know then was how, in the early years after my birth, his career was not advancing much faster than Sylvia's – and for that he put the blame on the scandal surrounding their affair.

Many years later, when he was writing his memoir *Forsyte*

and Hindsight, Jim sent me the short passage about my birth and asked for my approval: 'I had an affair with a much liked and older secretary,' he wrote. 'She became pregnant and I was cited as co-respondent by her husband, who had not even seen her for ten years. It became public knowledge and my career took a dive.'

He went on to say some lovely things about me and I told him that everything he had written was fine. But when after his death I read his personal file at the BBC Caversham archive and returned to my mother's letters, I was no longer sure that he had painted an entirely accurate picture. When they met, the 'much liked and older secretary' was acting up as a production assistant and floor manager and was senior to him. He had volunteered to be named as co-respondent because they wanted Richie to divorce Sylvia so that they could marry. And his Caversham file gives no clear sign that he was in the dog house.

His annual report for 1958 shows that just two months after my birth, he was given the chance to act up in the same role Sylvia had been doing the previous year:

Since the beginning of March he has been Acting Floor manager for the serial 'Starr and Company' [...] He has carried out his duties conscientiously, with efficiency and tact. His personality has strengthened since he has been given additional authority.

And in November came a rave review from the director and head of drama, Michael Elliott: 'His personality spreads a pleasant aura over all our work which everybody felt from the actors to technicians.'

There is a hint in December 1958 that young Cellan-Jones, for all his talents, presented a problem for BBC managers. A.G. Finch 'Establishment Assistant, Television' writes to Hywel Davies, head of Welsh programmes in Cardiff, about what they appear to have fixed up for the young man, promising, 'It will be all plain sailing now.'

It seems an attachment in Cardiff has been arranged for Jim, perhaps to get him away from the scene of an affair which has scandalised the drama department. But it is difficult to be sure because the document I read at Caversham 60 years later has a whole paragraph obscured by a thick black line. When I opened Jim's file a memo on top warned me that some documents had been censored and here was one example.

But if he had been sent away to Cardiff because of the scandal his exile only lasted a few months. By March 1959, he was back in London and the same A.G. Finch was writing to congratulate Jim on his forthcoming marriage, 'particularly as it is to another member of the family!' His bride was Margaret Eavis, who had followed much the same route through the drama department as both Sylvia and Jim and was now a trainee assistant floor manager. Another memo informed him that the Corporation was giving the couple a wedding present of £5.

Among my mother's files was a faded newspaper cutting, reporting the wedding at Pilton in Somerset, with a photo of the couple. 'Both bride and bridegroom hold appointments in BBC television and will reside in London,' the caption read.

It was the start of what was to be a long and happy marriage but Jim and Maggie would have to leave London again if he was to make progress towards his ambition of directing.

In November 1959, a memo makes it clear how, four

years after he had joined the BBC as a lowly call boy, Jim was getting impatient with what he regarded as his slow progress. His file shows him making repeated complaints about the pace at which his career was progressing and being told that if he wanted promotion he needed to look outside London.

Jim stayed in London through 1960, continuing to get good reports – 'an excellent year's work' said the drama department administrator. But he eventually took the advice to head to the regions in search of advancement towards a director's job and 1961 found him and Maggie in Bristol where they were to stay for the next two years. The West Region, based in the same Whiteladies Road headquarters where Sylvia had joined the BBC 20 years earlier, was best known for the Natural History Unit but was also a centre of drama production. It seems Jim made a favourable impression from the start. His annual report, written in the summer of 1961 as he turned 30, provides a compelling picture of what a charming and capable man he must have been:

> He works hard and his ebullient and apparently extrovert personality helps to give a Company an encouraging impetus. He is friendly both with artists and with crew.
>
> Intelligent and very catholic in his interests, especially in the entertainment world, he has his own prejudices in theatrical matters, as anyone connected with the theatre must have, but he readily forgets them if the producer's ideas in the current show run counter to his.

Jim's promotion to a permanent post in Bristol as a production assistant came with a handy pay rise, taking his annual salary above £1,000 for the first time. In early 1958, when I was born, he had been earning £625; by April 1961, his salary was £1,385. Nevertheless, Jim's frustration at what he saw as his slow progress towards the goal of becoming a producer/director continued to grow. It was understandable – most of the ambitious young men in the drama department (and it was still almost exclusively men) had made it into the key creative roles in a production by the time they were 30. Time was slipping away and if he wasn't given an opportunity soon he could end up marooned as a production assistant.

Jim and his wife Maggie both felt there was another reason why he was not being given a crack at directing, as he recounts in *Forsyte and Hindsight*:

> *I went on doing PA work and being demoted between jobs; I was getting very little money for a lot of hard work. This went on for three and a half years. Maggie, my wife and an outstanding AFM, went to see the Drama Administrator. Fiercely she asked, 'Is it because of the scandal that Jim isn't getting promotion?'*
>
> *'Yes I'm afraid it is,' he said shame-facedly, 'and it doesn't look as if he ever will.'*

Was this true? While the BBC had been a very puritan organisation under Lord Reith he was long gone and it is hard to believe that Jim and Sylvia were the only people in drama – one of the Corporation's more bohemian departments – to have had an affair. Perhaps, however, it was sheer embarrassment on the part of the administrators at the idea of the two former lovers brushing past each other on the fifth floor at Television Centre. 'Safer to keep him down in Bristol,' you can imagine them saying.

Eventually, he did break through, mostly thanks to *Lorna Doone*. Jim was the production assistant on an 11-part dramatisation of the nineteenth-century romantic novel set on Exmoor and was deputed to organise some filming of snow scenes. As luck would have it the brutal winter of 1963 was just getting into its stride, with much of the country covered in the deepest snow for 300 years. Jim found a farm in Somerset which had not been modernised and headed out into the snow with just two cameramen and a variety of clothes, mainly sheepskins, from the wardrobe department.

In what is the most vivid passage in *Forsyte and Hindsight* he describes how he not only directed the cameramen but played one of the characters in wide shot:

We dug the sheep out of the snow (some of them we'd dug in first), and everywhere we directed the camera, the land was sparkling white and glorious.

I saw a half-frozen waterfall above a pond which looked ravishing. I said to the cameraman, 'What we really need is for someone to get into the water and shoot upward.' 'You do it,' he said and handed me the camera. I did it, and bloody cold it was too. It was a beautiful shot, but it ended up on the cutting room floor.

This work did not go unnoticed in his annual report:

Recently he arranged in arctic conditions, to film some very useful snow sequences for Lorna Doone. *These demanded considerable initiative, imagination and plain endurance.*

Jim relates how on a visit to Bristol, the head of drama, Sydney Newman, said he didn't think much of the last episode of *Lorna Doone* except for the snow sequences, which were brilliant. 'Cue dagger looks from the director.'

A few months later, he was on a directors' course and from December 1963 he is listed on his file as based in London as first a trainee producer, then a few months later as a staff producer/director. Nine years after starting as a call boy he had finally made it.

By March 1964 he had already directed eight episodes of *Compact*, 'the worst sort of twice weekly romantically rubbishy serial about a woman's magazine' as he described it. His new job meant his salary topped £2,000 for the first time, but within a year, he would take the path followed by all ambitious young directors, leaving the BBC staff to go on a short-term contract – less secure, but much better paid. By 1966 he was the rising star of the drama department and about to take on the production that would make his name known more widely. The head of drama wrote in his report:

James Cellan-Jones is a most sensitive director. He combines the ability to communicate with actors (and improve them) with the technical knowledge essential to present them at their best. His filming is a particularly strong point. He is about to take over from David Giles as director of The Forsyte Saga *for the next few months. He is a man who is universally liked and respected and I am extremely glad he is in this department.*

By now, Jim and Maggie had two sons: Simon born in 1963 when they were still in the West Country and Deiniol, always known as Din, who was born in London in 1965. Their daughter Lavinia, or Vinny, came along in 1967. Jim's finances as a freelance director were never stable, veering between feast and famine, and at one point an ambitious house purchase and an ill-considered bridging loan pushed him to the brink of bankruptcy. But eventually the family settled in a large, comfortable house in Kew.

And what contact did Jim have during this period with Ruskin Park House? With me, none, and with Sylvia just a handful of letters, mostly agreeing to increase the weekly child maintenance payments in line with the law. Apart from the letter he wrote after his mother's death in 1962 imploring her not to contact his father, they were formal and businesslike.

When I wrote to him in the spring of 1981, I knew nothing of these letters and very little about my father. I had followed his career closely, watched his programmes and knew that I had three half-siblings, Simon, Din and Vinny. My view of his character came largely from my mother who never said a bad word about him, looking back on their affair with tenderness and blaming external forces – his parents, the lawyers – for its end. I cannot remember exactly what I wrote (unlike my mother, I didn't keep carbon copies of my letters) but I am pretty sure it carried no tone of resentment. After all, what was there to resent? I had been brought up by a loving mother, brother and my Parish family, and given a good education, even if money had been tight and our home quite humble. Yes, my dad's absence had been an embarrassment when I was younger but that was now being replaced by curiosity and pride in his achievements. So I think I explained that I was in my last term at Cambridge and it would be nice if he would come and see me before I graduated. I put the letter in the post and waited. Every morning I went to check my pigeonhole in the porter's lodge for a reply, but while over the next ten days there were several rejection letters from journalist training schemes, nothing arrived from my father.

By now, I was resentful. I wrote him another letter, this time an angry screed accusing him of walking away from his responsibilities. Finally, just as I had completed my exams, I found a letter in my pigeonhole. It was addressed from his house in Kew, though I had written to him at Yorkshire TV where he was working, not wanting to risk causing him any embarrassment at home:

'Dear Rory,' it began. 'Your letters arrived here together yesterday, both after being forwarded all over the place. I'm at present commuting between Yorkshire and Brighton and the mail gets diverted all over the place.'

I began to feel sorry for him. The repetition of 'all over the place' seemed to reflect his state of mind – flustered, embarrassed, perhaps even ashamed.

'I can understand the irritated tone of the second letter' – now I felt a little embarrassed – 'for all sorts of reasons I would have liked to come and see you in Cambridge before you went down, but I simply can't.' He explained that he was still working in Leeds and Brighton and couldn't get a day off but he could 'give you some lunch any day the following week, if you're free'.

He ended, 'You must be relieved that your finals are over: best of luck with them,' and signed off, 'Yours, Father.'

I can only imagine how he must have agonised over this letter – what to say, what to call himself – because once I got to know him I realised we shared a very English reticence about expressing our feelings, despite the deep Welsh emotions flowing beneath.

For whatever reason that first plan for a lunch in late June after I left didn't come off. The delay in arranging a meeting with my father was just one more thing making me anxious at an extremely nervous time for me. I left Cambridge with a good degree but no job in journalism – the latest faint hope was an interview for a short-term contract in the BBC's Leeds operation. While I continued to bang on doors, I needed to earn some money and found a temporary job in a City bank. The work involved proofreading banking documents and was mind-blowingly tedious but it paid £70 a week, which was better than the £50 I had earned selling socks in Selfridges, my Christmas and summer vacation employer for the last couple of years. A kind friend from Cambridge whose father was a director of the bank had got me the job. It was my first taste of the old boys' network in action, but I needed the cash for my £20 a week rent on a room in a house in Clapham I was sharing with university friends. To my mum's tearful dismay, I had decided not to return to Ruskin Park House.

That was the summer of Botham's Ashes, which I followed obsessively on the radio in the Clapham house with my great friend David, another cricket fan. At the bank I could not listen to the radio but with access to a telephone I discovered that by dialling 154 I could get the score. My dozens of calls to the premium rate number as the Headingley Test reached its dramatic conclusion must have eaten into the bank's profits that summer.

Then Jim wrote again saying, 'It sounds ridiculous and overbusy but the only day I can make sure to be in London and have lunch with you is Friday July 10th.'

And so it was in the lunch break from my job at Warburg Bank that I met my father for the first time.

When I walked into the City restaurant that Friday lunchtime to meet Jim, was the Ashes series on my list of opening conversational gambits? I hope not because as I later learned he did not share my interest in cricket or any other sport. The sad truth is that I remember very little about that lunch except that we were both a little shy, a little awkward and relieved to fall back on small talk about Cambridge and my job hunt rather than address the past. He was dressed casually in cords and the open-toed sandals he wore on all but the most formal occasions. I was trussed up in my one suit – dress-down Fridays had yet to arrive in the City.

What I do remember is that I liked him. He was clearly a nice man with a diffident charm and once we had got over our huge mutual embarrassment at the situation, he had a fund of amusing stories about his work – many of which I was to hear time and again over the coming years. After an hour, I hurried back to the bank, satisfied that at least the ice was broken, the deed was done.

A few weeks on, I was being shown around the BBC newsroom in Leeds, a place of clattering typewriters and shrouded in cigarette smoke. After failing at the final hurdle to get a place on the coveted News Trainee scheme, I had asked the personnel officer who had broken the news what else I could do. He'd advised me to write to all of the BBC's regional newsrooms and just this one had replied, saying they were looking for a researcher on a short-term contract to work on a new current affairs series fronted by Khalid Aziz, the presenter of their nightly news programme *Look North*. A few days after my interview, a letter arrived offering me the contract as a 'General Programme Assistant, starting on 1st September at a salary of £4,726.'

'I appreciate that you have other "irons in the fire",' wrote the personnel officer, 'but would be grateful if you could let me know as soon as possible whether you are able to accept this offer.' I did have one other iron in the fire – I had been offered a permanent job on the *TEFL Gazette*, a trade paper about teaching English as a foreign language based in Fulham. My mother told me it would be insanely risky to take a short-term contract in gloomy Yorkshire when a permanent job in London was on offer. But I was getting into the habit of ignoring her advice and so in September 1981, I began what was to be a 40-year career at the BBC.

I wrote to my father about my news and got a congratulatory letter – though I soon realised he knew as little about the news business as my mother. He also offered to take me out to dinner when he was next working at Yorkshire Television and a month or so later we were sharing sticky duck and pancakes at Leeds' finest Chinese restaurant. Once again, the conversation was limited to work – his and mine – and we avoided any mention of my mother or the past.

Over the next four years we fell into a pattern. We would exchange the odd letter – he started signing himself in self-consciously Victorian manner 'Yr affec Father' and then thankfully just 'Jim', which I called him ever after. Every few months, he would take me out for a meal, first in Leeds then in London when I got my big break as a sub-editor in the main TV newsroom. We got on well enough and he dropped into conversation the occasional morsel about his children, my half-siblings Simon, Din and Vinny. But somehow it all seemed rather unsatisfactory, our relationship stuck at a superficial level, as if he were a distant if amiable business acquaintance rather than my father. Then one day early in 1985 the phone on my desk in Television Centre rang.

It was only after he died, in 2019, that I learned how late Jim was in telling his and Maggie's children about the existence of their older brother. At the cottage on the site of the Glastonbury Festival in Pilton where their parents had spent many summers, I sat with Vinny and Simon talking for the first time at any length about how they learned about the big secret. Vinny, now a potter, lived in the cottage and was recovering from hosting 30 friends who had slept in the garden during the festival. Simon, whose career as a film and TV director had really taken off in the United States, was briefly home at the nearby Somerset farmhouse he'd bought a few years earlier. Our brother Din, a barrister, and a rather old-fashioned man of enormous wit and charm, had died in 2013, a terrible loss.

Simon was 16 when Jim took him into the garden at Kew. 'He said, "I've got some news, I've got another son." I was a gawky 16-year-old; I was quite thrown and wondered if it was something I should be ashamed about. Because they'd made it clear that they were ashamed.' Years earlier, someone had mentioned to Simon that there was a boy with the same unusual surname as him at Dulwich College. Jim told him it was a distant relative. And when a couple of years after the conversation at Kew he had tried to talk to his mother about me, she had quickly shut him down.

Vinny, four years younger than Simon, was told when she was 16, some time in late 1984. 'He was terribly, desperately awkward, he couldn't look me in the face. He sort of said, "I don't really know why I haven't told you, I've told the boys ... I've got a son."'

A year or so earlier, the mother of a school friend had seen my name in the acknowledgements of a book called *Paupers' Paris* for which I'd done some restaurant reviews and asked Vinny whether I was a relative. 'I instantly said – because I'd never heard of you – no, it's not a relation, I don't know who that is. It didn't even occur to me to say to Mum or Dad, "Is this a relation?" Because I'd have heard of you; they'd have told me about you.'

From the outside, I somehow assumed the Cellan-Jones clan with their artistic connections would be more gossipy and open about everything than my Parish relations. But Simon and Vinny said the opposite was true; there were plenty of things left unsaid.

Finally, when he was 21, Simon decided enough was enough – he was going to meet his brother. After all, by then we were both working in the same building. He had decided not to go to university, instead spending months in Beirut at the height of the Lebanese civil war with a school friend who went on to be foreign editor of *The Times*. But instead of journalism, Simon had set his heart on a career in film and television.

Like Jim, he had started at the bottom, although rather than call boy the bottom rung was now runner, an all-purpose dogsbody moving from one short-term contract to another and unpaid between productions. But after a couple of years, he got a more long-term contract as an assistant floor manager with the BBC working on an ambitious series called *Edge of Darkness*. By then, I had been at Television Centre for a couple of years and my career as a TV news producer was taking off. I had been appointed to a new Special Projects unit, handling coverage of major news stories at home and abroad and was soon to start work on a documentary about the Brighton bomb.

'How did you track me down?' I asked Simon when we talked about all of this nearly 40 years later. 'I just dialled 0 and said to the operator put me through to Rory Cellan-Jones.' We had a brief conversation and arranged to meet at Albertine's, the wine bar whose entire trade seemed to consist of BBC staff steeling themselves for a night shift or raucously celebrating a colleague's departure for a better-paid job.

It is strange meeting your brother for the first time in your twenties. We had no shared history and little in common – while he was younger and more junior in his BBC job than me, he was a more confident person, with the same easy charm as Jim but without the diffidence. We got on because we were interested in each other and wanted to make things work. And then Simon did something for which I will be forever grateful. He went home and told his mum and dad that they had to invite me round to the house in Kew. A few weeks later, I turned up on their doorstep in Kew bearing a pot plant for Maggie. Milliseconds after I rang the bell there was a fusillade of barking and two boxers slammed against the back of the door. It then opened to reveal Simon, Jim and Maggie trying to restrain the dogs, while Din and Vinny stood smiling somewhat nervously. I stepped over the threshold, handed the pot plant to Maggie, and began to get to know my new family.

CHAPTER 14

ENDINGS

Right up until the end of her life, Sylvia kept up her letter writing habit. Indeed, through the late 1970s and early 1980s the volume seemed to increase because she had a new correspondent – me. When I left Ruskin Park House, first for West Berlin, Cambridge and Paris, and then for my first job in Leeds, the only way I kept in touch with my mum – who still refused to get a telephone installed – was via weekly letters home. Their contents provide a heavily censored account of my six months in West Berlin at the height of the Cold War; my nine months teaching at the smart lycée on the fringes of Paris and the fantastic job I got reviewing cheap restaurants for the *Paupers' Paris* guidebook; my studies in Cambridge; and my first job in journalism in the smoky, noisy *Look North* newsroom. As I did not keep a diary, my anodyne scribblings and her lengthy screeds of what to me back then was deadly dull family news coupled with annoying maternal advice are the only record I have of that key period in my life.

Then, some time in the mid-1980s, she finally got a telephone, which meant I stopped writing to her, calling her instead once a week, often wandering around the house doing other things as a lengthy monologue about nothing in particular unspooled. Indeed, as the phone took over, first fixed line then mobile, I lost the habit of letter writing altogether. My life was recorded in emails, texts and increasingly in social media posts on Twitter or Facebook.

But Sylvia kept on writing and as I sorted through the bulky folders I have marked 'late 1970s' and '1980–1996' a wave of sadness washed over me. The last 20 years of her life were not happy and I realise now that this was largely because she felt that two of the mainstays of her life, the BBC and me, had abandoned her.

In February 1992, Sylvia replied to a letter from Stephen, by now 50 and finally making good headway in his career as a criminal barrister. Unlike me, he retained the letter writing habit, often dropping by Ruskin Park House on his way to or from court, and if Sylvia was not there putting quite a lengthy note through the door. Sylvia's letter started by saying that I had just left after bringing my 18-month-old son Adam over for a visit. Then, after an inconsequential ramble about reusing a 1975 diary because the dates fitted 1992, came this:

Re-reading your Wednesday letter I see that I missed the para. inviting me to lunch at a weekend of my choosing.

But I can't think I should be a welcome guest anywhere in my present deeply depressed state. There have been too many disappointments, major and minor, too much sadness since the beginning of 1986.

I sometimes get better in the summer so you might think of November. There are no certainties any more.

Looking back I think I've had around 35–40

interesting and rewarding years in my life and perhaps
that is as much or more than any of us have a right to
expect.

Just what, I asked myself, had happened at the beginning
of 1986, and why was it the start of so many disappointments,
so much sadness? She had been absolutely distraught when I
had broken up with a girlfriend who, typically, she had only
appreciated when she was gone. But that split had happened
in 1984 so unless she was getting her dates mixed up – entirely
possible – that did not match. Then I remembered what
had happened in January 1986. I had left London, my staff
producer job in the BBC TV newsroom and the flat in Balham
I'd just bought with a £30,000 mortgage, and moved to
Cardiff. I wanted to be a reporter, not a producer, and had
applied for a vacancy on *Wales Today*, the BBC evening news
programme for Wales. I got the job but that meant leaving the
staff and the pension scheme and going on contract. It was a
bit of a risk but it was made clear to me that I'd have to start
in local television and then try to fight my way back.

But my mother was appalled. How on earth could I give up
everything I had worked so hard for – my job in London, my
flat and above all my pension? And all for some flaky contract
on local Welsh television of all things! (Explaining that the
people at BBC Wales saw themselves as serving a nation cut
no ice.) What strikes me now is how strange this ultra-cautious
attitude was from someone who had been prepared to take
so many risks with her own life – learning to fly, leaving her
husband, heading off to London with an eight-year-old child
and nowhere decent for the two of them to live.

But she was just as cautious in her later years about her

older son's career choices. She wrote to Joan when Stephen was going through the nightmare of the Bar exams – one of the last people to do that without a university degree or even A levels – that she wished he had settled on a nice steady job in a bank instead of getting involved in the theatre and then the law.

Eventually, she forgave me – after all, in two and a half years I was back in London reporting for BBC breakfast television – but she never visited me in Cardiff and was rather sniffy about my job in Wales.

What was really missing from her life, though, was the institution that had given her an education, been at the centre of her social life, even given her a child – the BBC. In August 1974, she turned 60 and back then that meant retirement for women, no ifs, no buts. On her retirement day, she did receive what must be one of the most beautifully written and sensitive letters ever from a bureaucrat – except that Huw Wheldon was no apparatchik but a brilliant broadcaster who by then had become director of television. He told Sylvia that it was customary for the director general to write to long-serving staff when they retired but Charles Curran was away and when her file had been put in front of him he'd decided straight away that he would write on the DG's behalf:

You have been associated with so many memorable productions of all kinds. You have worked with so many people whose names are widely known and widely recognised.

All in all, you have given so much excellent service to the BBC since your early years in Bristol and over a whole period of over 30 years since then, that it simply would not do for you to leave without at least having in your possession a letter expressing formal gratitude and formal good wishes; to which it is a pleasure to add informal thanks and informal good wishes for your success in the future both for you and for your son.

Sylvia was clearly delighted with this letter. She wrote back that very same day to thank him, with reminiscences of them meeting at Alexandra Palace and Lime Grove when she worked for George Barnes who, like Wheldon now, was running the television service. She continued:

Life at the BBC has been so rewarding, exciting and full of varied and continuing interest, I can think of nowhere comparable.

I don't at all want to retire; it's like leaving home forever – being cashiered on one's birthday, stripped of identity (card), stopwatch and the ability to cash cheques!

But of course it's the whole atmosphere and the people I shall miss most.

She strikes quite a light-hearted tone but beneath the surface you can detect real hurt at her eviction from her Television Centre home. Two years earlier, in the spring and summer of 1972, she had what she later described to a doctor as a 'nervous breakdown' – the 1970s term for what we would now call clinical depression. I would come home from school to find her sitting in the armchair in the living room staring at the wall, seemingly incapable of movement. Aged 14, I felt helpless, so most weekends I got the bus round the South

Circular to Stephen's house in Barnes to escape the gloom enveloping the flat. It now seems to me that the depression may have been brought on by Mum's realisation that in the next few years she would be leaving the BBC and I would be leaving home. That summer, aided by medication, she did slowly pull out of her depression but she was on anti-depressants for the rest of her life.

For the first few years after she retired, Sylvia did the odd spell of freelance work for the BBC but this work became ever harder to find. I rather assumed that she had given up on the idea of paid employment – after all, with her BBC pension and quite substantial savings, she was no longer short of money. Then, buried in her correspondence from the late 1970s, I found a surprise – a letter on Clarence House notepaper:

Dear Mrs. Rich,

Thank you for your letter expressing interest in the vacant post of Daily Help at Clarence House.

I should like you to come here for an interview this Friday, 27th October, at 2.45 p.m. when further information about the position will be given to you.

Perhaps you would kindly telephone me (930-3141) to confirm that this is convenient or, if it is not, to arrange an alternative date.

In the meantime, I enclose an Application for Employment form which I shall be grateful if you will complete and return as soon as possible in the accompanying envelope.

The letter was signed by someone describing themselves as 'Clerk Assistant to Queen Elizabeth the Queen Mother'.

I laughed out loud when I found this. My mother's idea of cleaning involved a cursory tour of the visible parts of the carpet with the ancient Hoover, a quick flick of a duster and then shoving everything under the bed or the dressing table where a thick layer of dust accumulated over the decades, as I found when I cleared the flat after her death. (I'm afraid I have inherited this philosophy of cleaning.) She might have made a decent secretary for the Queen Mother – surely no more tricky a character than Joan Gilbert, the editor of *Picture Page* – but she was nobody's idea of a 'daily help'. Perhaps that became clear during the interview at Clarence House, but there are no further clues about what happened to Sylvia's quest, aged 64, to enter the service of the royal household.

But it is evident that in the decade after her retirement from the BBC she was desperate for something to get her out of the flat and to keep her brain ticking over. In 1980, she wrote to the editor of *Sale of the Century*, a TV quiz show that she and I had watched from time to time. 'I've often thought how much I should like to take part,' she wrote, 'but don't know how you select candidates and whether I might be eligible.'

She outlined her qualifications and interests:

> *I work as a freelance P A. with authors, archaeologists, poets and publishers, but am now semi-retired.*
>
> *Interests: travel, reading, crossword puzzles, children, skiing, surfing, watching television (selectively I hope).*

She did go on several skiing holidays and despite the fact that she never progressed beyond the nursery slopes I think we can allow her that. But surfing? An image of Sylvia catching a monster wave off some Hawaiian beach floats before my eyes – and then I laugh at the sheer chutzpah of my mother. Then, at the end, to cap it all, she signs herself Sylvia Parish and in the draft version she kept it says in brackets 'age 54' – a mere 12 years younger than her true age.

Money remained a constant concern, even when it no longer needed to be. Perhaps the rising rent on the flat was weighing on her mind. She refused to admit that turning down the chance to buy it from the council a few years earlier for £5,000 had been a mistake, while noting that some of those who had done so were now selling at a tidy profit. But so enraged was she by repeated increases in the rent that she went straight to the top, writing to Secretary of State for the Environment Michael Heseltine.

The letter is a complaint that Mr Heseltine has approved increases on council tenants' rents of up to 30 per cent, but around this Sylvia has wrapped what is in effect an autobiography, albeit an artfully edited one:

Dear Mr. Heseltine,

I'm a single parent, and when my son and I first came to live here, after five years with an alcoholic landlady and a mouse, it seemed utter bliss to have a clean flat of our own with hot water and a bath, and good schools nearby; that was about twenty years ago and we continued to be happy, with very infrequent and reasonable rent and rate increases.

Somehow Stephen and I have been merged – she doesn't want to be seen as a serial single mother. But why are rents rocketing for a flat barely big enough for two? 'I find it hard to understand why the increase for a small flat should exceed that for a family sized house with garden,' she says. She has been rejected for a rate rebate because she is in the poverty trap – in other words, her BBC pension and her investment earnings are too high. But that's not how she sees it, insisting she really is poor:

> *Now that I'm retired, with a BBC pension (not index-linked) and my son in his final year at University, I economise by giving up meat and doing little cooking in term time, and have reduced ironing and vacuum cleaning by about 80 per cent, which saves electricity.*

As for that son, well, things aren't looking too good for him either:

> *My son hopes to graduate next June, but a Modern Languages degree isn't linked to any specific vocation so I can't help fearing that he may join the ranks of the unemployed then.*

Now, she may have genuinely believed she was poor – after all, she certainly had been back in the 1950s and 60s – but I was on a full grant, earning decent money at Selfridges in the university vacations and, apart from the occasional short-term loan which she insisted was repaid, I was not costing her anything. Fifteen years later, she died leaving in the documents under the bed a six-figure sum in investments – government gilts, unit trusts and shares in the utilities privatised by the Thatcher government in which Michael Heseltine served.

But in the early 1980s, she was beginning her retreat into the past, constructing a story about herself and her world which had some truth to it – her father had liked a flutter – but which was embellished and romanticised. Yes, life had been a struggle but it was a better and more fulfilling life in every way. Take the BBC drama department, for instance. Just a week after the letter to Michael Heseltine, she wrote a long gossipy letter to Hilary Leeds, her wartime Bristol colleague, explaining why she probably would not be doing any more freelance work. Drama had moved on from the days when it was all broadcast live from the studio and, Sylvia thought, not in a good way:

> *I loved it when we did everything live and in the right sequence – since now everything is pre-taped and done in bits and pieces and then stuck together it's lost a lot of its interest for me and I don't think the end result is any better – and it must be considerably more costly in time and effort.*
>
> *Now sometimes a whole year is spent on one play, with pre and post filming, dubbing and post dubbing, for ever reshooting, editing and editing and re-editing.*

In fact, the move away from the studio towards shooting television drama on location, more like a feature film, had begun long before Sylvia's 1974 retirement. But for her, its golden age was the 1950s, when she was getting an elephant into a studio and meeting a charming young assistant floor manager on the set of *Who Goes There!*.

The trouble was that her obsession with the past – and in particular with the BBC as it once was – began to turn into long, meandering monologues which tested the patience of her relatives. In 1981 she went to stay for a few days with Bunty and her husband Bill at their Birmingham home. Bill, who had been quite friendly with Richie, had never had much tolerance for Sylvia's BBC gossip and it appears that this time, recovering from a major operation, he let that show. Sylvia wrote to apologise:

> *I'm truly sorry that I tend to talk about the past and irritate Bill.*
>
> *I've managed to keep a vow of chastity for 24 years with no trouble at all so I ought to be able to keep one of silence – or at least half silence, which, though its infinitely more difficult I really will try to do next time I visit you.*
>
> *Part of the difficulty is that my past life, in Bristol and then in London, was infinitely more interesting for me than the present.*

Mostly, her family tolerated the endless stream of consciousness which came pouring out of their increasingly eccentric relative. 'Your Aunty Sylvia is quite a character,' wrote Joan's daughter Dawn in a note to her teenage son Robert, giving him directions for a visit to Ruskin Park House and warning him not to expect much in the way of food. Somehow, Robert ended up showing this note to Sylvia, who then gleefully shared its contents with Joan.

While back then I found what I regarded as her constant inane wittering intensely irritating and embarrassing, I am now beginning to understand why she was like that. After all, she was now spending most of her time alone in the increasingly shabby flat. No wonder that when she did get out and meet people the floodgates opened and she talked and talked about the only thing that was on her mind – the past.

Perhaps I am giving too depressing a picture of Sylvia's final years. She did have two areas of her life which continued to make her happy – her holidays and her family. From that very first day trip to Le Touquet in 1934, she had looked forward to getting away and in her later years that meant package holidays to the Algarve, Crete or Majorca. There was always a lot of anxiety beforehand – she started packing many days in advance, then spent the night before even a lunchtime flight on the hard benches of Gatwick's departure lounge. 'What do you think I am, made of money?' she'd say when we suggested she book herself into an airport hotel. But she usually seemed to enjoy the holidays, returning with tales of the nice man who'd bought her a G&T at the hotel bar or the retired woman with whom she'd shared a table – and no doubt countless tales of life at the BBC.

But what was most valuable to her remained her family, and in particular her sisters Joan and Bunty. The three women remained extremely close throughout their lives, sharing joy and sorrow in their letters with barely a cross word. Joan and Bunty were the glue that kept the wider Parish family together, reminding the younger members of where we came from – 'your Grandma Jordan was one of 17' – and bringing us all together for important celebrations.

So when in August 1994 Stephen and I decided to hold a party at my Ealing home for Sylvia's eightieth birthday our first call was to our two aunts. They told us who absolutely had to be on the list and on the day a big crowd gathered in the garden – all four of Mum's siblings, many of their children, Warwickshire farming cousins, nieces and nephews, grandchildren and daughters-in-law and a couple of old BBC friends, including Hilary Leeds from Bristol. Stephen and I each made a speech, a very grand cake ordered from a patisserie was consumed and everyone seemed to have a good time.

One picture taken that day shows a group of us gathered around a table, all of us looking down at a photograph album someone has brought along. Stephen and I are wearing ties, as are all the men; the ladies are wearing smart flowery dresses, except for one. Mum, in the centre, is wearing quite a casual striped top and holding a glass of champagne, a slight smile on her face. Apart from Joan, she is the oldest person in the photo, but with her wavy brown hair she certainly doesn't look it. She loved being the centre of attention that day, heckling Stephen and me gently as we made our speeches. Afterwards, I drove her home across London and she chatted about her next holiday, a week in Crete in late September.

A month later, when Mum was nearing the end of her holiday, I was filming at a British Gas office in Reading. Someone came over to tell me there was an urgent phone call for me. 'Can't it wait?' I said irritably, but it couldn't. The call was to tell me that Stephen was in hospital after collapsing while out on a run. At 52, he was still a keen and pretty fast runner, having completed the London Marathon in his forties in 3 hours and 10 seconds – he had been furious about not breaking the three-hour barrier. I could not tell from the call how serious things were but when I arrived at Bart's Hospital I was told that my brother had suffered a cerebral haemorrhage, a life-threatening condition.

Suddenly, I found myself for the first time the head of our little family unit with important decisions to take, the first being what to do about Mum. A couple of months later, replying to a letter of condolence from an old BBC colleague, Sylvia related what had happened:

My return plane was delayed and my Travel Club rep. seemed to be taking extra care of me, checking my luggage in for me etc – I thought because of my advanced age. But when we got to Gatwick I was about to look for a taxi when Rory appeared so I was delighted – until he got me into the car and then told me that Stephen had had a stroke.

Rory had tried to get me on an earlier flight home but when that proved impossible he'd phoned my rep in Crete and asked her not to tell me.

So Rory took me to his house in Ealing – and to Bart's Hospital to see Stephen the next morning.

The nurse advised me to try and talk to him normally and said that he might understand but wouldn't be able to reply. When Pat first saw him earlier she told me he had been able to talk but since then had had a second cerebral haemorrhage.

Rory and I went to see him the following day but he died later that day.

The only consoling thing is that had he lived he would have had no quality of life and he'd always had such an active [life] *and varied interests.*

Sylvia stayed with us in Ealing while we organised the funeral at a church across from Stephen's beloved Lord's and for a few more days afterwards. Suddenly, she did look her age. I found her one morning standing half-dressed on the landing, confused as to where she was and what she needed to do. Her relationship with Stephen had at times been tempestuous but they had been through so much together – the custody battles with Richie, coming to London and managing in sordid accommodation, then exhilaration at the move to Ruskin Park House, the emotional drama of the affair with Jimmy, then the two of them coping together with a new baby. Yet another of the pillars of her life had gone.

By the following year it was becoming clear that, just like her sister Joan, Sylvia was losing her memory. That did not stop her writing letters but she seemed to be putting her affairs in order. She wrote to her solicitors in Bristol telling them of Stephen's death and asking them to draw up a new will dividing her estate – 'if it can be called that' – between me and her daughter-in-law Pat: 'There are one or two smaller legacies but I've decided to send cheques to them now – I never expected to last this long!'

That must have been the inspiration for 'Aunty Sylvia's lottery' which my Birmingham cousins told me about. Perhaps she was getting her affairs in order because she was aware that her memory was going. Her letter to my cousin Christine enclosing a cheque included this throwaway line: 'I'm getting like Joan, very forgetful. I can never remember what day it is.'

By December, as her second Christmas without Stephen approached, her memory problems were worsening, along with her isolation in the flat. When I was working in New York for a fortnight she wrote to Bunty:

I miss Stephen a lot especially at Christmas which was always so special to him – he used to come and see me

285

three times a week [...] Most of the time I am here alone with the radio or television for company. I just see the milkman once a week to pay him. My corridor is quite empty now.

Again, she says her memory is a bit like Joan's:

I never know what day of the week it is until I look at the Radio Times. I made a sort of list saying 'When you wake up it will be ie Friday, Saturday etc'. But if I forget to tick them off it doesn't work.

Later, as if it were a matter of little importance, she remarks: 'Following some tests I have to go to my Doctors this week because there is some abnormality – I've no idea what it can be!'

What she had forgotten or perhaps didn't know was that I had initiated those tests, increasingly worried about her health. In that letter to Bunty, she mentions having had 'quite a serious fire' after placing the new electric kettle I had bought her on a gas ring she kept lit for warmth. There had been several such incidents and I arranged an appointment early in 1996 at the Maudsley Hospital, just down the hill from Ruskin Park House. There, with great tact and gentleness, a consultant confirmed that Sylvia was in the early stages of Alzheimer's disease. She showed no great concern on hearing this diagnosis but then I'm not sure she took it in.

The last two letters among the thousands spread over six decades my mother left behind are dated February and March 1996 and are addressed to Bunty. One is typed, the other handwritten, with no sign that her illness was affecting her handwriting. Both describe visits to the hospital and at first sight are the work of someone in complete control of their faculties. In February, describing an upcoming CT scan, she tells Bunty it 'involves rotating an X-Ray beam around the head or body and enables the doctor to see inside your head or body without causing any discomfort (not a pretty sight!).'

In both letters she complains that the specialist asked for me to come along too – 'I don't know why and don't feel I need a "Minder".' She describes various memory tests and thinks she did reasonably well at counting backwards from 30 to 1 'which was simple' but completely forgot a name and address the doctor had told her to remember five minutes earlier.

She does recognise that she is suffering from 'memory loss' – the word Alzheimer's is never mentioned – and says 'about a year ago Rory told me quite gently that I had a tendency to repeat myself so I try to talk less!'

She is lonely, complaining that she sees nobody: 'I lead a very solitary life and Sundays seem so long I've thought of taking several sleeping tablets midday and dividing it into two days.' But she is stubbornly determined to resist attempts to improve matters. She mentions that I had discovered some sheltered housing in Ealing but that, while it would be lovely to live nearer me, she was relieved when the doctor advised against moving away from the two hospitals treating her.

Then she wonders whether if she collapsed in the flat she would be discovered within a week 'unless the milk bottles lined up (the milkman would probably just think I am away). Rory would be the one who would notice if he rang up once or twice and got no reply.'

While there's plenty of sadness in these two letters, there are still flashes of humour and moments of contentment: 'Must stop now,' she says at the end of the February letter, 'to have a small whisky and a cheese sandwich and watch Rory in *Working Lunch*'. I had been the reporter on the new lunchtime business programme for 18 months and she enjoyed 'seeing me' every day at a set time.

At the end of the March letter, she seems determined to rise above her troubles: 'Enough of my boring memory problems. I wish I'd never been told about them. The spring is on its way and then I can get out more.'

And her final written words: 'I came across my MENSA Certificate – which cheered me up a bit!'

I think when I was a teenager she mentioned to me that she had passed the Mensa intelligence test, for which you have to be above the ninety-eighth percentile, but I had filed it under 'tall tale', along with her claim to have been on the verge of becoming a pilot when war broke out. Yet again, I've a feeling I underestimated her.

I said that these two letters were the final documents in the Sylvia Archive, but I have in front of me one more. It is a brown envelope from the Department of Social Security and I found it when I climbed up a caretaker's ladder into the flat after failing one weekend in that spring of 1996 to get her to answer the phone – just as she had predicted in her letter to Bunty. She lay unconscious in bed, an empty bottle of sleeping pills on the bedside table and the envelope alongside it. On it she had scrawled this:

Darling Rory,
I love you – but I am tired of living in a capsule.

288

It's time for me to die.
Have a Happy life,
Love Mum

As it turned out, it was not time for her to die. She had not taken enough sleeping pills for that. She was taken down to the Maudsley where she spent a few days recovering before returning to the flat. But the incident seemed to have accelerated her decline – she was more confused and less coherent when I visited her or called on the phone.

It was the summer of Euro 96 and I called her one June Saturday to tell her I was off to Wembley to see England play Scotland. 'Will there be fighting, will there be riots?' she asked in an excited but mildly hysterical tone. I tried to reassure her that there would be no trouble. That was one of our last conversations. A few days later, with her doctor worried about her condition, she was taken back into the Maudsley for observation.

A couple of weeks later, on the day of the England v Germany Euro 96 semi-final, I was sitting in the *Working Lunch* office at Television Centre when the hospital rang. My mother had had a major stroke; I needed to get there as soon as possible. I drove to Camberwell to find she had been transferred across the road to King's College Hospital. I was told there was no hope that she would recover and sat by the bed for a couple of hours, listening to her jagged, somewhat disturbed breathing. I reflected that less than two years earlier I had sat by Stephen's deathbed – now with the other half of my little family unit slipping away I was effectively orphaned. I drove home to Ealing, distracted by the football commentary, even parking up guiltily at a petrol station to hear the outcome of the dramatic penalty shootout. I sat there, tears streaming down my face. I suppose any passer-by who peered in must have thought a grown man was taking England's defeat rather too much to heart.

Sylvia survived another two weeks, during which time Joan and Bunty came to sit by her bedside and say their goodbyes.

Then it was time to plan a funeral and clear the flat.

Two years after her eightieth birthday party in our Ealing garden, the Parishes assembled again, a great crowd of them filing into the church a few hundred yards from our home. The service was conducted by our own family vicar, Bob Stroud, the husband of Joan's daughter Dawn. I read a Shakespeare sonnet, just about making it through 'Shall I Compare Thee to a Summer's Day'. Afterwards, as we gathered for the wake back at my house, my Birmingham relatives slightly starstruck by the presence of my friend Adrian Chiles, there was laughter as well as tears as we remembered Sylvia's many eccentricities.

One mourner did not come back to the house but his presence meant a huge amount to me. Six years after I first saw my dad alongside my mum at my wedding, he was there for her funeral. As I came out of the church he gave me a great bear hug, whispered 'Dear, dear boy' in my ear and slipped away.

A few weeks later, we met for lunch. By then, I had begun sifting through the mountain of letters I had retrieved from Ruskin Park House and was increasingly gripped by the story they told. I explained to Jim a little of what I'd found, not in a spirit of recrimination – I really didn't blame him for anything – but to start a conversation. He blushed, looked down at his plate, and muttered something like 'the guilt, the guilt'. As embarrassed as he was, I changed the subject and we never discussed the matter again.

* * *

A month or so after her death, an obituary for Sylvia Rich appeared in the BBC staff newspaper *Ariel*. It said she had served the BBC for 33 years and 'worked with some of its most memorable characters', running through a brief summary of her career from wartime Bristol to the drama department at Television Centre. The obituary concluded with this paragraph:

> *Throughout all but the first five years of her career she brought up two sons on her own. When being a single mother was even harder than today, Sylvia Rich's achievement in combining the two roles was all the more remarkable.*

Underneath was the name of the author, Rory Cellan-Jones.

I had lobbied hard for my mum to be remembered in *Ariel*, despite the fact that she was 'a mere secretary'. When I got the go-ahead, I realised that far too often I had switched off when she had reminisced about her career and, even though I had begun skimming through the boxes of letters I had brought home, there were big gaps in my knowledge. So I rang Hilary Leeds in Bristol and she took me through the years with Geoffrey Grigson in radio talks and beyond with her usual efficiency. It mattered to me that she and a few of Mum's other BBC friends were pleased with the obituary but I now felt I had done my duty by my mother and could move on.

I crammed the collection of letters into a filing cabinet in my tiny, cluttered study at home and over the next 25 years barely looked at them. When I returned to them to write this book they were thick with dust and in a somewhat chaotic state, stuffed in no particular order into bulging folders. The task of building a compelling narrative from them seemed daunting. Then, as I started reading again and going beyond the contents of the red box which had been my focus in the weeks after my mum's death, I was soon gripped. I would go to one file in search of a particular letter and two hours later I would be sitting on the floor of my study still reading, surrounded by new discoveries.

The correspondence with the Midland Aero Club on the eve of the Second World War, the letter left on the kitchen table telling Richie she was leaving him, the description of her first production as a floor manager and the challenge of getting an elephant ridden by Stephen into the studio are just three out of countless examples which gave me a new view of my mother.

Time and again, I would dash along the corridor to Diane's study clutching my latest find to read out to her. I felt like a researcher finding ancient documents buried in some forgotten corner of a library which changed the way the world saw some historical figure. Diane would listen patiently, perhaps not quite as gripped as I was.

But then for me, this was a voyage of discovery, both exciting and at times deeply painful. I was finding out that the mother I had found neurotic, silly, sometimes deceitful and often deeply annoying had been a quite remarkable woman. She was a better writer, a more perceptive observer of the world around her, of the people that she met and of her own foibles, than I had ever imagined.

Above all, she was brave, fiercely determined to bring up her two sons as she saw fit and to give them the best education she could possibly afford. Stephen and I were the two great loves of her life, followed by the BBC, and, when she was in a sentimental mood, Jim.

But as I read through the BBC job applications, the legal file which documented the biggest drama of her life and the later letters where she told of her depression and her longing for the past, I realised we had all let her down in different ways. The BBC had opened a door into a whole new world for her but then shut it when she tried to climb the ladder and use her undoubted gifts in a more challenging and better-paid job. Her sons had grown tired of her long, involved tales about her past and had too often failed to give her the respect she deserved. As for Jim, well, the legal file appeared to show that he had made promises to her that he had been unable to keep.

Writing this book has at times been a gruelling experience as I lived through Sylvia's struggles and the emotional trauma of her custody battles with Richie, her love affair with my father and then the drama of my birth. But by leaving behind such a frank and detailed account of her life she has done what she intended when she slipped that note into the box containing her most intimate and painful secrets.

Yes, Mum, I think I do now understand how it really was.

Thank you.

A LETTER FROM JIM

By the time my dad died in 2019 at the age of 88 I had known him for 38 years and, while we had steered clear of discussions about the circumstances surrounding my birth, we had developed a fond, easy-going relationship. After the initial awkwardness about what I should call him we had settled on Jim – 'Father' was much too formal and 'Dad' seemed … well, a bit weird for someone I had first met at 23. Thanks to my brother Simon breaking the ice I became a regular visitor to the big house in Kew, which was the Cellan-Jones family home for many years. It was a far cry from Ruskin Park House – an eight-bedroom Victorian home, ramshackle but comfortable, filled to the brim with slightly battered furniture and seemingly every inch occupied by the antique china and glassware which Jim and Maggie loved to hunt down at car boot sales.

Once, we brought American friends to the house with us for a Guy Fawkes Night party. I could see as the evening wore on, with mulled wine and sausage rolls around the fire and a couple of distinguished actors chatting with Jim, that the American couple felt they had stepped into a scene from a Richard Curtis movie. As we left, the husband turned to me and said, 'There is just one word to describe that ... charming!'

I too was susceptible to that charm and the thrill of finding a new family. It was particularly rewarding to get to know my two new brothers, Simon and Din, and my sister, Vinny. It took time – we were, after all, complete strangers with no shared past – but gradually we learned to relax and enjoy each other's company. Din, shy beneath the outward self-assurance of a Westminster and Oxford educated barrister, found it hardest, I think. So I was touched when he invited me to his stag weekend at a cottage in the Berkshire countryside. It involved long walks – that was fine – but also heroic quantities of alcohol which I struggled to consume at quite the rate that his friends could manage.

Once Diane and I had children, Jim proved to be an excellent if eccentric grandfather, always guaranteed to come up with an unusual Christmas present. One year, our six-year-old son opened a parcel and his eyes widened. It was some sort of rocket. We inspected the box to find huge safety warnings and the instruction 'Do Not Launch Within Five Miles of an Airport'. As we were not that far from Heathrow, we decided that what was effectively a surface-to-air missile might not be a suitable toy and binned it.

There were limits to how smoothly I adapted to my new family. Every Christmas Eve we would head over to Kew to hand over and receive presents from the Cellan-Joneses. (Christmas Day was reserved for my mum and after her death, for Stephen's widow, Pat, and my nephew, Sam.) There would be mince pies and later a lethal gin and tonic or two, mixed by Din, in a sitting room with a roaring fire in front of which two boxer dogs lay snoring and farting. One year, early in our marriage, we took Diane's parents, Joe and Kathleen, who had come to stay with us for Christmas. In the sitting room we found Marlene, an American who had been an au pair for the kids back in the 1970s and had become a close friend of the family. She was now an academic at a New England college and she could be both very funny and extremely profane.

When I told her that I was going to be cooking Christmas dinner for the first time, she had a warning: 'You'll fuck it. Everyone fucks their first turkey! You will absolutely fuck it.' There was a moment's silence, then Kathleen laughed nervously, while Joe looked puzzled, as if he could not quite believe what he had heard. The couple lived in Ramsbottom, a Lancashire textile town and both worked in the mills for many years. They might have heard that kind of language at work but never at home – after all, Joe was an elder of the Presbyterian church. While I could eff and blind with the best of them – I was, after all, a journalist – I too had grown up in a family where bad language was frowned upon. But for the Cellan-Jones household, slightly higher up the social scale and a lot more bohemian than the Parishes, there was no difference between what was acceptable on the studio floor and in the living room.

While I might have been embarrassed on that one occasion, I was still rather enchanted with this new Cellan-Jones world. It was a place where you might hear some scurrilous anecdote about an actor you had assumed was a pillar of society, where the downstairs loo was home to Jim's framed award certificates and where you could barely see across the sitting room, such was the fug generated by a family where everyone seemed to smoke incessantly.

I was also proud of my dad's work and increasingly of Simon's blossoming career as a TV director. While once a friend's question about a Cellan-Jones in the credits would have me stuttering in embarrassment as I tried to explain the connection, now I would proudly say '*Fortunes of War*? Yes, that's my dad.' Or '*Our Friends in the North*? Yes, that's my brilliant brother Simon.' Equally, as I began to make my name as a television reporter, my dad was proud of me, joshing me that I was now better known than him and that people asked him whether he was related to that Rory Cellan-Jones.

As Jim entered his seventies, his directing work dried up, though he kept himself busy, lecturing about TV drama and writing his memoir, *Forsyte and Hindsight*. When he wrote a short novel, *Heartsease*, in which characters gather at a remote farmhouse for a creative writing weekend, he asked me to help him get it published. I was both flattered that he had asked me and daunted – it was never going to be picked up by a mainstream publisher so we'd have to go down the DIY route. I put quite a lot of effort into understanding Amazon Kindle Direct Publishing, which allows you to bring out a book in digital form. He seemed moderately pleased when, after consulting Twitter and getting help from an experienced self-published author, I finally managed to get *Heartsease* into the right format and published on the Kindle store. But it was clear that he did not think that a digital version was the real McCoy and a few weeks later, he called to enquire about getting it printed as a 'proper book'. I promised, somewhat wearily, to look into it but having seen what it would cost quietly dropped the idea, hoping rather shamefully that he would forget about it. He did – or perhaps he sensed my grumpiness and thought better of raising it again.

As old men do, he became repetitive, telling the same (only quite) amusing anecdotes about this actor or that disaster on location time and again. Just as I had done with my mother, I began to tune out during these long monologues about TV people I didn't know. But then in 2010 something happened to remind me of what a distinguished career he'd had. The BFI mounted a James Cellan Jones retrospective with screenings over several days at BFI South Bank. Diane and I went along on the Sunday when Jim was being interviewed on stage. Yes, some of the hoary old anecdotes were trotted out, but his diffident charm and obvious passion for his craft won the audience over. Then we sat and watched some of his work. By then I had it in my mind that he had been a good, solid, middle-of-the-road director – classic series like *The Portrait of a Lady*, lush period pieces such as *Jennie: Lady Randolph Churchill* and later, the gentle sitcom *A Fine Romance*. Nothing there to frighten the horses or lead to outraged headlines in the *Daily Mail*.

It soon became clear that I had underestimated him too – in the early 1970s he had been responsible for some groundbreaking television of a kind that would never see the light of day today. *The Roads to Freedom*, the dramatisation of a Sartre trilogy where the characters agonise at length about their lives and loves as war approaches, was demanding television but made such an impression on some young viewers, including the polemicist Peter Hitchens, that 50 years later they mounted a passionate and ultimately successful campaign to get the BBC to show it again. The haunting theme tune 'La Route est Dure', sung by Georgia Brown, was composed by Jim and was played at the end of his funeral.

Even more striking was *Eyeless in Gaza*, his 1971 five-part serialisation of an Aldous Huxley novel. There is a scene in the book where a dog falls out of an aircraft and lands next to a couple sunbathing on a roof, covering them with blood. Many a director might have cut that but Jim set about finding a way to film it that involved a biplane, a revolving mirror, a quarter-inch model of a fox terrier and a lot of fake blood. He managed to convey the horror of the scene without making it look either so silly or so gruesome that it would have to be ditched. We walked out of the cinema marvelling at how our expectations of an afternoon of tepid television had been confounded.

Over the years, then, Jim and I built a relationship of both love and respect. What we lacked, however, was the emotional connection, for good or ill, of a father and son. He had never disciplined me or shouted at me when I was growing up. I had never rebelled or sworn at him or told him, like my own kids told me, that he was boring and his jokes weren't funny. Most of all, we had never really opened up to each other or cried in each other's arms.

That changed a little near the end of his life because of something we had in common – Parkinson's disease. For Jim, it came along in his eighties and, as with many elderly people, it was just the latest in a series of maladies, including an aortic aneurysm which very nearly killed him in his early seventies. A couple of years after he was diagnosed with Parkinson's, he and Maggie sold the house in Kew and moved to Wells in Somerset. They bought a pretty but wildly unsuitable house spread over three floors with steep stairs. Maggie fell ill and died, and a year or so after losing his wife of more than 50 years, Jim broke his leg badly after tripping over. If he hadn't had Parkinson's the doctors might have been able to get him back on his feet but his tremor meant they were never able to set the bone properly. From then on, he could only get about very slowly with a walking frame and eventually needed a full-time carer.

In the summer of 2018, while on holiday in Italy, I noticed that I was dragging my foot as I was walking. A month or so later, a neurologist wrote to the BBC after seeing my hand shaking during a live television broadcast and suggested I get that checked out. It took me four months to get a hospital appointment but in January 2019, I was told that I had Parkinson's. Like Jim, I had had another serious illness, a malignant melanoma behind my left eye, for which I had been receiving treatment since 2005. That had originally seemed life-threatening, whereas Parkinson's was a slow burner, so it was a few weeks before I began to tell friends and family about my diagnosis, eventually telling the world via Twitter in May after another live broadcast where my tremor was very evident.

I can't remember if I even told Jim – I was unsure whether it was worth burdening him with the news. But in July, shortly after I had sent him a bottle of whisky for his eighty-eighth birthday, he wrote to me, the first letter I could remember getting from him since the early years after I met him in the 1980s. It was written on a scrap of lined paper, apparently torn from a notebook, in the tiny spidery handwriting which is a symptom of Parkinson's. 'Dear Rory, I feel guilty at not taking the time to talk to you about Parkinson's Disease,' he began, before going on to list some of the many symptoms of the condition:

Shaky hands
difficulty in walking

tendency to fall (never since broken leg!)
difficulty in climbing
tiredness walking
overactive salivary glands
forgetfulness – *names, faces, places, mathematical*
stupidities
Sleeplessness

He told me that all of these were 'beatable' with the right
medication – quite an optimistic view – while warning that
the danger was that you thought any unfamiliar symptom was
due to Parkinson's when it might not be. He had an anecdote
about how he'd won one battle against the disease:

The other day I had as Patron (!) to give a speech of
welcome to the drama festival. I had an attack of
salivary overproduction and said I couldn't do it. They
panicked and said I had to (meaning they couldn't get
anyone else). So I did. It went ok and got well reported
in the local press. I seem to bluff my way through things.

And he ended on a positive note:

I intend to carry on at least until the end of the century.
  Thank you for the delightful whiskey!
  I do hope you'll come and see me soon,
Love,
Jim

I was touched by the letter which came at a time when I
was suffering from another Parkinson's symptom, depression,

302

and thought I must make the time to go down to Wells to see him. But I never managed it. One night at the end of August, Simon, who lived not far from Jim in Somerset, rang to tell me that our father had suffered a major stroke and was not expected to live. I arranged to travel down the next morning to the hospital in Bath in the hope of seeing him. But by the morning he was dead and I travelled instead to Castle Cary railway station where Simon collected me, greeting me with a hug. I spent the day with him, his wife Star and three children, and with Vinny, sharing our different memories of Jim.

But it was not until a couple of years later that I talked to Vinny about that final letter from Jim and found out about the deep current of emotion underlying it. 'When he first heard about your Parkinson's he just cried and cried,' she told me. He was an emotional man but I wondered why this news had hit him so hard. Was it because he felt that, after being absent for my childhood, his last gift to me had been to pass on this wretched disease? If so, he was wrong to feel any guilt. I did not hold him responsible for my Parkinson's, or for anything else. I had come away from reading the intimate account of my parents' affair and its aftermath with a feeling of great sadness for two people trapped by circumstances, boxed in by the social mores of the times and by his parents.

Sixty years on, I did not blame him, I loved him.

How I wish I could hug him and tell him that now ...

ACKNOWLEDGEMENTS

I first read my mother's extraordinary treasure trove of letters in 1996 and have been mulling over the story they tell ever since, but it was only in 2021 that I first considered that there might be a book in them. That was after a call from the journalist Catherine Pepinster which resulted in a feature in the *Sunday Telegraph*, so I am grateful to her.

My agent Elly James, whose calm and wise advice I have learned to value over the years, then helped me to shape a book proposal. I was then lucky enough to meet Hannah MacDonald of September Publishing who had her own vision of how the story should be structured and persuaded me to think more deeply about my feelings about my parents. Hannah has been the perfect editor, supportive but also acute in her advice about how to weave the source material into a compelling narrative. Charlotte Cole and Liz Marvin were also eagle-eyed in spotting inaccuracies, repetition and clumsiness and were invaluable in making my prose read better.

I also owe a huge debt to my friend Lindsay Shaw who, after a conversation about the book, offered to help, transcribing hundreds of letters and researching subjects ranging from wartime in Swansea to illegitimacy and adoption in the late 1950s.

But this is a book about families – three of them, the Parishes, the Cellan-Joneses and the BBC.

My mother's family, the Parishes, provided a loving refuge from Ruskin Park House during what could have been a lonely childhood. Thanks in particular to Bunty and Bill Harlow's daughters, my cousins Susan, Christine and Jane, who shared their memories of my visits and our family. Thanks also to my nephew Sam Rich and my sister-in-law, Stephen's widow Pat Starr, for jogging my memory with photographs ranging from the 1930s to the 1990s.

It was my brother Simon who first invited me to the Cellan-Jones family home in Kew, where I met Vinny and Din, my two other new half-siblings. Ever since they have welcomed me to all manner of family events, both happy and sad. I am hugely grateful to Simon and Vinny for being prepared to open up about what they knew about me before we met, and I look back with immense fondness on Din, taken from us far too young.

As for the BBC, the team at the Caversham Written Archives helped me dig out memos about broadcasting during air raids in Bristol in the war and I was delighted to meet the distinguished TV director Alvin Rakoff who told me what it was like to work for BBC Drama in the 1950s.

Finally, I could not possibly have gone on the emotional journey this book has entailed without the support of my wife Diane. Many a time I've rushed into her study waving a letter with some new discovery, interrupting her research into the value of data or her work on reshaping GDP. Thank you, Diane, for listening so patiently and for putting up with me for all these years.